LAURA INGALLS WILDER

Laura Ingalls Wilder wrote stories that have defined the American frontier for generations of readers. As both author and character in her own books, she became one of the most famous figures in American children's literature. Her award-winning *Little House* series, based on her childhood in Wisconsin, Kansas, Minnesota, and South Dakota, blended memoir and fiction into a vivid depiction of nineteenth-century settler life that continues to shape many Americans' understanding of the country's past. Poised between fiction and fact, literature and history, Wilder's life is a fascinating window on the American West.

Placing Wilder's life and work in historical context, and including previously unpublished material from the Wilder archives, Sallie Ketcham introduces students to domestic frontier life, the conflict between Native Americans and infringing white populations, and the West in public memory and imagination.

Sallie Ketcham is an independent scholar and writer from Minnesota.

ROUTLEDGE HISTORICAL AMERICANS

SERIES EDITOR: PAUL FINKELMAN

Routledge Historical Americans is a series of short, vibrant biographies that illuminate the lives of Americans who have had an impact on the world. Each book includes a short overview of the person's life and puts that person into historical context through essential primary documents, written both by the subjects and about them. A series website supports the books, containing extra images and documents, links to further research, and, where possible, multi-media sources on the subjects. Perfect for including in any course on American History, the books in the Routledge Historical Americans series show the impact everyday people can have on the course of history.

Woody Guthrie: Writing America's Songs
Ronald D. Cohen

Frederick Douglass: Reformer and Statesman
L. Diane Barnes

Thurgood Marshall: Race, Rights, and the Struggle for a More Perfect Union
Charles L. Zelden

Harry S. Truman: The Coming of the Cold War
Nicole L. Anslover

John Winthrop: Founding the City upon a Hill
Michael Parker

John F. Kennedy: The Spirit of Cold War Liberalism
Jason K. Duncan

Bill Clinton: Building a Bridge to the New Millennium
David H. Bennett

Ronald Reagan: Champion of Conservative America
James H. Broussard

Laura Ingalls Wilder: American Writer on the Prairie
Sallie Ketcham

Laura Ingalls Wilder
American Writer on the Prairie

SALLIE KETCHAM

NEW YORK AND LONDON

www.routledge.com/cw/HistoricalAmericans

First published 2015
by Routledge
711 Third Avenue, New York, NY 10017

and by Routledge
2 Park Square, Milton Park, Abingdon, Oxon OX14 4RN

Routledge is an imprint of the Taylor & Francis Group, an informa business

© 2015 Taylor & Francis

The right of Sallie Ketcham to be identified as author of this work has been asserted by her in accordance with sections 77 and 78 of the Copyright, Designs and Patents Act 1988.

All rights reserved. No part of this book may be reprinted or reproduced or utilized in any form or by any electronic, mechanical, or other means, now known or hereafter invented, including photocopying and recording, or in any information storage or retrieval system, without permission in writing from the publishers.

Trademark notice: Product or corporate names may be trademarks or registered trademarks, and are used only for identification and explanation without intent to infringe.

Library of Congress Cataloging-in-Publication Data

Ketcham, Sallie.
Laura Ingalls Wilder : American writer on the prairie / Sallie Ketcham.
    pages cm. — (Routledge historical Americans)
  1. Wilder, Laura Ingalls, 1867–1957.   2. Wilder, Laura Ingalls, 1867–1957.
Little house books.   3. Wilder, Laura Ingalls, 1867–1957—Political and social
views.   4. Wilder, Laura Ingalls, 1867–1957—Criticism and interpretation.
5. Autobiographical fiction, American—History and criticism.   6. Authors,
American—20th century—Biography.   7. Women pioneers—United States—
Biography.   8. Frontier and pioneer life—United States.   I. Title.
    PS3545.I342Z73 2014
    813'.52—dc23
    [B]
    2014012611

ISBN: 978-0-415-82019-6 (hbk)
ISBN: 978-0-415-82020-2 (pbk)
ISBN: 978-0-203-40915-2 (ebk)

Typeset in Minion and Scala Sans
by Apex CoVantage, LLC

For Steve,
who makes all things possible

CONTENTS

Acknowledgments		ix
Introduction		1
PART I		
Laura Ingalls Wilder: American Writer on the Prairie		**5**
Chapter 1	A Home in the West: The 1860s	7
Chapter 2	Wandering the West: The 1870s	27
Chapter 3	Settling the West: The 1880s	52
Chapter 4	Leaving the West: The 1890s	73
Chapter 5	Writing the West: 1911 to 1943	94
Chapter 6	I Am Your Laura: 1943 and Forward	111
PART II		
Documents		**121**
Bibliography		163
Index		167

ACKNOWLEDGMENTS

As a Minnesota children's writer researching the life and legacy of Laura Ingalls Wilder, I quickly realized that nearly everyone I encountered had a Laura story. I will always be grateful to the many individuals who generously shared their stories with me, who explained their reasons for loving the Little House (or not), and who listened patiently to my own ideas about the significance of Wilder's work.

I owe a huge debt of thanks to Paul Finkelman, the series editor, and to Kimberly Guinta, senior editor at Routledge. Their close reading and smart editorial comments greatly improved this book. Thanks also to Genevieve Aoki and Rebecca Novack at Routledge for their assistance and support. Michael McNally, religion chair at Carleton College, provided invaluable advice on Native American history, tradition, and scholarship.

To the legendary Jean Coday and to the entire staff of the Laura Ingalls Wilder Historic Home and Museum in Mansfield, Missouri, who encouraged me to wander Rocky Ridge and who so kindly took the time to answer all my questions—thank you. I am also grateful for the research assistance I received from directors, staff, and volunteers at all the Laura Ingalls Wilder home sites, especially Cheryl Palmlund in De Smet. Equally dedicated and probing staff members at the Wisconsin, Minnesota and South Dakota Historical Societies were instrumental in helping me locate documents pertaining to the early lives of the Quiner, Ingalls, and Wilder families. Thanks also to the librarians at the University of Utah who retrieved the records of The Holy Cross Hospital regarding the death of Rose Wilder Lane's son for me and to Robert Spangler of the Iowa Braille and Sight Saving School in Vinton, Iowa.

Expert archivists Spencer Howard and Matthew Schaefer at the Herbert Hoover Presidential Library and Museum in West Branch, Iowa, greeted

x • Acknowledgments

me in a blizzard and then proceeded to turn the time I spent studying the Rose Wilder Lane Papers into one of the genuine highlights of my Wilder research. I am indebted to Noel Silverman, Esq., The Little House Heritage Trust, and Nancy Koupal at the South Dakota Historical Society Press for their generosity regarding the use of primary documents, particularly the excerpt from Wilder's unpublished autobiographical memoir "Pioneer Girl."

Finally, I am more grateful than I can say for the contributions of my mother, Sally Johnson Ketcham: former curator of history at the Nebraska State Historical Society, historic preservationist, walking encyclopedia of the West. I could not have written this book if it were not for all the things she has taught me, over so many years.

INTRODUCTION

"Once upon a time, sixty years ago, a little girl lived in the Big Woods of Wisconsin, in a little gray house made of logs."

It is the opening line of an American classic, beloved by millions, so culturally iconic that it is immediately recognizable even to those who have never read the book. From the outset, Laura Ingalls Wilder framed her childhood as a frontier fairy tale. And like all fairy tales, Wilder's story is complex and cautionary, full of trials and enchantment. Part love song to the plains, part coming-of-age story, part traditional Western, part social and domestic history of the West, Laura Ingalls Wilder wrote stories of the American frontier that were as unique as her life and as vivid as her vanishing voice, the authentic voice of a covered-wagon pioneer.

In *The Uses of Enchantment: The Meaning and Importance of Fairy Tales,* child psychologist Bruno Bettelheim describes both the characteristics and the purpose of great children's literature:

> For a story truly to hold the child's attention, it must entertain him and arouse his curiosity. But to enrich his life, it must stimulate his imagination; help him to develop his intellect and to clarify his emotions; be attuned to his anxieties and aspirations; give full recognition to his difficulties, while at the same time suggesting solutions to the problems which perturb him. In short, it must at one and the same time relate to all aspects of his personality—and this without ever belittling but, on the contrary, giving full credence to the seriousness of the child's predicaments, while simultaneously promoting confidence in himself and his future.[1]

2 • Introduction

Laura Ingalls Wilder's series of *Little House* books have held the attention, enriched the lives, and stimulated the imaginations of children for nearly a century. In all of American literature, only a handful of characters—Huck, Jo, Holden, Dorothy, and Laura, the eponymous heroine of Wilder's novels—can claim such an intimate, first-name hold on millions of readers over multiple generations. *Little House in the Big Woods,* which debuted in 1932, has never been out of print. It has been translated into dozens of languages, including Hebrew, Farsi, and Japanese. Wilder's work launched Ronald Reagan's favorite television series, created a cottage tourist industry, generated reams of biographical and critical analysis, produced countless commercial spinoffs, and even renamed highways across the Midwest.

Laura Ingalls Wilder wrote semi-autobiographical fiction for children. Her explicit, stated purpose (unusual and generally suspect in any author) was to detail pioneer life and explain the development of the Western frontier as she experienced it—in effect, an early and original attempt to provide context for America's westward expansion and for the pioneer experience itself. Her life was the subject of her work, and yet Wilder remains a relative cypher. Literary, psychological, or existential biographers have been frustrated by Wilder's personal reticence. Compared to her compulsively self-analytical daughter, the writer Rose Wilder Lane, Wilder retained few personal letters and kept a journal only sporadically. Instead, she left an eight-volume series of prize-winning children's books and insisted on their veracity, their "truth," but the personal incidents and other material she omitted in her fiction, sometimes intentionally, sometimes not, and sometimes at the behest of her editors as material inappropriate for children, is fundamental to understanding Wilder's life and legacy. The *Little House* books concluded with Laura's marriage at eighteen, leaving millions of children and literally hundreds of scholars to pose the same persistent question: *And then what happened?*

Wilder's work represents a singular achievement in children's literature, but her social and cultural significance remains controversial, divisive, and politicized. Even the question of Wilder's sole authorship has come under question, as biographers attempt to evaluate the role that Rose Wilder Lane played in editing, fostering, and promoting her mother's work. Like Mark Twain, another writer who straddles the line between adult and children's literature, the novels of Laura Ingalls Wilder generate heated academic debate—and the occasional call for book banning. There is no question that Wilder's *Little House* books influenced generations of American school children, shaping their understanding of Western history, frontier life, Plains Indian culture, and the mythos of the unbroken West. So did Roy Rogers, but thousands of his fans don't go on pilgrimage to his birthplace every year.

Interestingly, Wilder is both the subject and the author of Western history (albeit fictionalized). In an era in which a respectable woman's name was presumed to appear in the newspaper three times—to document her birth, marriage, and death—Wilder carved out a thriving career as a farm journalist in her mid-forties. She was no amateur, naïf genius, or Grandma Moses. She knew her material. By the time she began writing her groundbreaking series for children, she had already subsisted on frozen bear meat, witnessed the forced removal of the Osages, sewed shirts to survive, taught school at the age of fifteen, hand-harvested wheat, delivered two children in a shanty, raised and decapitated her beloved prize chickens, cleared a Missouri farm with a crosscut saw, founded a local literary society, and watched the frontier pass before her eyes. "Memories!" she wrote in 1924. "We go through life collecting them whether we will or not! Sometimes I wonder if they are our treasures in Heaven or the consuming fires of torment when we carry them with us as we, too, pass on." Laura's life, like the Golden West itself, was full of contradictions.

Above all, Wilder was the product of a specific time and place. By mining her everyday childhood experiences, she crafted a richly detailed portrait of frontier life and settlement, effectively defined Manifest Destiny for generations of readers, and inspired them to read and learn more, which in turn led many of them to discover different voices and different sources. Laura Ingalls Wilder was her own primary source. "All I have told is true," she later admitted, "but it is not the whole truth." She told her story, her way—often to the frustration of her readers, biographers, and critics. Wilder was fully aware that she had outlived the West of her memory and her art. Near the end of her life, she began calling her childhood home in South Dakota, "The Land of Used to Be." The same countryside she had first glimpsed through the puckered canvas at the back of a covered wagon, she would eventually view from the window of an airplane.

The study of Wilder's work overlaps multiple academic disciplines. She is claimed and explained by conservatives, libertarians, environmentalists, feminists, revisionists, literary historians, childhood experts, performance artists, new western historians, entomologists, and television critics. Their disparate narratives and interpretations of Wilder's legacy are as varied, contradictory, and tumultuous as the Western experience itself. Wilder's own explanation for her work may sound slightly disingenuous today (and it is far from the whole truth) but in the end it is her detailed, specific reading of the West—at once both supremely domestic and heroic—that remains the foundation of her continuing appeal and is responsible for the continual reinterpretation and reinvention of her work.

"I wanted the children now to understand more about the beginnings of things, to know what is behind the things they see—what it is that made America as they know it."

For Laura Ingalls Wilder, the songs of the cradle went down to the grave.

NOTE

1. Bettelheim, Bruno. *The Uses of Enchantment: The Meaning and Importance of Fairy Tales.* New York: Knopf, 1976, 5.

PART I

LAURA INGALLS WILDER: AMERICAN WRITER ON THE PRAIRIE

CHAPTER 1

A HOME IN THE WEST: THE 1860S

In the settlement of every new country there are always transient settlers who make their appearance, perhaps to take advantage of cheap land, a small tract of which they cultivate for a few seasons, and then tire of even the faint dawn of civilization, and press on to some wilder frontier region, where they exist by hunting, trapping and fishing, thus spending an aimless, worthless life . . .

The History of Westmorland County Pennsylvania, 1906

As I looked about me I felt that the grass was the country, as the water is the sea . . . and there was so much motion in it, the whole country seemed, somehow, to be running.

Willa Cather

Long after her father's death, Laura Ingalls Wilder wrote to her daughter, fellow writer Rose Wilder Lane, "Pa was no business man. He was a hunter and a trapper, a musician and a poet."[1]

Charles Phillip Ingalls may have been no businessman, but to his admiring daughter (and likeminded, globetrotting granddaughter), he was the consummate pioneer: an undaunted farmer and jack-of-all trades; an optimistic man brimming with energy and talent; a devoted husband and father; a respected citizen; and a fast friend. But perhaps his most significant personality trait, at least in terms of his daughter's future development, was what Wilder would describe in her novels as Charles's "wandering foot." For it was Charles Ingalls's impulsivity, restlessness, and faith in greener pastures that led to Wilder's own itinerant childhood on the western frontier and, ultimately, to the transformation of her experiences there into landmark American literature.

On February 7, 1867, when Laura Elizabeth Ingalls was born by the fire in the little log house her father had constructed near Lake Pepin, Wisconsin, Charles Ingalls had already spent a lifetime moving west. Born in Cuba, New York, to Lansford and Laura Colby Ingalls, Charles had moved with his parents and siblings from Cuba to the open prairie near Elgin, Illinois, from Illinois north to the village of Concord, in southeastern Wisconsin, and finally, about 1862, when Lansford Ingalls lost the title to his Concord farm, from Concord to the Chippewa River Valley of western Wisconsin. It was here, on the edge of the dwindling Big Woods—the French explorers' *Grand Bois*—that Charles purchased eighty acres of land and built the first of many little houses for his bride, the proverbial girl-next-door whom he had met and married in Concord in 1860.

For Caroline Quiner Ingalls, Charles's genteel and retiring wife, a home of her own and a modicum of privacy probably came as a welcome relief. At the age of twenty, she had embarked on married life in the Concord home of Charles's parents, shoehorned in with Charles's eight siblings. The couple's first child, Mary Amelia, was born in the small, secluded log house on her father's birthday, just short of her parent's fifth wedding anniversary. Laura Elizabeth arrived two years later. Both girls inherited their father's intense blue eyes, eyes that dominate every surviving photograph of Charles's handsome narrow face—his whisk-broom beard and untamed hair notwithstanding. Tiny, rough-and-tumble Laura—Pa's Half-Pint—inherited her mother's lustrous halo of dark hair, if not her mother's mild-mannered disposition. In almost every photograph of Wilder's parents, Charles and Caroline lean in close to one another or are physically touching. In an era of stiff and formal photography, it is an uncommon and unselfconsciously affectionate pose.

The couple's enduring frontier marriage was also notably egalitarian by nineteenth-century standards. As Wilder later noted, "Ma did follow Pa wherever he went, but Pa never went anywhere that Ma wouldn't follow."[2] In feminist writer Kathryn Adam's words:

> The beautiful quality of the Ingalls' marriage, and surely part of the books' great charm, was that Ma and Pa regularly acknowledged one another's contributions in front of their children. Pa was quick with praise for Ma's housekeeping, for her endurance, for the way she could improvise in a tight situation. In the Ingalls family, "women's work" was seen as a matter of skill and achievement, and it could be a legitimate source of a woman's self-esteem. While it is true that Laura, for one, found a woman's traditional role limiting for someone of her energy and interests, at least womanly achievements were held in high regard by her family and the larger community, not only because they signified the performance of an appropriate role but also because the things women knew how to do made a respected contribution to family and community life.[3]

The 1860s had been an eventful and turbulent decade for the Ingalls and Quiner families. At the outbreak of the Civil War, while the neighboring families still resided in the southeastern Wisconsin county of Jefferson, three Ingalls–Quiner marriages had taken place in rapid succession: Henry Quiner (Caroline's brother) to Polly Ingalls (Charles's sister); Charles to Caroline; and Peter Ingalls (Charles's brother) to Eliza Ann Quiner (Caroline's sister). As the war dragged on, Joseph Quiner—Caroline, Henry and Eliza's eldest brother—joined the Union Army. Four months later, he was dead. Shot through the arm at the battle of Shiloh, Joseph Quiner's wound reopened in a Tennessee army hospital, where he bled to death before the surgeon could attend him.[4] Caroline believed the shock of her brother's needless death was going to kill his inconsolable widow, Nancy. Only a few months before the death of Joseph, Caroline's mother Charlotte had barely survived an attack of what her doctor termed "scarlet dyphtheria." A surviving letter from Caroline to her sister Martha Quiner Carpenter, written in Caroline's elegant copybook script, paints a graphic picture of their mother's illness. "She was of a scarlet red from head to foot and of a burning heat, and when she began to get better the skin came off all over her—she could peal it off in large pieces; all her fingernails came off and as I told you before she has not the full use of (two fingers) yet."[5] It was not the first time Caroline Ingalls had witnessed the suffering caused by lethal epidemics and the casual hazards of frontier life, and it was far from the last.

In 1838, Caroline Ingalls's Yankee father, Henry N. Quiner,[6] had been in the vanguard of white settlers who pressed into Wisconsin Territory from Michigan and Illinois. Like Lansford Ingalls, Quiner had left New England and made several interim moves west before buying land near Milwaukee, where Quiner farmed and traded with the Ho-Chunk Indians and others who remained in the Great Lakes region after the Black Hawk War. The Quiner family prospered until disaster struck. In early November 1845, Quiner and his brother-in-law Captain Alexander McGregor set sail on Lake Michigan in McGregor's schooner *Ocean,* a small stout ship of the Milwaukee fleet. The schooner, loaded with lumber, sailed into a November gale and capsized near St. Joseph, Michigan, with the loss of all on board. The steamer *Champion* found the wreckage two miles from shore. The *Ocean* had lost her mainmast, her hatches had given way, and her sails were torn "to rags." Also hauling lumber and headed for Chicago, the sloop *James K. Polk* and her crew of seven disappeared without a trace, probably in the same violent storm. A writer at the *Milwaukee Gazette* reported:

> In the loss of the Schooner OCEAN, four of our citizens have passed from time to eternity. Just before the OCEAN sailed from this port, Capt. McGregor came to our office, subscribed for our paper, and with buoyancy of health and

spirits good humeredly [sic] contrasted the varied and exciting life of a sailor with the monotony of a printer's existence, and his hearty laugh and jovial voice still ring in our ears. He has left a wife and 1 child. The Mate, Mr. Russel, has also left a wife and child. The second mate, Quiner, has left a wife and 5 or 6 children to mourn his loss. The cabin boy, an Irish lad, has left a mother who was partially dependent upon him for support. We hope the tears of widows and orphans will incite government to some action in favor of our Lake harbors.[7]

With the death of her father, Caroline's world turned upside down. All her prospects—for security, education, even marriage—were substantially diminished. Wilder would later assert that her mother was "well educated for her time and place and rather above Pa socially."[8] When the adult Wilder wrote to her Aunt Martha Quiner Carpenter asking for details of her mother's upbringing, Carpenter said the circumstances of their impoverished childhood "made one's heart ache" and were rarely discussed. "I remember when the folks came from Milwaukee to tell us about father," Martha wrote. "I can see them getting out of the wagon, they were dressed in black." She remembered too much, she said. She had never been able to forget how the family, destitute and fatherless, had survived on cornmeal and water after the flour ran out. "They say to forget the past, but I don't see how."[9]

While it is possible that Caroline and her siblings received some financial support or assistance from their prominent uncles, Edwin and Elisha Quiner—at least until Charlotte Tucker Quiner remarried neighboring widower Frederick Holbrook in 1848—the early years of privation had taught Caroline hard lessons in prudence, self-reliance, and the art of making do. The Quiners were a proud, well-educated, and decidedly literary family. Caroline's uncle Edwin Bentley Quiner was a pioneer journalist, editor, and clerk of the legislature. He transformed his meticulous 4,000-page scrapbook of newspaper clippings into *The Military History of Wisconsin*, the definitive account of Wisconsin's role in the Civil War.[10] His brother Elisha was a well-regarded printer. Caroline's mother Charlotte was also better educated than the vast majority of her peers. She had attended a private female seminary in Massachusetts, taught school, and worked as a dressmaker before her marriage.[11] Caroline began teaching school at the age of sixteen. The university education afforded to her strong-willed cousin Emilie Quiner (Edwin's daughter and a Civil War nurse) was far beyond the Holbrooks' means, but it is indicative of a family that placed an unusually high value on the education of its daughters. Caroline prized literature and maintained a small library of books, newspapers, quarterlies, and sheet music in all of her homes, even in the most primitive of dugouts. She was her daughters' first teacher, encouraging them to read before they were old enough to attend school, and supervising their education when school was

A Home in the West: The 1860s • 11

not accessible. Although the Ingalls's household was cash poor, it provided greater intellectual stimulation than the average pioneer home and seems to have stirred Laura's imagination from an early age.

In Concord, the Ingalls family lived just across the Oconomowoc River from the Quiner-Holbrooks, which accounted for the many marriages, close family ties, and working relationships. During the Civil War, however, this comfortable situation suddenly changed. In 1862, Charles's father Lansford Ingalls was unable to repay a $500 loan he had secured against his property and lost title to the family farm. This reversal of fortune profoundly altered the future path of newlyweds Charles and Caroline, as well as the couple's extended family. The Ingalls family decided to quit staid Jefferson County and move en masse to Pepin, Wisconsin, on the state's western border. They joined Caroline's sister Martha and her husband Charles Carr Carpenter, who had arrived years earlier to take and break wild land. A descendant later recalled that the Ingalls lived and ate beside their wagons until they erected a single cabin to accommodate all the children and grandchildren, close to twenty family members.[12] In choosing Pepin County, the entangled Ingalls–Quiner clan had picked an exceptionally beautiful area in which to start over, a landscape dominated by rocks, hawks, and rivers. "One cannot imagine a more lovely expanse of water than Lake Pepin in quiet clear weather," wrote artist Henry Lewis in 1848. "And no wilder scene than when, whipped by the storm, its waves bound against the rocky cliffs." Wilder, with her lyrical sensitivity to the natural world, would later describe Lake Pepin as "legend-haunted."[13] As a child, she must have heard tales of the great lake monster said to lurk in Pepin's dark waters.

Charles Ingalls and Henry Quiner needed cash to buy land in Pepin County, so they hired out as harvest hands across the lake in Minnesota, possibly within the bounds of the former Dakota Indian reserve known as the Half-Breed Tract. After the harvest of 1863, they had saved enough money to purchase two adjoining 80-acre parcels of land. Working side-by-side allowed the two men to pool their resources and stretch their subsistence farm incomes. Their wives tended large vegetable gardens, pigs, chickens, and cows. Charles hunted game for the table, set traps, and traded furs. He was also a skilled carpenter who typically sought odd jobs. By the time Laura was born in 1867, the Ingalls were enjoying a period of comparative stability and comfort in a cabin of their own in a tranquil valley called Lost Creek.

By all accounts, Laura's family life was affectionate and supportive. The domestic detail Wilder recorded in her first novel *Little House in the Big Woods* continues to engage young readers in part because Wilder's earliest childhood memories of life in the Big Woods read like a fairytale. Like Little Red Riding Hood, Laura lives in a lonely cabin in the darkening woods, where wolves that "eat little girls" prowl just outside the walls.[14] Pa is a woodcarver who makes wonderful gifts for Christmas. Mother is good and gentle and kind. Wild bears, stalking panthers (or cougars as they are more commonly called today), and talking owls haunt the woods at night, but Pa's magic fiddle dispels the fear and the darkness. Sleigh-bells ring out in the frosty air as beautiful young women pile into cutters and race over the snow-covered hills to a glorious "sugar ball," the great celebration of the maple sugar harvest. Naughty, sullen children receive their just rewards—like young cousin Charley who cries wolf once too often, is stung by a swarm of angry bees, and nearly dies from the attack. Wilder would carefully mine these and other real-life experiences, then spin them like gold into "Laura's" quintessential frontier fairytale.

Wilder claimed she wrote *Little House in the Big Woods* to preserve her father's stories; in fact, she preserved her own. The domestic detail she recorded in her first novel captivated readers and would become a recurring leitmotif in all her writing. In the book, as in life, Laura and Mary each had a climbing tree of their own, and they spent countless hours playing in and under the branches. Mary's tree was lightning scarred. But for all the romance in which she wrapped Laura's life in the Big Woods, Wilder's lost world could be exhausting, unflinching, and harsh. When the big butcher knife appears in the fall, Laura runs and hides and plugs her ears. She doesn't want to hear the pig scream again. From very early childhood, children on the frontier were expected to assist with dirty, physically demanding, and time-consuming tasks. Young children of both genders fed and watered livestock, picked fruit and berries, weeded gardens, hauled water in buckets to the house, collected kindling, and helped clean dead fish, birds, and game. Children as young as five were often placed in charge of their younger siblings, taxed with keeping them safe from falls, open fires, wells, snakes, and each other. Girls performed the daily round of domestic chores. They swept, sewed, boiled laundry, washed dishes, made beds, collected cooking grease and ash for soap-making, and, in an era before packaged or processed foods, helped with the never-ending task of food preparation and preservation.

Western historian Glenda Riley points out that because highly skilled frontierswomen processed the raw material produced in the field and on the farm, they were critical to the frontier economy. Girls were expected to learn by doing, as quickly and thoroughly as possible. "By the time a frontier girl was of marriage age," Riley explains, "her greatest personal assets centered around her abilities as a domestic manufacturer. She was rated as a worker in the same way that men were graded as 'providers' . . . Mates, then, were chosen in large part as economic partners. It was considered a bonus if they were also compatible. For the typical frontier couple, their wedding day marked not only the beginning of a shared life but the beginning of a shared business venture as well."[15]

A Home in the West: The 1860s • 13

Maple sugar-making, vividly described in *Little House in the Big Woods,* was a reliable way to generate cash in the boom-and-bust Civil War economy and post-war years. In 1932, Wilder's contemporary Angela Haste Favell recalled events from her own childhood in the Wisconsin woods that bear an uncannily similarity to Wilder's experiences:

> My father took a homestead in the midst of a forest. He had to cut down trees to clear a space to build the cabin. We lived in a tent while building it. By the time he had the house built and a barn to shelter our two cows and four oxen and chickens, winter and deep snow were with us. Winter brought an addition to our already large family . . . There was no work to be had. As everyone was too poor to hire, they did their own work. Father, though, thought himself lucky to have a good many pine trees on the homestead, and with the help of my two brothers, 12 and 14 years old, he cut down the trees and made them into shingles for which he found ready sale . . . He also found he had over 1000 sugar maple trees on the place, which he tapped in the spring, and, with the help of the older children, he boiled down the sap into sirup and sugar. They sold these products at a nearby village and this helped to keep the wolf at bay . . . I loved to stand in the maple forest and listen to the drip, drip, drip of the sap of 1000 trees dripping into buckets and listen to the harsh call of the blue jay, the drumming of the woodpecker on some dead trees and the friendly notes of the chickadees.[16]

The impact of the Civil War on the Ingalls family, both economic and personal, is alluded to only obliquely in Wilder's novels. Charles did not enlist in the war; two of his younger brothers volunteered at the very end of the conflict in 1865. Clearly for white settlers in Wisconsin in 1862, there were far more pressing military issues than the remote battlefields of the south, issues with broader implications for Wilder's formative beliefs and later work. In the late summer of 1862, with local militias decimated by army enlistments and the threat of conscription, the Dakota War exploded in Minnesota, sending shock waves throughout the entire region. The war— generally referred to as the "Sioux Uprising" at the time, a euphemism that underscored the state and federal governments' denial of any responsibility for the outbreak of hostilities—and its bloody aftermath coincided with the Ingalls's removal to the Minnesota–Wisconsin border.

Angela Haste Favell's narrative sheds light on how quickly rumor and panic gripped white settlers in the region, even those as far from the front as Wisconsin and Iowa.

> For a while we didn't know but we would all be scalped. There were a good many Indians roaming around, hunting and fishing, but they were always friendly. Now, they acted differently. They held powwows and war dances, and

everybody thought they were getting ready to massacre the white people. The Indian agent found that he couldn't control them.

It was a rather sorry time, as there were no men left to protect their families. It got to be so serious that the Indian agent sent a messenger around to the homesteads, telling people to take as few household goods as they could possibly get along with, and go to Waupaca, the county seat of that county. There was a temporary fort there and a company of soldiers who hadn't gone to the front . . . I will always remember it.[17]

As would Caroline Ingalls. Her memories of Indian conflict and Indian removal would play a defining role in the writing of *Little House on the Prairie*, Wilder's most dramatic and controversial work.

The Dakota War raged for a month and a half in the late summer and early fall of 1862, reducing parts of southern Minnesota to a smoking cornfield. Treaty violations, graft, lies, and the late arrival of annuity payments had pushed the starving Dakota to one last, defiant effort to drive off the white newcomers and take back their land. By the time the war ended, hundreds of encroaching white settlers lay dead. Assessments of the death toll on both sides vary greatly, but one recent estimate indicates that if the same percentage of Minnesota's population had been killed today, 15,000 people would have died in the conflict.[18] Refugees, some of them orphaned children, raced east to flee the violence; they poured into the capital of St. Paul, not far from Pepin. It is likely that tales of these events, later referred to as "the Minnesota massacres" in *Little House on the Prairie*, left a psychic scar on Caroline Ingalls and influenced Wilder's own beliefs, which may account for the depiction of Ma's fear and loathing of all Indians and Wilder's more-conflicted twentieth-century perspective. Caroline was a reader. Newspapers and periodicals of the time carried sensational headlines and graphic illustrations of white settlers defending their homes in isolated communities like German-settled New Ulm, followed by lurid "captivity narratives," long a popular staple of American literature.

For the Dakota, the consequences of defeat were catastrophic. On the day after Christmas 1862, thirty-eight Dakota warriors were marched through the streets of Mankato to a massive platform gallows specially designed to accommodate their number. It was the largest mass execution in American history, although paradoxically (and despite vehement public outcry for vengeance) due to President Abraham Lincoln's politically risky executive decision to reprieve 265 condemned Dakota men from execution, it was also the nation's largest mass clemency.[19] Eyewitness accounts of the execution ran nationwide, including a gruesome report in *The New York Times*. While some surviving Dakota braves and their families who had been rounded up were placed in a military internment camp at Fort

Snelling, state government officials began the process of commandeering Dakota reserve lands, opening the land to homesteaders and expelling Indians from the state. In 1863, the Dakota were removed west to what is now South Dakota. The Dakota Diaspora was only the most recent in a long history of forced removal. The Winnebago of Wisconsin were also removed to what is now South Dakota following the Dakota War, where conditions proved so harsh that most of the tribe quit South Dakota for a reservation in Nebraska in 1865. In 1874, when the Homestead Act was extended to Native Americans, many Winnebago returned to Wisconsin and took homesteads in the central portion of the state. The removal of the Osages from Kansas, the organizing theme of dispossession in Wilder's third novel *Little House on the Prairie*, occurred seven years after the Dakota War of 1862.

For the Ingalls, who had witnessed the Dakota Diaspora as it actually occurred, a valuable lesson had been learned. Forced Indian removal meant military protection for new settlers in previously remote or inhospitable locations and the immediate expansion of prime homestead land, something in increasingly short supply in the decade following the Civil War. At the end of the Civil War, thousands of veterans returned home, repacked their kits, and headed west in search of "free land." The Homestead Act of 1862 granted 160 acres (one quarter section) of federal land to anyone who had not taken up arms against the United States government, was over 21 (including freed slaves and women), or was the head of a household. Homesteaders who resided on the land for five years and improved it were granted title for the cost of the filing fee. The Homestead Act followed The Preemption Act of 1841, which had allowed settlers who were already living on public domain lands—technically squatters—the right of first purchase, usually at $1.25 per acre. Although both acts had resulted in widespread fraud and abuse by land and railroad speculators, they were also responsible for the frantic "get there first" approach among settlers on the frontier. For many returning soldiers, immigrants, day laborers, widows, second sons, the adventurous, and, as was frequently the case, less-experienced farmers, the lure of "free land" was impossible to resist.

However, at least initially, Charles Ingalls was not among them. Although Laura later stated that her parents had lost all their savings in a bank failure after the Civil War (and there were several contemporary bank failures in Pepin Country), when Charles Ingalls decided to leave Wisconsin in 1868, he felt secure enough to buy land, instead of choosing to break raw ground as a homesteader. In the winter or spring of 1868, he and Henry Quiner met with a traveling salesman representing the Missouri railroad and land speculator, Adamantine Johnson.[20] Johnson had fallen on hard times and needed to raise quick capital. Charles and Henry Quiner obliged him: each signed a promissory note agreeing to purchase 80 acres of Johnson's land in

Chariton County, Missouri, for $900. They bought the land sight unseen. As Laura later admitted, albeit with grudging affection, her father was "inclined to be reckless."[21]

Charles immediately agreed to sell his Pepin property on installments to Gustaf Gustafson, one of the many Swedes who lived up Lost Creek. On paper, Charles made a profit on the transaction. He then loaded his wagon, tied the billowing canvas like a hoopskirt over the top, and drove his young family 400 miles south to their new farm near Rothville, Missouri. It would have been an exhausting journey with small children, lasting several weeks, culminating in an unfamiliar destination and a strange social environment. Laura was too young to remember her family's brief sojourn in Missouri. She omitted the move in her novels and little is known of the time her family spent there or why they left so abruptly. In 1868, much of Chariton County was raw prairie riddled with swampland, better suited to cattle than to crops.[22] The railroad had bypassed the county seat of Keytesville (near the site of the Ingalls's new property), one of several blows to the local economy. Charles and Henry Quiner arrived too late in the season to plant a crop. They may have counted on carpentry and day labor to carry them through the winter, but found no work. However, it seems more likely that Charles suddenly realized he could not afford to pay for the land. Not long after the Ingalls left Pepin, Gustafson stopped making payments on the Ingalls's Big Woods property. Charles needed cash for seed, staples, livestock, and his promissory note to Adamantine Johnson. He may have made a new calculation, based on his deteriorating finances. If he was willing to break raw land—no small feat without sons or extended family to assist—and if he was convinced he could "prove up" on his claim in five years, then 160 acres were his for the cost of the filing fee. Every year, thousands of homesteaders made the same bet and lost. But for Charles Ingalls, now far from his Wisconsin home, spending $900 he didn't have to purchase 80-acres of swampy Missouri farm ground he could not afford to plant probably no longer looked like an option or a bargain. After a year in Missouri, Charles Ingalls and Henry Quiner called it quits. Henry took his family and returned to his wooded acreage in Wisconsin, leaving Charles to pursue his quest for a home in the West.

Whatever his primary motivation, when Charles Ingalls left Missouri, he immediately joined the horde of white settlers swarming over the Kansas border, building cabins and staking out claims on the Osage Diminished Reserve, a highly fertile tract of land belonging to the Osage Indians. By 1870, the Ingalls were living in Rutland Township, Montgomery County, Kansas—well inside the boundaries of the Diminished Reserve—about thirteen miles southwest of the town of Independence.[23] There, despite the general lack of trees, Charles culled timber (all of which legally belonged to the Osages) from a nearby creek to build a new house, installed glass windows, planted a garden, dug a well, sat down with his fiddle, and proceeded to wait out the forced removal of the Osages. The Ingalls were squatters on the Osage Diminished Reserve, poised to preempt or homestead land the instant the Osage Indians were removed from Kansas to "Indian Territory," in what is now Oklahoma. The Sturges Treaty of 1868, which provided for the sale of the Osage Diminished Reserved and the removal of the Osages south of the Kansas border, had been negotiated but never ratified, and the Osages were understandably outraged by the host of newcomers streaming onto their land and poaching their resources. Thanks to railroad land grants, private holdings, school lands and other set-asides, the most desirable land for homesteading in Kansas was no longer plentiful. Charles had a powerful incentive to stay in Montgomery, Kansas, legally or not. In *Little House on the Prairie,* Wilder depicted Pa's decision to settle within the bounds of the Osage Diminished Reserve as an inadvertent error and costly mistake, carefully explaining how he had accidently selected land just three miles inside the unmarked border of the reserve. However, the claim that Charles located the family's new homestead on Osage reserve land entirely by accident is simply not credible; all he had to do was ask the neighbors. Rutland Township was rapidly filling with land-hungry settlers when the Ingalls arrived, so much so that the frustrated 1870 census-taker specifically noted that he was refusing to record property values on his census form for newcomers like the Ingalls because "the lands belonged to the Osage Indians and the settlers had no title to said lands."[24]

For many young readers, the events Wilder narrates in *Little House on the Prairie* provide a first introduction to Plains Indian culture. Consequently, the book has come under considerable scrutiny for its characterization and description of the Osages. Wilder, who was barely three years old when the Ingalls lived in Kansas, relied almost entirely on family oral history to reconstruct the story of their time there. Wilder was compelled to revise her own personal history and skew the timeline of her childhood when she wrote *Little House on the Prairie.* This confusion, compounded by Wilder's unwavering insistence that all of her books were "true," historical and strictly autobiographical, led biographers to investigate similar discrepancies between Wilder's life and art. In the *Little House* series of novels, *Little House on the Prairie* is the chronological sequel to *Little House in the Big Woods.* It is the Kansas chapter of the Ingalls's story and it takes place *after* the incidents Wilder described in *Little House in the Big Woods.* In terms of Wilder's own life story however, the events she narrated in *Little House on the Prairie* actually occurred *before* the events she recalled and described in *Little House in the Big Woods.* When she wrote *Little House in the Big Woods,* Wilder did not foresee the demand for her further adventures. To

18 • Laura Ingalls Wilder: American Writer on the Prairie

resolve this discrepancy in the sequel, she advanced the age of her heroine by two years. Wilder's "Indian story" as she and others generally referred to the manuscript version of *Little House on the Prairie* while she was drafting it, tells a darker story for an older child and it is set against a backdrop of fear, violence, and the threat of dispossession (of both the Osages and the Ingalls).

In Wilder's writing, the Ingalls were among the newcomers—"oppressive trespassers" in the words of federal Indian Agent Isaac Gibson[25]—who hoped to preserve peaceful relations with the Osages. Considered progressive for its depiction of Indians in 1935, many critics find *Little House on the Prairie* offensive and unreadable today. Ma's fear and loathing of all Indians—an aversion, according to Wilder's aunt Martha Carpenter, that she and Caroline had developed in childhood[26]—is contrasted with Pa and Laura's more conflicted views.

Although she was a diligent researcher, carefully fact-checking names, dates, and locations, Wilder herself seemed perplexed by specific details regarding the family's time in Kansas, including the actual site of their home and why they abandoned it. By the time she wrote the novel, no family members were still alive who could verify the sequence of events. In *Little House on the Prairie,* the Ingalls decide to abandon their new house and claim because they are threatened with removal by federal troops. In the novel, Wilder mistakenly located her family forty miles southwest of Independence, Kansas—which would have placed them squarely, if inadvertently, in what was then "Indian Territory" and is now Oklahoma. The inconsistency between her memory and her family's oral history must have piqued Wilder's curiosity. Before the publication of *Little House on the Prairie* in 1935, she went searching for the remains of the cabin site, but was unable to find it. She was looking in the wrong place. In fact, the family did settle on Indian land—and deliberately—but in Kansas.

By the time the Ingalls left Missouri, crossed the Verdigris River and, with Caroline's dogged assistance, began heaving logs to erect their newest little house, tensions between the Osages and the encroaching settlers had intensified. For the hungry Osages, the situation was no longer tolerable. When they returned from their disappointing summer buffalo hunt to their camps along the river, the Osages encountered hundreds of newly-arrived squatters busily cutting timber, erecting cabins, tilling soil, trapping animals, and shooting game on Osage land. As was the case in Minnesota in 1862, the annuity payments owed to the Indians by the federal government were also in arrears.

Against this historic backdrop of disorder and unrest, Wilder introduces the Osage Chief Soldat du Chene. Wilder spent a considerable amount of time and effort trying to find the name of the Osage chief her father attributed to saving all the white settlers in the area by his refusal to go to war, but

A Home in the West: The 1860s • 19

the name she was given by a member of the Oklahoma Historical Society's staff was clearly incorrect. In her autobiographical memoir "Pioneer Girl," Wilder provides a stripped-down account of the removal of the Osages, which she greatly expanded and dramatized in *Little House on the Prairie:* "In the spring, the Indians came back. I sat on the doorstep one day and watched them pass on their path which went right by the door. As far away as I could see, they were coming, riding their ponies. First came the big Indians. On black ponies and gray ponies and spotted ponies and yellow ponies and red ponies they rode past. Behind them came the women and children, riding too. Then, as far as the eye could see, in both directions on the flat land, were Indians riding one behind the other."[27]

Despite the undertone of fear and sadness, Wilder packs the narrative of her childhood in Kansas with vanishing details of domestic life on the frontier. Even on the sweltering prairie with no one to notice, Ma feels compelled to keep up appearances and iron all their clothing on the wagon seat. Wilder relates how pioneers constructed a homestead cabin and provides a myriad of detail: how to improvise a roof with the wagon canvas; how to peg a door, fit a latch, and make a windlass for the well; how to build a chimney out of rocks and mud. In Laura's lost world, the gift of a tin cup and a candy cane makes for an overwhelming Christmas. Children sleep on sacks of "dry, clean, dead grasses," then spend their days exploring an Edenic wilderness. But it is also a world in which children do not speak unless spoken to and quickly learn that uncomfortable or provocative questions terminate conversation. Ma instantly shuts down any discussion of the "Minnesota massacres"—even among adults—by immediately changing the subject. She flatly refuses to define the word *massacre* for Laura. After Laura repeatedly asks Pa if the government will make the Indians move west, Pa finally answers her:

> "When white settlers come into a country, the Indians have to move on. The government is going to move these Indians west, any time now. That's why we're here, Laura. White people are going to settle all this country, and we get the best land because we get here first and take our pick. Now do you understand?"

> "Yes, Pa," Laura said. "But, Pa, I thought this was Indian Territory. Won't it make the Indians mad to have to . . ."

> "No more questions, Laura," Pa said, firmly. "Go to sleep."[28]

Sleep proved hard to come by in Kansas. In both "Pioneer Girl," Wilder's unpublished biographical memoir and in *Little House on the Prairie,* Wilder records nights of blind terror caused by the sound of Indian war-cries and drumming as the Osages held their councils. "A great many Indians had come and camped by the creek, and in the nights we would hear them screeching and screaming. It was a far more frightening sound than the wolves' howling. Pa said the Indians were having their war dances."[29] Recent research supports the location of a Claremont Band Osage camp close to the Ingalls's cabin. The cabin's location just yards from an important Osage trail probably accounts for the family's frequent encounters with Osage hunters.[30]

In Wilder's novel of the period, the departure of the Osages on their semi-annual buffalo hunt provided Laura with the rare opportunity to explore an unoccupied Osage camp with Mary and her father, where the girls collected colorful beads. It is possible that the event took place in real life. Pioneer children were usually diverted from home during childbirth. On August 3, 1870, Laura and Mary likely arrived home from some relatively remote location only to discover their mother in bed with a new baby sister, Caroline Celestia. Dr. George Tann and/or a neighboring matron are the most likely candidates to have delivered the frail new baby in Laura and Mary's absence. A homeopathic doctor, George Tann would later establish a reservation hospital to serve Indians in Oklahoma. In *Little House on the Prairie*, Dr. Tann is noted as the first black American Laura Ingalls had ever seen. Although African American homesteaders had begun migrating to Kansas immediately after the Civil War to escape racism and oppression, in 1870 when the Ingalls lived in Kansas, their numbers were still small. By 1879 (two years after President Rutherford B. Hayes ended Reconstruction and withdrew federal troops from the South), their numbers had swelled into the thousands. Members of the great black migration to Kansas in 1879 became known as the Exodusters.

Childbirth on the isolated prairie was always painful, frequently deadly, and rarely mentioned (along with other taboo subjects like sexuality, pregnancy, menstruation, prostitution, illegitimacy, and privies). Even diapers were considered unmentionable, although on the wagon trail where countless young women gave birth, it appears new mothers simply scraped used diapers, air dried them and reused them. Three years after Carrie Ingalls's birth, Mormon convert Emma Batchelor Lee (seventeenth wife of John D. Lee) broke ranks with her sisters and gave a blunt account of her own, fairly common, experience of frontier childbirth:

> (She) was alone with her five children when she realized her sixth was about to be born—several weeks earlier than predicted. Instructing her eldest son, Billy, to ask his younger brother to take the three youngest children out "under the tamarack bushes by the corral," well out of earshot of the house, she then explained to Billy that he mustn't be scared if she made a noise since "that always goes with it." After folding a pad and securing it to the bed with safety pins, she

got out scissors, string, and a bottle of olive oil; heated a teakettle of water on the stove; and browned flour in the oven. Longing for the company and assistance of "sweet competent Rachel," one of her husband's senior wives, who had helped her through the birth of her twins, she "prayed she wouldn't die" knowing that "with all those children playing happily outside, she MUST NOT DIE."

In time, the baby was born, and with the help of her son she tied and cut the umbilical cord, then rubbed the newborn all over with olive oil, sprinkled parched flour on the navel, and pinned on the "belly-band." Billy then carried the placenta outside in the chamber pot and buried it—far from his siblings who were still unaware of the activities in the house. Upon his return, his mother asked him to write his baby sister's birth date—October 25, 1873—"in the Book," then had him invite the younger children in to meet the newest member of the family.[31]

Unlike many pioneers, Charles Ingalls spent money on doctors for his family willingly and without hesitation. Dr. Tann probably visited the Ingalls's home a second time, not long after Carrie's birth, bearing bitter quinine when the Ingalls were struck down by malaria, the debilitating "fever and ague" of frontier life. Spread by mosquitoes, malaria often left entire families like the Ingalls incapacitated by severe fever and alternating chills. For those who survived, the uncontrollable shaking and other symptoms of the disease could persist for weeks, which in turn jeopardized planting and harvest schedules and the very survival of the homestead itself. But despite poverty, illness, and uncertainty, many of Wilder's memories of the period are joyous, especially Christmas. Long summer evenings spent out of doors resulted in some of her most lyrical writing. The evocative moonlight duet between Pa and "the nightingale" is just one example:

Everything was silent, listening to the nightingale's song. The bird sang on and on. The cool wind moved over the prairie and the song was round and clear above the grasses' whispering. The sky was like a bowl of light overturned on the flat black land.

The song ended. No one moved or spoke. Laura and Mary were quiet, Ma and Pa sat motionless. Only the wind stirred and the grasses sighed. Then Pa lifted his fiddle to his shoulder and gently touched the bow to the strings. A few notes fell like clear water into the stillness. A pause, and Pa began to play the nightingale's song. The nightingale answered him. The nightingale began to sing again. It was singing with Pa's fiddle.

When the strings were silent, the nightingale went on singing. When it paused, the fiddle called to it and it sang again. The bird and the fiddle were talking to each other in the cool night under the moon.[32]

It is a passage that underscored the mythos of the American West for generations of readers, written in simple direct prose and yet so poetic that it still retains the power to seduce. Ironically, the passage has been used to question Wilder's memory as inauthentic or to discount the experience as an "artistic interpolation" because the nightingale is a European bird, not native to Kansas.[33] Wilder, however, is nothing if not a Westerner, and in this case her authenticity is bolstered by her word choice. On the Great Plains, the "nightingale" is another name for the Northern Mockingbird, a bird known for its intelligence, mimicry, and complicated songs. Although there are instances of Wilder suppressing, supplementing, or rearranging the facts of her life to fit her fiction, this is not an instance in which she appears to have blurred the line between literal and artistic truth.

In 1937, Wilder gave a speech at a Detroit book fair in which she provided an example of the type of material she omitted from *Little House on the Prairie* on the basis of its unsuitability for children, even though Wilder admitted she had wanted to tell the story and had been well aware of it when she was a child. The story throws light on frontier crime and the real dangers travelers faced, often from their own ranks, by transporting every dime they owned on their bodies or in wagons loaded with goods. Wilder chose to tell her sedate audience the ripping story of the Bloody Benders, a serial-killing family of innkeepers on the road between the Ingalls's cabin and the town of Independence.

> We stopped there [the Bender's inn] on the way to the Little House, while Pa watered the horses and brought us all a drink from the well near the door of the house. I saw Kate Bender standing in the doorway. We did not go in because we could not afford to stop at a tavern.
>
> On his trip to Independence to sell his furs, Pa stopped again for water, but did not go in for the same reason as before.
>
> There were Kate Bender and two men, her brothers, in the family and their tavern was the only place for travelers to stop on the road south from Independence. People disappeared on that road. Leaving Independence and going south they were never heard from again. It was thought they were killed by Indians but no bodies were ever found.
>
> Then it was noticed that the Benders' garden was always freshly plowed but never planted. People wondered. And then a man came from the east looking for his brother, who was missing.
>
> He made up a party in Independence and they followed the road south, but when they came to the Bender place there was no one there. There were signs of hurried departure and they searched the place.

The front room was divided by a calico curtain against which the dining table stood. On the curtain back of the table were stains about as high as the head of a man when seated. Behind the curtain was a trap door in the floor and beside it lay a heavy hammer.

In the cellar underneath was the body of a man whose head had been crushed by the hammer. It appeared that he had been seated at the table back to the curtain and had been struck from behind it. A grave was partly dug in the garden with a shovel close by. The posse searched the garden and dug up human bones and bodies. One body was that of a little girl who had been buried alive with her murdered parents. The garden was truly a grave-yard kept plowed so it would show no signs.[34]

Wilder went on to suggest that her father might have been a member of the vigilante group that went hunting for the Benders, but in this instance she was mistaken: the Ingalls left Kansas well over a year before the Benders' disappearance. She also neglected to mention, but must have known, that two of the Benders' victims were her family's closest neighbors in Kansas.[35] Thirty-year-old George Longcor (also Loncher) had only recently buried his young wife and infant son when he stopped at the Bender's inn with his surviving toddler, Mary Ann. Both bodies were found in the Benders' garden. Searchers, gagging at the scene, indicated that Mary Ann had been buried alive.[36] Although Wilder omitted the story, it suggests just how much of her family's oral tradition regarding their time in Kansas had been saved, preserved, and passed down, as well as just how much specificity—like the names of Soldat du Chene[37] or George Longcor—had been lost.

Wilder was no Pollyanna. She would write unflinchingly of poverty, hardship, illness, and fear. She described her family as "fatalists,"[38] who accepted setbacks with a minimum of fuss and simply did their best to carry on. She had limited patience with despair, surrender, or complaint. All her life, Wilder took comfort in her family and viewed her childhood home as a source of strength and inspiration. At the Detroit book fair, after referring to the Benders and to the death of a family of children in a terrible blizzard, she added:

Sister Mary and I knew of these things but someway we were shielded from the full terror of them. Although we knew them to be true they seemed unreal to us for Ma was always there serene and quiet and Pa with his fiddle and his songs.[39]

But for the Ingalls in the spring of 1871, fatalism was clearly in order, as was the family's customary decision to just get on with it. Although in both her adult autobiography and *Little House on the Prairie* Wilder attributed her father's motive for leaving Kansas to his conviction that federal soldiers were about to remove him from Indian Territory, the historical record is less straightforward. Federal removal is the story Wilder remembered and it is likely the account her parents repeated over the years. And, in fact, troops were in the region for a variety of purposes: to keep order, to remove squatters from the Cherokee Strip (just about three miles south of the Ingalls cabin), and to facilitate the removal of the Osages. But by conflating the threatened removal of the Ingalls family from "their" land with the forced removal of the Osages from theirs, Wilder invited comparisons between the two disparate stories and united the Ingalls and the Osage Indians as victims of a common oppressor—the federal government.

Anti-federal views, shared to some degree by all members of the Ingalls family, have a long history in the West. New Western historian Patricia Nelson Limerick provides context:

> Western emigrants understood not just that they were taking risks but also that risks led to rewards. When nature or natives interrupted the progression from risk to reward, the Westerner felt aggrieved . . . Blaming nature or blaming human beings, those looking for a scapegoat had a third, increasingly popular target: the federal government. Since it was the government's responsibility to control the Indians, and, in a number of ways increasing into the twentieth century, to control nature, Westerners found it easy to shift the direction of their resentment. Attacked by Indians or threatened by nature, aggrieved Westerners took to pointing accusingly at the federal government. In effect, Westerners centralized their resentment much more efficiently than the federal government centralized its powers.[40]

However, it seems that the primary reason for the Ingalls's abrupt departure from Kansas was far less dramatic and political than federal intervention. In 1871, Charles received a letter from Gustaf Gustafson in Wisconsin. Gustafson could not afford to pay for the land he had purchased from Charles in 1868. He wanted to return the property to Charles and he wanted Charles to take possession immediately.[41] For the second time in less than three years, the Ingalls packed their wagon. They relinquished their little house with the extravagant glass window to the tall grass and the wolves. In her novel, Wilder said a lonely nightingale sang them out of Kansas as they turned their backs on the frontier and reluctantly rode away.[42]

NOTES

1. Rose Wilder Lane Papers, Herbert Hoover Presidential Library, West Branch, Iowa. LIW Series, Box 13. Correspondence, LIW to RWL, 1937.
2. Donald Zochert, *Laura: The Life of Laura Ingalls Wilder* (New York, NY: Avon Books, 1977), 104.

A Home in the West: The 1860s · 25

3. Kathryn Adam, "Laura, Ma, Mary, Carrie and Grace: Western Women Portrayed by Laura Ingalls Wilder," in *The Women's West*, eds. Susan Armitage and Elizabeth Jameson (Tulsa: University of Oklahoma Press, 1987), 101.

4. Civil War "Widows' Pension" File, (WC10479) Joseph C. Quiner, National Archives.

5. Laura Ingalls Wilder Family Correspondence, 1861–1919, Wisconsin Historical Society manuscript collection Stout SC 142.

6. Usually cited as Henry Newton Quiner, Caroline's father is listed as "Henry Newcomb Quiner" on his March 1843 Wisconsin land patent. Bureau of Land Management General Land Records.

7. *Daily National Pilot,* Buffalo; Nov. 22, 1845.

8. Lane Papers. LIW to RWL, 1936 Correspondence. Folder 19.

9. Lane Papers. Martha Quiner Carpenter to LIW, 10–9–1925.

10. See *Dictionary of Wisconsin Biography,* "E. B. Quiner" (Madison, WI: Wisconsin Historical Society Press, 1960), 295.

11. John E. Miller, *Becoming Laura Ingalls Wilder* (Columbia, MO: University of Missouri Press, 1998), 17.

12. Zochert, 15.

13. "Let's Visit Mrs. Wilder" interview with John F. Case, *Ruralist* editor, February 1918, reproduced in Stephen W. Hines, ed., *Laura Ingalls Wilder, Farm Journalist: Writings from the Ozarks* (Columbia, MO: University of Missouri Press, 2007), 3–4.

14. LIW, *Little House in the Big Woods* (New York: Harper & Bros., 1953), 3.

15. Riley, Glenda. *Frontierswomen, the Iowa Experience* (Ames, IA: Iowa State University Press, 1981), 57.

16. Angela Haste Favell. "A Girl Pioneer in the Wisconsin Wilderness," *Milwaukee Journal,* Aug. 7, 1932.

17. Ibid.

18. Curt Brown. "In the Footsteps of Little Crow," Part 1, *Star Tribune,* August 15, 2012.

19. Paul Finkelman. "I Could Not Afford to Hang Men for Votes," *William Mitchell Law Review,* 2013, 39, no. 2, 405–49.

20. Zochert, p. 23.

21. LIW, Detroit Book Fair Speech, 1937 in William Anderson, ed., *Little House Sampler* (Lincoln, MO: University of Nebraska Press, 1988), 220–21.

22. *History of Howard and Chariton Counties, Missouri: Written and Compiled from the Most Official Authentic and Private Sources, Including a History of Its Townships, Towns, and Villages, Together with a Condensed History of Missouri* (St. Louis: National Historical, 1883), 378.

23. 1870 US Federal Census, Rutland Township, Montgomery, Kansas.

24. Ibid.

25. Penny T. Lisenmayer, "Kansas Settlers on the Osage Diminished Reserve," *Kansas History: A Journal of the Central Plains* 24, no. 3 (2001), 168–85.

26. Lane Papers, Martha Quiner Carpenter to LIW. Sept. 2, 1925.

27. Lane Papers, LIW's "Pioneer Girl" manuscript, Brandt Draft, 5. (Hereafter, LIW, "Pioneer Girl").

28. LIW, *Little House on the Prairie* (New York: Harper & Bros., 1953), 237.

29. LIW, "Pioneer Girl," 3.

30. Linsenmayer, 175.

31. Linda Peavy and Ursula Smith, *Pioneer Women: The Lives of Women on the Frontier* (New York: Smithmark Publishers, 1996), 77.

32. LIW, *Little House on the Prairie,* 70.

33. Anita Fellman, *Little House, Long Shadow* (Columbia, MO: University of Missouri Press, 2008), 87.

34. LIW, Detroit Book Fair Speech, 1937, in *Little House Sampler,* 220–21.

26 • Laura Ingalls Wilder: American Writer on the Prairie

35. 1870 Federal Census, Rutland Township, Montgomery County, Kansas.
36. David McCormick. "The Bloody Benders Grim Harvest," *Wild West Magazine*, March 30, 2012.
37. One overlooked candidate for the much-debated "Soldat du Chene" is Wa Tse ki he ka or "Star Chief," also known as Governor Joe. Star Chief was appointed Governor of all the Osages in 1869 by Indian Agent Isaac Gibson. See Louis F. Burns, *A History of the Osage People* (Tuscaloosa, AL: University of Alabama Press, 2004), 55, 134, and passim.
38. Lane Papers, Box 13. Undated letter LIW to RWL.
39. LIW, *A Little House Sampler*, 222.
40. Patricia Nelson Limerick, *The Legacy of Conquest: The Unbroken Past of the American West* (New York, NY: Norton, 1987), 44–45.
41. Zochert, 46.
42. LIW, *Little House on the Prairie*, 326.

CHAPTER **2**

WANDERING THE WEST: THE 1870S

During the summer of their first visitation, the demons left behind them evil enough to pollute a whole continent . . . often the locust clouds would coming drifting across the sun, very much like streamers of snow, floating lazily by for days on end; then, all of a sudden, as if overcome by their own neglect, they would swoop down, dashing and spreading like an angry flood, slicing and shearing, cutting with greedy teeth, laying waste to every foot of the field they lighted in.

Ole Edvart Rolvaag

After three ineffectual years and one long elliptical journey, the Ingalls returned to friends and family in Wisconsin. But the Big Woods would not be home for long. Times were tough in Pepin. The town's initial logging boom had passed and the economic center of the area had shifted across the river to Lake City, Minnesota, which had the better boat landing and new rail connections.[1] Over time, the increase in settlers had reduced the amount of game in the woods. This was a serious drawback to hunters such as Charles Ingalls, who depended on venison, bear meat, and wildfowl to feed their families. In October 1873, Charles sold his land in Pepin County for the second time and made a handsome profit on the $1,000 transaction.[2] He was actively planning another move west, this time with his elder brother Peter. Peter intended to rent a farm in southern Minnesota, near the Zumbro River; Charles was moving farther on, to the naked, black-dirt prairies of western Minnesota. In order to cross Lake Pepin before ice-out, they planned to leave Wisconsin in February—an unlikely month for wagon travel and open camping, but necessary if Charles and Peter had any chance to plant that spring. Their departure date was delayed when

28 • Laura Ingalls Wilder: American Writer on the Prairie

the young Ingalls cousins, all living together in Peter's house in preparation for their move west, contracted scarlet fever. When, as an adult, Laura wrote about this period in her family's history, she remembered it as a tense time for everyone. As Caroline and her sister Eliza nursed eight sick children, all sprawled together in makeshift beds on the floor, Charles and Peter anxiously toe-tapped the spongy ice along the shoreline. The children recovered just in time for their parents to drive teams across the booming ice. Laura recalled being bundled into the wagon and that her ears hurt so badly she was unable to play with her cousins.[3] In general, pioneers dreaded crossing frozen lakes and rivers, knowing that any miscalculation of the thickness or stability of the ice could potentially claim their wagons, their teams, all their worldly possessions, or even their lives. As the Ingalls drove their creaking wagons across the lake on the treacherous ice road, over the snowy embankment, and through the streets of Lake City on the far side of the Mississippi River, they must have been aware it was unlikely that they would ever see their parents or the woods of Wisconsin again.

The Minnesota winter proved too harsh for travel. Charles and Peter located an abandoned cabin, moved in, and waited for the thaw. They parted company when Peter's family branched off for the farm near South Troy. Charles drove on alone for nearly two hundred miles, paralleling the brand new railroad tracks that ran due west to the depot town soon to be known as Walnut Grove. Laura would later portray the journey as an extended camping trip. The Ingalls would stop for the night by a sheltered creek bottom, feed and water their horses, collect sticks for a campfire, and cook dinner in an iron spider set over the flames. Laura and Mary would fall asleep listening to the evening bird calls and the sound of the Ingalls's hardworking horses, David and Sampson, crunching oats on the opposite side of the canvas. Sometimes, Charles took out his fiddle and played it under the stars. They passed Indian burial mounds and the ruins of several structures destroyed in the Dakota War of 1862, but no Sioux—nearly all of whom had been removed in the aftermath of the war. There was no road to follow west of New Ulm, where some of the fiercest fighting of the Dakota War had taken place, just wagon tracks in the broken grass. One night, Laura started bolt upright from sleep at an amazing and unrecognizable sound. It was "a clear, wonderful call" and it carried for miles over the prairie. Caroline called to Laura in the twilight and told her to hurry if she wanted to see the source. She caught a glimpse of the first locomotive she had ever seen as the train disappeared with the engine's fading whistle. "We were all silent, looking at them," Wilder later wrote.[4]

Although the first transcontinental railroad had been completed five years earlier, on May 10, 1869, in Promontory, Utah, when the "golden spike" finally linked Omaha to Sacramento, the Union Pacific's tracks lay

Wandering the West: The 1870s • 29

roughly three hundred miles south of the Ingalls's final destination. The transcontinental railroad had been built in large part to accommodate the rush of settlers moving west with their families and supplies (at the same time providing rapid return service for western goods and raw materials). The Ingalls were typical of the majority of farm families in the 1870s; they traveled west by wagon. If feasible, many pioneer families loaded their wagons onto barges and "took the river route" for at least part of the long journey, to save time and expense. Depending on the destination, even the expense of provisioning the trip could prove prohibitive. When Pamelia Fergus of Little Falls, Minnesota (who had been living on her own for four years with four children before her husband finally summoned them to the Montana Territory), set out by wagon, she was instructed by her husband to purchase "600 pounds of flour, 300 of meal, 50 of beans, 100 of rice, 50 of cheese, 50 of butter, and 400 of sugar, plus two barrels of crackers, 20 gallons of syrup, and specified amounts of black tea, coffee, salt, bacon, ham, dried beef, codfish, and dried fruits and vegetables."[5] Many ingenious pioneer women did not purchase butter. If they kept a cow on the trail, they would milk it in the morning, skim the cream, pour the cream into a churn, and let the all-day rocking of the wagon beat the cream into butter. If an over-loaded wagon broke down or proved too heavy for horse or oxen to pull, families would abandon their precious personal possessions, but not their food. The tall grass prairies were littered with keepsakes: hand-painted fur-niture, immigrant trunks, porcelain dishes, books, and old familiar paint-ings. Laura's first train trip did not take place until 1879, when crews of the Chicago & North Western Railroad were furiously extending tracks from western Minnesota into the Dakota Territory.

The Ingalls had no predetermined stopping point once they reached western Minnesota. As they approached what is now the town of Walnut Grove, they turned north, riding along the ridgeline of a winding creek. Charles stopped at the farm of Norwegian immigrant Eleck Nelson and inquired about land for sale. Nelson, in turn, directed him to another Nor-wegian farmer who wanted to sell his quarter section on Plum Creek and move farther west. According to Laura, Plum Creek was "the prettiest creek we had ever seen."[6] It roared with yellow foam during the spring snowmelt, but otherwise the shallow creek meandered softly through open country and teemed with tiny fish. Dense thickets of wild plums bent over the slop-ing banks. The grove of walnuts for which the town was named was an unusual feature on the flat, treeless landscape.

For less than $500, Charles purchased 160 acres of virgin black-gold loam, a sod barn, and a sod house of sorts. Tunneled into the creek bank like a badger den, the sod dugout was the Ingalls's new home. Plum Creek ran at the foot of the door. The pioneer dugout was the crudest of sod houses, but it was well adapted to the extreme climate of the Great Plains. Dirt cheap, tightly constructed, and well insulated, the dugout was warmer in winter and cooler in summer than timber homes or board and batten cabins. The Ingalls's new dugout sported a grease-paper window by the door. Inside was a single room with a hard-packed earthen floor. The walls had been whitewashed with lime to increase light and reduce the amount of dirt that crumbled from the sod; whitewash also acted as a primitive disinfectant. Many pioneers attempted to line their walls and ceiling with muslin, but this had little effect on the hordes of fleas and bedbugs, much less the mice and other writhing creatures that burrowed through the roof and dropped on unsuspecting sleepers in the night. A sod roof, waterlogged after a storm, could leak for days. Pioneers regularly piled damp quilts atop their belongings in the center of the room to avoid dripping ceilings and puddles on the floor. One dugout settler attested to these conditions with a hint of tongue-in-cheek humor. "After the storms, we carried the water out with buckets, then waded around in the mud until it dried up. Then to keep us nerved up, sometimes the bull snakes would get in the roof and now and then one would lose his hold and fall down on the bed, then off on the floor. Mother would grab the hoe and there was something doing and after the fight was over Mr. Bull Snake was dragged outside. Of course there had to be something to keep us from getting discouraged."[7]

In 1876, homesteader Mattie Oblinger made an inventory of the typical sod house: one cook stove and a bare minimum of utensils, a small sink, two short benches, dishes enough to set a small table, one bedstead, a lounge, a sheet-iron trunk, a blue chest, two pictures, two chairs "brought from home," and a homemade table.[8] The Ingalls arrived without a bedstead. Whatever Caroline's true feelings regarding her new home, according to Laura she met the challenge with her usual aplomb, cooking meals, improvising beds, and sewing curtains.

Lack of basic sanitation was a perennial danger in the overcrowded sod house. Dr. Cass G. Barnes, a noted horse-and-buggy physician on the plains, gave his assessment:

> It was not wholly the fault of the sod houses that contagious diseases and epidemics were common. The common drinking cup, the open dug well, the outdoor toilet, or no toilet at all, shared the blame with the lack of ventilation and crowded quarters of the sod house . . . the floor of the dugout, or sod house was commonly the clay dirt, innocent of joist or board flooring. It is not possible to scrub it or disinfect it of the millions of germs that found a breeding place in the dirt trodden underfoot. Food in open dishes, milk, butter, and the table dishes were easily contaminated by the germs raised in the dust if an attempt to sweep the floor was attempted . . . the wooden pail in the corner held the

supply of drinking water, and the drinking cup in common use went days at a time without being sterilized by boiling water. Disease germs were here, there, everywhere and anywhere.[9]

Although Laura later admitted she believed her family had hauled all their drinking water directly from the creek, she created a fresh stream for the Ingalls to enjoy in *On the Banks of Plum Creek;* she didn't want her readers to assume that her family was somehow careless or "dirty."[10] Wilder avoids the subject in her novels, but on the treeless prairie, cooking and heating fuel came from one of two sources: coal or cattle. Coal cost real money. The majority of homesteaders burned cow dung, and the first thing Pa does is put a cow in the sod barn.

What the new farm lacked in creature comforts, it made up for in wild beauty. With the sparkling creek rushing past their doorstep, the prairie in full bloom, and nearby tableland to explore, the Ingalls new farmstead had its compensations. For the first time in Laura's life, a town with shops, a school, and a fledgling Congregational Church was well within walking distance. Like her father, Laura was happiest out of doors and treated the prairie as a vast living addition to her mother's tiny, underground dugout. It is a distinction that would become increasingly important in her later life and work. Ma and Mary were homebound, seemingly content. Laura, however, was restive and frequently slipped the bonds of domesticity for the wider world beyond the door.

To what degree Laura's nascent nonconformity inconvenienced or distressed her more-conventional mother is a matter of debate. As Western historian Glenda Riley suggests:

> In a sense, frontierswomen were themselves deviants from "women's sphere" because they agreed to disrupt homes and families to move them to a situation where high standards of domesticity would be unattainable. But because these women paid lip service to standards of domesticity, while rejecting them by their actions, does not automatically indicate distress and strain on their parts. As historian Julie Roy Jeffrey points out, "Assenting to ideas was not the same as living up to their prescriptions. Domesticity described the norms and not the actual conduct of American women." Jeffrey adds that "perhaps frontierswomen were even repaid for their defection from the ideal by regaining an economic importance to the family that many women in settled regions had lost, as well as becoming the shapers of culture rather than its symbolic arbitrator."[11]

Either way, Laura clearly preferred to abandon her protective sunbonnet, assist her father with outdoor chores, explore the creek, or wander the flowering tableland behind the dugout. Wilder scholar Dolores Rosenblum

32 • Laura Ingalls Wilder: American Writer on the Prairie

describes Laura's evolving relationship with wide-open spaces as "intimate immensity," a theme that will suffuse almost all of Wilder's work and become central to her vision of the Western frontier. "The basic 'human' plot of all the narratives . . . is 'to survive,' that is, to learn the rules—and internalize them so that you can enjoy life as a civilized human being . . . Wilder's central metaphor for the process of human survival and development involves the problem of inhabiting space: how do you fill with your presence an emptiness that threatens to affect you? The narratives thus are organized around a variety of habitations constructed against and in compliance with the vast outer space surrounding the human figures."[12]

Throughout the summer and harvest of 1874, Charles (who did not plant a crop that year) worked for his ambitious neighbor from Norway, Eleck Nelson. Laura tagged along. She spent a great deal of time with Nelson's twenty-two-year-old wife Olena, who apparently enjoyed Laura's lively company, and the Nelson's toddler daughter Anna. Laura probably assisted Olena Nelson by minding Anna, a task she likely performed without compensation. Childcare was an important collective task on the frontier and, like tending cattle, it was a task invariably delegated to older children. Olena Nelson took a special interest in Laura and taught her how to milk a cow, a skill Laura would use to startle her parents in the sod barn. By the 1870s, Scandinavian farmers were thronging to Minnesota, dispatching letters home in praise of the rich black soil and urging family and friends to join them (and advising them in more candid moments to "bring warm clothes"). In Wilder's memoir, Charles joked that his daughter spent so much time with the Nelsons she spoke English "like a Swede." No doubt his comment would have baffled the Norwegian Nelsons.

Due to the proximity of Walnut Grove, winter in the dugout was less isolating for the Ingalls than were previous years in Kansas or Wisconsin. The town consisted of two small stores, a blacksmith shop, a schoolhouse, and a few raw-looking houses peppered with knotholes made from lumber hauled in by train. Laura and her family were finally able to attend church on a regular basis, a welcome change for devout and sociable Caroline. Initially, Sunday services were held in the home of James Kennedy. Kennedy's redheaded daughter Nettie became Laura's close friend. The Reverend Edwin Alden, a mission church organizer and great favorite of the Ingalls, established the town's Congregational Church not long afterward. The first two baptisms performed in the new church were those of Charles and Caroline Ingalls. Although adult baptism was common among Protestant denominations in the nineteenth century, it seemed to mark a turning point for Laura's parents. Both became sincerely attached to Alden, his work, and the Congregational Church. Charles donated his time to help construct the building. According to church records, he contributed a princely $26.15 to

Wandering the West: The 1870s • 33

the new bell fund—an amount so large for a man of Charles's limited means that it almost seems to be a transcription error—and was elected one of the first trustees. Caroline became part of a larger, active community again, eager to participate in church and social activities. In her novel, Wilder gives an account of her first magical Christmas Eve in the new church, complete with a dazzling Christmas tree and unexpected gifts for the children from Alden's home church in Waseca.

By spring, Caroline, now 36, knew she was pregnant again. With a fourth child on the way, the Ingalls abandoned the dugout. Optimistic as ever, Charles bought lumber on credit against his fall wheat crop and built a sturdy, golden-pine house on the opposite side of the creek. He outfitted the house with glass windows, a "boughten-shingle roof," and new cook stove. As their wheat ripened under the roasting sun, the Ingalls looked forward to a providential harvest.

The rippling wheat was just days from cutting when the locusts arrived. Rocky Mountain locusts had chewed through a swath of Minnesota in 1873 and 1874, but the voracious swarm that arrived in time to consume the Ingalls's wheat crop was of an entirely different magnitude. Entomologist Jeffrey Lockwood illustrates the enormity of the invasion:

> After a swarm had departed, one Minnesota farmer went into his field to see how many eggs had been left behind. Digging into the loose soil the poor fellow was flabbergasted to find that no matter where he dug the ground was packed with egg pods. Turning over a shovel full of soil and making a careful count, he found that there were 150 eggs per square inch. Perhaps he'd been an accountant before becoming a farmer because he determined, "at this rate there will be 940,896,000 eggs to the acre, or the nice little pile of 6,586,272,000 on seven acres of my farm."

> We might be tempted to discount this exercise in rural mathematics, except that twenty years earlier a similar calculation had been made during the locust invasions of Utah. Two of the settlers, Taylor Heninger and John Ivie of Sanpete County, made their estimates with painstaking precision, noting that "by actual count and careful average we found 118–28/54th eggs to the square inch of ground; making a total of 743,424,000 eggs to the acre, or a total of 2,973,696,000 to the four acre piece." Certainly not all these eggs yielded locusts, and not all the hatchlings survived the course of development, but even if 1 in 100 reached adulthood their four-football-field-sized farm would have produced 30 million locusts—about the human population of the country at that time.[13]

They ate flesh, they ate fabric, they ate fence posts. As the locusts devoured Redwood County, the settlers fought back. Farmers tried driving them off with great pyres of smoking manure. They dug pits, hoping to trap the slimy nymphs as they writhed from the ground and marched across their fields. In her memoir, Wilder captures the gruesome invasion. "When they [the locusts] came to the creek, they walked steadily into the water and drowned. Others came on, walking over the drowning ones, until they drowned. And others walked over them, until the creek was choked with dead grasshoppers and more grasshoppers walked safely across on the bodies."[14] Farm families were advised to jump up and down, waving their arms about their heads, shaking sheets and banging on pots to frighten the devils away. A few farmers blasted the egg beds with dynamite which, to quote one observer, "surely did far more good to their sense of vengeance than it did harm to the locusts."[15]

The Ingalls were ruined. Saddled by debt, his cash crop gone, and, most significantly, with nowhere else to go, Charles made a last-ditch effort to finance the farm for another season. Leaving the care of the farm to heavily pregnant Caroline, Charles packed up and headed east. His destination was Peter Ingalls's farm on the Zumbro, where he planned to hire out as a harvest hand in fields unaffected by the locusts. In "Pioneer Girl," Wilder makes it clear that her father made the entire journey on foot, nearly 200 miles, because he could not afford train fare. As Lockwood points out, "his journey echoes our culture's canonical story of a people wandering in the wilderness seeking the promised land. Laura learns from her mother's reading of Scripture that locusts played a pivotal role in the time of the Egyptian pharaohs. And so the tale of the pioneers became interwoven with Western culture's most deep and abiding literary account of locusts. Perhaps the Ingalls sensed that they were part of a great human migration—an American exodus—across the continent. But what they did not know while watching their farm disappear under a blanket of locusts that summer of 1875 was that no people on earth, not even a pharaoh, had ever witnessed a swarm of such immensity."[16]

Charles earned a dollar a day working as a field hand alongside hundreds of other men and boys displaced by the infestation. Eleck Nelson assisted Caroline in Charles's absence, most notably when a prairie fire threatened the Ingalls's barn and property. When Charles returned to Plum Creek in the fall, Caroline was near delivery. Although his employment opportunities would have been limited, Charles moved the family into rented rooms in town for the harsh, isolating winter. It was a pattern he would often repeat—wintering in town, returning to the farmstead in early spring. As discouraged settlers began leaving Walnut Grove, they sold out at "grasshopper prices" to the next wave of less-experienced, but more-enthusiastic farm families. Charles, however, held on to his land and his dogged determination to plant again.

Wandering the West: The 1870s • 35

The Ingalls lived directly behind the Reverend Alden's new Congregational Church, which afforded easy access to both school and Sunday school. With its emphasis on Bible reading and the competitive memorization of Bible verses, Sunday school played an important auxiliary role in Laura's early education. Although Laura later noted that she and Mary "didn't care much for school,"[17] her classroom memories of the period have less to do with academics than playground politics, a theme to which she would return many times in her work. Selfish, condescending Nellie Owens, the daughter of Walnut Grove's most comfortable merchant and one of the inspirations for Nellie Oleson in Wilder's novels, was the primary target of Laura's ire, but anyone who had the temerity to comment upon the Ingalls's limited means was a target of Laura's wrath and creative retribution. In her novel (as in life), when Laura lured Nellie into the crayfish and leech-infested mud flats of Plum Creek, sympathetic observers cheered her on.

Coming home from school one dark November afternoon, Laura and her sisters found Caroline in bed with a baby once again. It was a boy this time, Charles Frederick, called Freddie for Caroline's kind but sickly stepfather who had died the previous year, his health long compromised by the lingering effects of "fever 'n ague." Laura recalled that she and Mary were proud of their baby brother and that they hurried home from school every day to see him. The snow was still on the ground when Charles moved the family back to the frame farmhouse in preparation for another planting season. At best, it promised to be an expensive high-risk venture. Western Minnesota farmers planted wheat; it was their most reliable cash crop, well suited to Minnesota's soil and climate. But by ramming their sod plows through the matted prairie grass and furrowing the newly exposed black dirt into wheat fields, Minnesota homesteaders had unwittingly produced the ideal, porous breeding ground for locusts, the next generation of which was already firmly seeded in the soil, simply waiting for warm weather to spew from the ground. Short of cash and chastened by locusts, Charles sowed only one small field of wheat that spring. He could not withstand two crop failures in a row.

As usual, the spring snowmelt caused Plum Creek to overflow its banks. The spring flooding marooned the Ingalls on their farm and coincided with a severe, but unexplained, illness for Caroline. Wilder would later recall how, in obedience to her father, she raced into the surging creek to summon Eleck Nelson for help. When Nelson spotted her, he desperately waved her off and rode into town to call for the doctor. Apparently, Charles had forgotten about the high water when he dispatched Laura. When she returned in her dripping, muddy clothes, Charles was still so distraught that all he could manage was a choked, "Good girl." Caroline must have been very ill. Wilder wrote that her mother was moaning and did not recognize her. The doctor, who had to be rowed to the house in a fishing boat, was summoned twice—an expense Charles could ill-afford—so it is clear that Caroline did not recover quickly. It is difficult to know what effect Caroline's illness had on her nursing infant, Freddie, but Laura and her sisters probably assumed full responsibility for his care at the time. If he was weaned to cow's milk during his mother's illness, as was often the case, then his own health and resistance to disease may have been compromised. A pioneer mother usually nursed her baby for at least two years. Not only did prolonged nursing provide a safe source of nutrition for the infant, but it also was the most common method of birth control.[18]

In 1873, the Comstock "Chastity" Laws made selling or distributing information regarding contraception or abortion a federal crime. Abstinence, withdrawal, and the use of "pessaries" (used for uterine prolapse but which functioned like a crude diaphragm) were methods used by some exhausted mothers to space or limit the number of births, albeit with varying degrees of success. A number of women on the frontier, usually experienced midwives or prostitutes, were aware that herbal potions mixed with ergot (a fungus of rye) could be used to induce abortion. But the vast majority of frontier families, especially on the farm where children were viewed as economic assets, were large. As a small child, pioneer Martha Gay Masterson remembered being "awakened from a nervous sleep by the wailing of an infant. I asked Mother whose baby was crying. She said it was hers. I said not a word for some time, fearing I might have to welcome another brother. I already had nine brothers."[19] The high rate of infant mortality also played a role in the propensity to create large families.

Caroline was still recovering when the pale green wheat began to spring up in the small field. This time, the locusts hatched directly under the seedlings and consumed the wheat as it rose from the ground. Horrified state governors began calling for days of public prayer, fasting, and humiliation in response to the crisis.[20] In Minnesota, limited public relief in the form of food aid was finally made available to affected farmers, but many refused to sign the state's mortifying oath attesting to their destitution. They would rather starve than sign. This stubborn, even self-defeating, trait among frontier farmers was accepted as a matter of course by Laura and her family. In Lockwood's words, "the agrarian ideal was starting to crack, but the cultural values of hard work and fierce independence had not yet crumbled."[21]

There was no cash, no crop, and, in the depressed regional economy, no work, which left the Ingalls with no option. They found an irrationally exuberant buyer for the farm and sold out, probably at a loss. Charles was nearing forty, with four small children; his days as a traveling harvester were numbered. By the time the locusts departed, he and William Steadman, a fellow member of the Congregational Church, had come up with a new business plan. Steadman wanted to buy and operate a hotel in Burr Oak, Iowa, on what had once been the major wagon route for pioneers heading south and west across the state. It is likely that the Ingalls were familiar with Burr Oak. They probably had driven through the town on their way to Kansas and would have remembered the hordes of covered wagons they had seen camping and provisioning in town. Burr Oak offered another advantage. It was located not far from Peter Ingalls's farm on the Zumbro River and the unaffected wheat fields. Charles decided to "backtrail," to head east. The Ingalls would reunite with Peter and Caroline's sister Eliza in southeastern Minnesota, stay throughout the late summer and fall while Charles worked the harvest, and then join the Steadmans at the Burr Oak hotel.

Once again, the family loaded the wagon and set out for pastures new. Laura was happy to be on the road again, but she hated moving east. East was a capitulation. Her family was heading in the wrong direction; she wished they were riding west, all the way west, as far west as Oregon. She was not alone. As the Ingalls rolled through central Minnesota, they met a devastated beekeeper who, baffled by the locust disaster, was on the verge of tears. The locusts had denuded the prairie for miles around his rows of beehives. They had consumed every blade of grass and flower. Even the bees had given up hope. With no pollen to feed their young, the bees had killed their own. After removing their dead young from the hives, the surviving bees fled their homes.[22]

In Wilder's memoir, her family's reunion and respite at Peter and Eliza Ingalls's farm reads like a summer idyll. Laura, Mary, and Carrie had not seen their double cousins since the families had parted company two years earlier after crossing frozen Lake Pepin. The children spent the long summer days outdoors, playing by the river, roasting crabapples, and herding cattle. Caring for livestock was a task commonly assigned to pioneer children. Laura relished the gentle cows and the time she spent searching for them barefoot in the cool meadows by the river at the end of the day.

News of Charles and Caroline's latest misfortune had reached Charlotte Quiner Holbrook, Caroline's increasingly anxious mother in Wisconsin. She wrote to Caroline's sister, Martha Carpenter, seeking information. "Did you see Charles and Caroline when you were at Peter's . . . I will be very glad when they find a stopping place. They have had a hard time of it since they left Pepin."[23] For Laura and her family, the unthinkable had just transpired. Wilder would omit the entire year to come from her novels, if not her memoir, in large part because the events were so at odds with the hopeful, uplifting story she intended to tell. As she later told her daughter Rose, "it is a story of its own and does not belong in the picture I am painting of the family."[24]

Summer heat and humidity on the plains could be remorseless. Great Plains writer Mari Sandoz described the pioneer frame house of her childhood as "hot as an iron bucket in the sun."[25] Milk and food spoiled rapidly in the heat and was considered a contributing factor to "summer complaint," a form of dysentery that disproportionately affected infants, often resulting in rapid dehydration and death. In July or August, Freddie Ingalls fell ill with severe diarrhea, although the cause remains unknown. Once again a doctor was called, but his treatment had no effect. Laura, like her parents, seems to have been utterly unprepared for the fact her brother "got worse instead of better, and one terrible day straightened out his little body and was dead."[26] Preparing bodies for burial was women's work; Caroline almost certainly washed and dressed Freddie's body herself before placing it in a tiny coffin. Although undertakers maintained a full stock of infant caskets, Freddie's coffin was most likely built by his carpenter father, taken to an unmarked burial site, and placed in the ground while the family offered graveside prayers. It was Laura's first, traumatic experience with death and it haunted her. Death, especially the death of children, was a subject she assiduously avoided all her life. Not long after Freddie's death, the Ingalls left for Burr Oak. Writing fifty years after the death of her brother, Wilder's account of the brief trip south to Iowa was terse: "It was a cold, miserable little journey."[27]

Burr Oak was no longer a bustling wagon-train town. In the fall of 1876, the town appeared "old and dark" to Laura. The town's main street boasted mature shade trees and two hotels: The Burr Oak House (also called the Masters Hotel) now operated by William Steadman and Charles Ingalls, and the more imposing American House. There were established churches in town, tidy homes with cottage gardens and climbing roses, a solid red brick schoolhouse and the imposing home of the Pfeifer family, with its formal entry, marble fireplace, wool carpets, and beeswax-burnished staircase. To Western homesteaders, Iowa represented a measure of Eastern sophistication, replete with Victorian architecture, private colleges, pianos, and debating societies. Burr Oak was less posh than many Iowa villages, but to the Ingalls it represented a town on the prairie, but not of it. Charles and Caroline Ingalls, in the throes of grief over the loss of their son, seem to have regretted their attempt at inn-keeping from the outset. It was a demanding, round-the-clock family-run business. If Charles had any ownership interest at all, he was clearly the junior partner. The expectation of ten-year-old Laura's contribution to the family's income changed overnight. Household chores, child care, and running errands for pennies gave way to a new economic reality in which Laura and Mary were expected to work almost as hard as their parents. The girls attended school, but spent virtually all their free time in the hotel's kitchen, where they helped Caroline prepare food, serve meals, take orders, scrub dishes, and wash laundry. At night, they crammed into the family's cramped sleeping quarters on the ground floor. Laura and Mary also were responsible for the care of the Steadman's youngest child, Tommy. Laura did her best to keep him happy and comfortable, but admitted that she found him disagreeable. His presence may have been a constant reminder of her own dead brother. Running the hotel kitchen was grueling work for Caroline Ingalls, a fact that did not escape Laura's notice. Her mother, Laura later recorded, was always tired; her father always busy. Caroline, pregnant again with her last child, had good reason to be tired after toiling on her feet all day.

The Burr Oak House featured two entrances, one for guests and "steady boarders" like young William Reed the schoolteacher, and one for patrons of the bar. For the teetotalling Ingalls, the saloon was an irritant and the source of increasing apprehension. The Ingalls lived, worked, and slept just steps away from the barroom, where strange, cigar-smoking men loitered at the door. The bar was noisy at night when the weary Ingalls needed sleep. It was a dramatic departure from Laura's semi-cloistered childhood in the country, but initially she found the new living situation exciting. There was a bullet hole in the kitchen door, a souvenir of a violent domestic dispute between young William Masters and his wife, Nancy. In "Pioneer Girl," many of the episodes Laura relates from her time in Burr Oak involve violence, drunkenness, vulnerability, or death. Significantly, she took to wandering the quiet, flower-strewn cemetery on the edge of town. She liked spending time among the gravestones, reading the names of the dead. Like all prairie cemeteries, Burr Oak's graveyard was packed with infants and young children, many of whom, unlike Freddie Ingalls, were buried under elaborately carved headstones of white lambs or resurrection angels. It seemed, she thought, "like a very pleasant place to lie and sleep forever."[28] She never lingered after sundown though. She was still pensive and grieving the loss of her brother at Christmastime. It was an unusual, unhappy Christmas for the Ingalls. In her memoir, Laura noted that even the "special present" Mrs. Steadman promised her as compensation for the long hours Laura had spent caring for Tommy (who had proved no substitute for Freddie) failed to materialize, an omission Laura accepted with a hint of bitter resignation.

Mr. Bisbee, the hotel's wealthy steady boarder "who had to be pleased," took a particular, somewhat unsettling interest in ten-year-old Laura and insisted on giving her private singing lessons.[29] An unmarried male "boarder" who could afford to do so often contracted with a hotel or local family to provide his meals, even if the boarder did not actually reside where he dined. Cooking and serving meals to transient men was an important source of supplemental income for many pioneer women, including Caroline Ingalls. Laura had no choice but to accommodate Bisbee's daily lessons at the hotel. Documenting few other activities or new friendships during her stay in Burr Oak, she spent much of her time with her mother and Amy, the hired girl who assisted in the hotel kitchen, preferring their company to that of the irritating Steadman boys.

The Burr Oak House turned out to be a cramped and disagreeable place to have the measles. When the Ingalls and Steadman children all came down with the disease, they were quarantined together in a darkened room. Not surprisingly, long days in the dark did nothing to improve the children's mutual and growing antagonism, a resentment mirrored by their parents. Mary Ingalls was hardest hit and slowest to recover. Although physically small and delicate in appearance, young Laura was, as her father put it, "as strong as a little French horse."[30] All throughout her life, Wilder benefited from her hardy constitution and took pride in her ability to work alongside men—clearing rocks, throwing hay, or holding up her end of a crosscut saw. While his daughters recuperated, Charles quietly took a second job at the local feed mill, where he used his team to grind corn. His partnership with Steadman was unpleasant, uneven, and unprofitable; Charles wanted out of the hotel business. He moved his family out of the hotel and into rented rooms above Kimball's grocery store.

Laura was glad to go, relieved that her mother no longer worked in the hotel and could return to housekeeping while the family awaited the birth of the new baby. Laura returned to school with renewed interest and fewer distractions. Burr Oak's substantial brick and stone schoolhouse was a new experience for her. Reading, arithmetic, and history formed the core of the curriculum, with a heavy emphasis on rote memorization (a skill at which Laura excelled). Books and supplies would have been in short supply and shared among students, but Laura and her sisters had one great advantage—a highly literate mother passionately committed to their education. Laura and Mary often read aloud from Mary's copy of the *Independent Fifth Reader*. With its focus on elocution, patriotic verse, and love of the West, the book ranked high among Laura's early literary influences. The rest are more speculative. Her later writing demonstrates that, like Abraham Lincoln, she was well acquainted with the Bible and Shakespeare. She read newspapers, the *Youth's Companion, The New York Ledger,* and other periodicals on a regular basis. In 1876, the newspapers she unfolded would have been full of banner headlines: the divisive, disputed "Stolen Election" of 1876 resulted in a one-vote electoral victory for President Rutherford B. Hayes; the Washington Monument was under construction and the Statue of Liberty's torch-bearing arm arrived from France; Alexander Graham Bell successfully tested and patented his telephone; in a sensational robbery on the bank of Northfield, Minnesota, several members of the Jesse James Gang were killed or captured; General George Armstrong Custer was defeated at the Battle of the Little Bighorn. Laura must also have been familiar with Louisa May Alcott's ubiquitous *Little Women,* first published in 1868. Mary, Laura, Carrie, and Grace bear unmistakable similarities to the four March girls: Meg/Mary, the mature and dutiful eldest daughter; Jo/Laura, the literary tomboy; Beth/Carrie, the frail sister, fiercely protected by Jo; and Amy/Grace, the indulged golden baby of the family.

Reading aloud and listening to Charles play his fiddle provided the Ingalls with entertainment on long winter evenings. Years later, Charles told Laura that their impromptu recitals often drew a crowd, as lonely men gathered downstairs to hear his two pretty, earnest daughters recite verse from the *Reader:*

> Talk not of the town, boys—give me the broad prairie;
> Where man, like the wind, roams impulsive and free;
> Behold how its beautiful colors all vary,
> Like those of the clouds or the deep-rolling sea!
> A life in the woods, boys, is even as changing:
> With proud independence we season our cheer;
> And those who the world are for happiness ranging;
> Won't find it at all if they don't find it here.
> Then enter, boys; cheerily, boys, enter and rest;
> I'll show you the life, boys, we live in the West.[31]

Life in the West wasn't always so carefree and, despite the general impression created in Wilder's fiction, children weren't always immured from rage, addiction, or acts of cruelty. In the grocery store below the Ingalls's rented rooms, after the men who gathered to eavesdrop on the Ingalls's evening entertainment had quietly dispersed, the alcoholic grocer and his wife were prone to loud arguments. One night, the woman's screams compelled Charles to intervene. Charles pulled on his pants in the dark and ran down the stairs, where he discovered the drunken grocer hauling his wife around the floor by her long hair with one hand. In his other hand, he clutched a flaming overturned lantern, which was dripping kerosene over his wife and the wooden floorboards. After separating the couple and dumping the grocer in bed, Charles returned upstairs. He said they were lucky the store hadn't burned down over their heads. When the nearby saloon did catch fire, Charles took part in the bucket brigade that saved the bar, but claimed he would have let it burn if he hadn't thought the fire would spread. Alcohol abuse, long a problem on the frontier where liquor was traded in lieu of cash, was common among traumatized Civil War veterans. Temperance campaigners often made the case for abstinence as much on the basis of the financial toll rot gut alcohol exacted on already hard-pressed families as they did on moral or religious grounds. Carrie Nation, the temperance movement's most famous crusader, had been the miserable impoverished wife of an alcoholic doctor. Shouting "Glory to God! Peace on Earth!" Carrie Nation eventually took her ideological battle directly to the barroom, where she used her trusty hatchet to smash shot glasses, whiskey bottles, bar stools, and mirrors.[32] Although Carrie did not launch her "hatchetations" until 1900, the Women's Christian Temperance Union was established in 1873. It quickly became a fixture of small town society in the Midwest and on the frontier, and its members helped pave the way for Prohibition in 1920. In "Pioneer Girl," Wilder included the story of Amy, Caroline's assistant and hired girl at the Burr Oak House, whose beau died during an episode of binge drinking.

Not long after the drunken domestic dispute in the grocery store, Charles moved his family to a small brick house on the edge of town. He rented the house from wealthy Mr. Bisbee, Laura's ersatz music instructor. Charles bought a cow, much to his daughter's delight, and Laura was given the task of driving it to pasture in the morning and home again at dusk. At eleven, Laura was considered a "great girl" and expected to wear shoes, but she could drive the cow in her bare feet and spend time wandering outdoors on her own, a freedom she cherished. Her sensory memory was always strong. She would record how much she liked the feel of the cool wet grass beneath her feet and the rain that fell on her face and soaked her thin summer clothes.[33]

In May, Caroline gave birth to Grace Pearl Ingalls. It was the last time Laura would arrive home from some long gratuitous "errand" to find her mother propped up in bed like the Madonna with her new child. Grace delighted Laura, who enjoyed caring for her, and Laura was even allowed to stay home from school for a time to assist her recovering mother. This may have been allowed in part because Laura, although highly intelligent and verbal, had recently faced her first academic setback. She had trouble learning how to multiply, which aggravated her and prevented her from advancing with the other students in her class. Never one to waste time or accept defeat, Laura's response was characteristic: she used the time at home to drill multiplication facts with Caroline until she had committed them to memory.

At home, Laura saw clearly just how hard her parents were struggling to make ends meet. The brick house was quiet and comfortable, removed from the bustle of Main Street. It also cost far more than Charles Ingalls could afford. As summer approached, all the livestock in town were sent out to pasture and the demand for feed from the gristmill dried up, taking with it Charles's livelihood. The financial strain on the family did not go unnoticed. Eunice Starr, the wife of Burr Oak's physician, a woman who knew the family and whose husband had almost certainly delivered Grace, went so far as to approach Caroline about the possibility of bringing Laura into Starr's own home as an adopted daughter and lady's companion, an arrangement not uncommon among overburdened families on the frontier. Laura was actually present when Caroline politely declined the offer, but the very suggestion of it would make an indelible impression on her. Throughout her life, Wilder displayed a decided touchiness at any suggestion of her family's neediness or, even worse, their perceived social inferiority. In "Pioneer Girl," she made a point of noting that the wealthy Pfeifer daughters, who lived in the marvelous mansion across from the Burr Oak House, often came to call and "sit with" Caroline, thereby validating her mother's respectability and social significance in the eyes of the townspeople. It is a recurring theme for Wilder, who will draw a line in the sand between lack of wealth and lack of social status, two entirely different things.

The Ingalls's financial situation, however, was approaching a crisis point. Charles Ingalls was used to living off the land, supplementing his farm income with day labor when necessary or convenient. In Burr Oak, Charles had no land, no steady job, few prospects, and mounting debt from rent, grocery, household, and medical bills. Many of the Ingalls and Quiner relations were still living relatively close to Burr Oak, but this time Charles did not turn to his brother Peter or to his extended family for assistance. The entire family had been hard hit. Caroline's brother, Henry Quiner, had been wiped out by locusts in central Minnesota. Caroline's widowed mother, Charlotte Holbrook, wrote that one of her grandsons had been reduced to chopping wood "for shares" (just a portion of the wood itself).[34] It was, Charlotte reluctantly conceded, better than nothing. Charles could not afford to stay in Burr Oak and he could not afford to leave. With his rent in arrears to Bisbee, Charles grew increasingly impatient and anxious to leave Iowa. In the spring, he approached his landlord with trepidation and asked if Bisbee would allow him to send the rent payment after Charles reestablished himself in the West. Bisbee flatly refused. In fact, he threatened to seize Charles's team of horses, the Ingalls's last asset, as compensation.

What Charles did next illustrates just how precarious the Ingalls's finances had become after their disastrous stint as hotel keepers. One evening after his confrontation with Bisbee, Charles hitched his threatened team to the wagon and loaded it. Then he and Caroline woke their daughters from a sound sleep, silently bundled them into the wagon, and skipped town in the dead of night. Laura later noted that, "when we left there was not enough money to pay the last month's rent and feed us on the way back to Walnut Grove."[35] But when Laura woke the next morning, she was exultant. They had crossed the county line and they were back on the open trail. Her mother was frying breakfast beside the wagon, the sun was rising in the east, and Laura was heading west, "the direction that always brought the happiest changes."[36]

44 • Laura Ingalls Wilder: American Writer on the Prairie

They drove straight back to Walnut Grove where John and Luperla Ensign, old friends from the Congregational Church, took them in. Charles found work in town and shared living expenses with the Ensigns until he could afford to move out. The families were compatible, despite Wilder's sweeping rejection of her first marriage proposal from smitten eleven-year-old Howard Ensign. John Ensign was twenty years Charles's senior, but the two men had much in common. Both were New York natives and early Wisconsin settlers. They had been farming side by side in North Hero Township when the locusts arrived. During the Civil War, John Ensign had served in Wisconsin's 12th Infantry as a musician. Wilder wrote of the Ensigns with fondness and gratitude.

Charles bought a lot and lumber to build a small house in town entirely on credit. He built the house in the pasture behind the town's hotel, owned by William Masters. Masters also owned the lumberyard. Charles was heavily in debt to Masters, for whom he did carpentry work. He worked briefly on a local farm, probably as a day laborer. Wilder remembered Charles's stint as a butcher in the "tiny butcher shop in town." There was no refrigeration, no ice in the shop. "When meat would be getting to its last chance, Pa would take some home on his wages."[37] Like the feed mill in Burr Oak, butcher work provided only part-time and seasonal employment.

On the fickle and leveling prairie, where so many families struggled to survive in primitive living conditions, a family's "respectability" often proved as determinative of social status as wealth, profession, or position. The Ingalls's poverty had little effect on the respect and affection they engendered in Walnut Grove (although Laura's prickly sensitivity to perceived slights and her scorn of the pretentious were well-established personality traits by the time she returned to Minnesota). Charles had experienced more than his share of financial reversals, but he was intelligent, charismatic, well liked, and impartial. Moreover, as a competent musician, he and his violin would have been in high demand at church and social affairs. In Walnut Grove, he served as justice of the peace from the front room of his house in the cow pasture. Curious and observant, Laura, in the kitchen, would listen to the cases brought before her father. At one point, their old friend and neighbor Eleck Nelson was nearly brought before Charles's makeshift court. Nelson had opened a saloon in the locust-decimated town. When frequent fights broke out at the bar, the constable decided to arrest Nelson and bring him before Charles. Nelson was discovered dead drunk in his wagon. While Olena Nelson "used some dreadful language" and hurled invectives at the constable, Charles quietly agreed to let Nelson go.[38] Like his daughter, Charles rarely forgot a kindness or a slight.

The Ingalls's sojourn in Iowa and their return to Walnut Grove coincided with a major economic depression triggered by the Financial Panic of 1873.

This severe and international economic downturn lasted from 1873 until 1879, greatly complicating the efforts of frontier farmers and laborers to get ahead, as banks and businesses failed, building and railroad construction stagnated, wages were cut, credit dried up, and interest rates rose. Charles Ingalls was a skilled carpenter and a seasoned, reliable worker, willing to accept any job he could find, but economic conditions were decidedly against him.

Twelve-year-old Laura attempted to pick up her life in Walnut Grove where she had left it, a life she had loved before the locusts, the loss of the farm, and the death of Freddie shattered it. Her daily activities still revolved around home, church, and school. Many of her old playmates remained in town, including the deliciously nasty Nellie Owens. Laura's strong will and self-assurance made her a leader among the girls at school, despite her marked preference for playing with the boys. According to Wilder's memoir, she outran her male counterparts, joined their baseball team, and hurled herself into their rough-and-tumble games at recess. None of this endeared her to her obedient older sister or the town's watchful matrons. Baseball may have been the final straw. Mary was appalled. When winter came and Mary tried dragging Laura by the hair from a snowball fight, Mary took several ice balls to the face. After Mary informed Caroline, Laura was ordered back inside the schoolhouse for the duration of the term. Laura openly resented the unchallenged advantages and greater freedoms her male counterparts enjoyed. Girls were expected to speak softly, defer to male authority, assist their mothers in the home, read quietly in the evening, and sew. When she and Howard Ensign tied for a prize in Sunday school, Ensign was awarded the beautiful reference Bible, "because he was a boy."[39] Howard's public prayer and testimony also offended Laura's sense of personal privacy. "It seemed to me that the things between one and God should be between him and God, like loving one's mother," she explained. "One didn't go around say, 'I love my mother, she has been so good to me.' One just loved her, and did things that she wanted one to do."[40]

Pioneer children grew up quickly. At twelve, with one foot still firmly planted in childhood, Laura went back to work. William Masters, who had sold the Burr Oak hotel to William Steadman and who now owned the hotel in Walnut Grove, needed help. Mrs. Masters hired Laura to wash dishes and wait tables for fifty cents per week. The Masters's eldest son Will (best known for shooting holes in hotel doors) and his long-suffering wife Nancy were living at the hotel. While Will drank and Nancy scrubbed in the hotel kitchen and laundry, Laura took care of their baby Nan when called upon.

In *Little Town on the Prairie,* Pa reacts indignantly to the very suggestion of his daughter working in a hotel. It was a fastidiousness the real Ingalls

46 • Laura Ingalls Wilder: American Writer on the Prairie

family could not afford. In Walnut Grove, Laura wanted to take the job at the hotel. Other than waiting on tables, she enjoyed her duties. When her work was done and baby Nan was asleep, Laura curled up with the latest edition of the *New York Ledger,* dreamed of someday making extravagant hats like the hats she saw in the window of the town milliner, and began focusing her keen powers of observation on the people around her. At the hotel, Laura realized, "interesting things were happening all the time."[41] Like all small towns, Walnut Grove had its share of secrets, gossip, and drama. Laura's memoir illustrates her growing awareness of adult behavior, particularly sexuality, including an incident she recorded in "Pioneer Girl" in which she watches Will Masters's smug sister, Matie, outwit a rival for the affections of the town's eligible doctor. She seduces him, becomes pregnant, and forces the wedding. Laura overhears Caroline, who helped with the rushed sewing of Matie's trousseau, murmuring to Charles that it would have been better for Matie to lose the doctor to her rival, "than to have gotten him that way."[42]

Laura rarely discusses sexuality in her work or surviving correspondence, but even as a child her reticence was not based on ignorance. She developed a fleeting crush on Silas Rude, the charismatic new boy in town. Dismissed out of hand as "a sissy" by Charles Ingalls, Silas left town in disgrace after staging an abduction hoax in which he claimed to have been tied up and beaten. Stories of small town sexual jealousy and revenge are shot through Wilder's "Pioneer Girl" narrative of this period in her life, culminating in a predatory incident she recorded in the manuscript. After working with Nancy Masters at the hotel for some time, Laura was hired to stay with her at night. Nancy suffered from "fainting spells," which posed a danger to herself and baby Nan. Will Masters was no help. He spent his evenings in the new saloon operated by Eleck Nelson, the Ingalls's young neighbor from Plum Creek. One night, Will returned and woke Laura from a dead sleep. As he bent over her, she could smell the sour whiskey on his breath. She sat up quickly. "Is Nannie sick?" she asked. "No," he answered, "lie down and be still." Laura refused and told him to leave or she would "scream for Nannie." She left their apartment the next day and did not return.[43]

Not yet thirteen, Laura was assertive enough to slam the door on Will Masters, but it is doubtful she informed her parents of the incident. She may have been reluctant to say anything that might compromise her ability to augment her family's income, because soon after leaving the Masters's employ, she was living out of the house again, this time working as a night nurse for Nannie Masters's convalescent sister, Sadie Hurley. The money Laura earned was never hers to keep; most of it went directly into the Ingalls's general fund for living expenses. Although she was a diligent, responsible, and uncomplaining worker, Laura despised living and sleeping away from home. Laura was still boarding with the Hurleys on the morning her father showed up at their doorstep looking for day work, and proceeded to spend hours making corn brooms for sale in town. Charles found sporadic employment mending fences, doing carpentry, and tending cattle, but the Ingalls had no farm and their future remained uncertain.[44]

They were not alone. Even before the locust invasions, thousands of frontier landholders and homesteaders had already played the risky game of farming and lost. Dispossession of the land, usually driven by extremely high interest rates on mortgage, planting, and general loan debt (often at rates topping 20 percent), resulted in the failure of many previously landed farmers to attain even the status of tenant farmer in the West. Men who had fallen into the uncomfortable position of landless farmers (like Charles Ingalls) were often relegated to the unsettled lives of itinerant farm laborers—a poorly compensated and precarious situation from which many could not recover. It was the "silent anger" of these disillusioned men and their families, according to historian James M. Marshall, that would, in the 1890s, fuel the Populist movement in the West and lead to the creation of the short-lived, but influential "People's Party."[45]

That winter, Mary felt so unwell that she stopped attending Sunday school. In *By the Shores of Silver Lake,* Wilder attributed Mary's life-altering illness to scarlet fever, perhaps because it was such a common disease and familiar to her readers, but recent research points to viral meningoencephalitis as the cause.[46] Wilder was aware of the difference. In a 1938 letter to her daughter Rose, Laura revealed that Mary had suffered from "spinal meningitis—a sort of spinal sickness."[47] Mary's illness began with the severe headache often diagnosed as "brain fever." When she became delirious, Caroline shaved Mary's head, believing this would cool her brain. Delirium usually preceded death and when Mary became delirious, the Ingalls prepared for the worst. Instead, Mary somehow rallied. One morning, Laura noticed that half of Mary's face was "drawn out of shape." Caroline told her that Mary had suffered a stroke. Wilder's powerful memory of the event is both tender and evocative, "as I looked at her I remembered her oak tree way back in Wisconsin that had been struck by lightning all down one side."[48] For both girls, Mary's illness marked childhood's end.

Friends and neighbors followed Mary's condition in the *Redwood Gazette.* "Miss Mary Ingalls has been confined to her bed about ten days with severe head ache. It was feared that hemorrhage of the brain had set in in [sic] one side of her face became partially paralyzed. She is now slowly convalescing."[49] But a month later, Mary was still bedridden and her eyes were beginning to fail. "Miss Mary Ingalls is still confined to her bed, and at times her sufferings are great."[50]

Nursing a critically ill child in a board-and-batten shack with two beds and no privacy meant that Laura was acutely aware of Mary's distress.

Laura spent the spring by Mary's bedside, saw none of her friends, and spent the rest of her time caring for Carrie and Grace. Charles called in Dr. Welcome from Sleepy Eye to consult with Dr. Hoyt. The doctors agreed that Mary's optic nerves were "dying," but thought her illness might have been a complication of her earlier bout with measles. Although Mary's facial paralysis resolved itself, her loss of vision did not. By summer, she was blind.[51]

Years later, Wilder expressed guilt and frustration over Mary's blindness, confiding to close friend Irene Lichty that she believed Mary's sight might have been saved if her family had been able to afford better medical care.[52] But in reality, there was no effective treatment for meningoencephalitis in 1879. Later, when Charles was able to take Mary to see a specialist in Chicago, the doctor informed them there was no chance of Mary ever recovering her vision.

Bad news traveled fast, but this time help was on the way. When the close-knit Ingalls–Quiner clan heard of Charles and Caroline's latest hardship, they responded. Mary was finally out of bed, growing stronger and able to spend most of the day sitting up in a chair when Laura Ladocia Ingalls Forbes—Charles's decisive sister and Laura's "Aunt Docia"—arrived at the door. She had driven her buggy all the way from Wisconsin to Walnut Grove, across the prairie alone, with a job offer for Charles. Docia's husband, Hiram Forbes, was a grading contractor for what would become the Chicago & North Western Railroad. West of Walnut Grove, the railroad had set up a temporary campsite for the workers who were extending tracks deep into Dakota Territory. Forbes offered Charles a seasonal, but salaried, position as bookkeeper and paymaster for the camp. Charles would also run the company store, a singularly thankless job, until the railroad crews disbanded for the winter. But by far the most important benefit of Forbes's offer was the location and timing of the job itself: Charles would be perfectly positioned to select, claim, and file for a prime Dakota homestead months before the onset of the highly anticipated land rush the following spring.

Charles accepted on the spot. Less than forty-eight hours later, he left town in Docia's buggy. This time, he was leaving Walnut Grove for good. As in Kansas and Burr Oak, Charles was drowning in debt. Unable to pay for both Mary's medical expenses and interest on the new house in the Masters's pasture, Charles returned the property for debt—"as usual getting the worst of the bargain," Wilder noted.[53] Interest rates were high and, as Wilder later explained, "a man once in debt could stand small chance of getting out."[54] With an offer of steady income from the railroad and the prospect of a fresh start on a pristine Dakota homestead, Charles seized the lifeline his brother-in-law had thrown him. Caroline and the girls were to join him as soon as he established himself in camp. Because they were taking the train as far as Tracy, Caroline and the girls pared their belonging. They could take no more than they could carry, a task that posed little difficulty. Laura said goodbye to her friends Anna Ensign, Nettie Kennedy, and Maud Blair. Laura had particularly fond memories of Nettie Kennedy. She noted one drowsy summer afternoon in particular, in which the girls spent the day on Nettie's farm, curled up with Nettie's books and pictures. Nettie and her little brother Sandy walked Laura halfway home that day, their bare feet padding down the dusty path beside the trail of blowing wildflowers they followed back into town. "I never saw them again," Wilder wrote simply.[55]

It was a short, ten-mile train ride from Walnut Grove to Tracy, the end of the line. Caroline and the girls waited quietly in the Tracy hotel parlor for Charles, who pulled up in a lumber wagon. The next morning, the reunited family started for the railroad camp. Wilder recalled the monotony of the journey, traveling over the level, treeless, unchanging land, "as though the horses were on a treadmill, trotting steadily and never moving forward."[56]

Homesteader accounts of wagon travel tend to chronicle the perfunctory and the prosaic. However, as a child, the writer Willa Cather made the long overland journey from Virginia to the West in 1883. Like Laura Ingalls Wilder, Willa Cather later drew on her own experience to describe the eerie feeling of traveling over unmarked, unbroken, and seemingly unlimited prairie, a feeling so many of her fellow travelers struggled to articulate:

> There seemed to be nothing to see; no fences, no creeks or trees, no hills or fields. If there was a road I could not make it out in the faint starlight. There was nothing but land: not a country at all, but the material out of which countries are made. No, there was nothing but land—slightly undulating, I knew, because often our wheels ground against the brake as we went down into a hollow and lurched up again on the other side. I had the feeling that the world was left behind, that we had got over the edge of it, and were outside man's jurisdiction . . . the wagon jolted on, carrying me I knew not whither. I don't think I was homesick. If we never arrived anywhere, it did not matter. Between that earth and that sky I felt erased, blotted out. I did not say my prayers that night: here, I felt, what would be would be.[57]

Night had fallen when Laura and her family finally reached the campsite, a collection of shanties shining in the darkness, lit by blazing kerosene lanterns. Docia Forbes met the weary travelers at the door and welcomed them with a hot supper. The Ingalls had left the settled States behind and crossed into Dakota Territory, the new frontier, willing to gamble one more time on the Golden West. Laura's greatest adventures, triumphs and disasters—the raw material of her art—were about to unfold.

NOTES

1. Miller, *Becoming Laura Ingalls*, 20.
2. Ibid., 30.
3. LIW, "Pioneer Girl," 24.
4. Ibid., 26.
5. Linda S. Peavy and Ursula Smith, *The Gold Rush Widows of Little Falls: A Story Drawn from the Letters of Pamelia and James Fergus* (St. Paul, MI: Minnesota Historical Society, 1990), 171.
6. LIW, "Pioneer Girl," 26.
7. Joanna L. Stratton, *Pioneer Women: Voices from the Kansas Frontier* (New York: Simon and Schuster, 1981), 53.
8. Letter from Mattie V. Oblinger to the Thomas Family, August 8, 1876, Nebraska State Historical Society Archives.
9. Cass G. Barns, *The Sod House* (Lincoln, NE: University of Nebraska Press, 1970), 245–46.
10. Miller, *Becoming Laura Ingalls*, 212 and notes.
11. Riley, *Frontierswomen*, 52.
12. Delores Rosenblum, "Intimate Immensity: Mythic Space in the Work of Laura Ingalls Wilder," in *Where the West Begins: Essays on Middle Border and Siouxland Writings*, eds. Arthur R. Huseboe and Willian Geyer (Sioux Falls, SD: Center for Western Studies Press, 1978), 74.
13. Jeffrey A. Lockwood, *Locust: The Devastating Rise and Mysterious Disappearance of the Insect that Shaped the American Frontier* (New York: Basic Books, 2004), 11–12.
14. LIW, "Pioneer Girl," 34.
15. Lockwood, 54.
16. Lockwood, 16.
17. LIW, "Pioneer Girl," 35.
18. Cathy Luchetti, *Children of the West: Family Life on the Frontier* (New York: Norton, 2001), 60.
19. Peavy and Smith, *Pioneer Women*, 42.
20. Lockwood, 40.
21. Lockwood, 71.
22. LIW, "Pioneer Girl," 40.
23. Laura Ingalls Wilder Family Correspondence, 1861–1919, Wisconsin Historical Society manuscript collection Stout SC 142.
24. Lane Papers, LIW to RWL, Box 13, undated.
25. Mari Sandoz, *Sandhill Sundays and Other Recollections* (Lincoln, NE: University of Nebraska Press, 1966), 8.
26. LIW, "Pioneer Girl," 41.
27. Ibid., 41.
28. Ibid., 47.
29. Ibid., 43.
30. Ibid., 11.
31. *The Independent Fifth Reader* (A. S. Barnes and Company, New York, 1868), 210.
32. Peavy and Smith, 135.
33. LIW, "Pioneer Girl," 46.
34. Laura Ingalls Wilder Family Correspondence, 1861–1919, Wisconsin Historical Society manuscript collection Stout SC 142.
35. Lane Papers, LIW to RWL, March 23, 1937. File 261.
36. LIW, "Pioneer Girl," 67.
37. Lane Papers, LIW to RLW, March 23, 1937. File 261.
38. LIW, "Pioneer Girl," 53–54.

Wandering the West: The 1870s · 51

39. Ibid., 62.
40. Ibid., 62.
41. Ibid., 51.
42. Ibid., 57.
43. LIW, "Pioneer Girl," Folder 3, LIW Papers, 1984–1943, Western Historical Manuscript Collection, Ellis Library, University of Missouri, Columbia, MO.
44. LIW, "Pioneer Girl," 63–64. Lane Papers, Hoover Presidential Library.
45. James M. Marshall, *Land Fever: Dispossession and the Frontier Myth* (Lexington, KY: University Press of Kentucky, 1986), 14 and 94–95.
46. Sarah S. Allexan, Carrie L. Byington, Jerome I. Finkelstein, and Beth A. Tarini, "Blindness in Walnut Grove: How Did Mary Ingalls Lose Her Sight?" *Pediatrics* 131, no. 3 (2013): 404–40.
47. Lane Papers, LIW to RLW, March 23, 1937. File 261.
48. LIW, "Pioneer Girl," 66
49. *Redwood Gazette,* April 24, 1879.
50. *Redwood Gazette,* May 15, 1879.
51. LIW, "Pioneer Girl," 66.
52. Irene Lichty, *The Ingalls Family from Plum Creek to Walnut Grove,* monograph, Minnesota Historical Society Archives (Private printing, 1970).
53. Lane Papers, LIW to RLW, March 23, 1937. File 261.
54. Ibid.
55. LIW, "Pioneer Girl," 67.
56. Ibid., 68.
57. Willa Cather, *My Antonia* (New York: Houghton Mifflin, 1954), 8.

CHAPTER **3**

SETTLING THE WEST: THE 1880S

I began to think what a wonderful childhood I had had. I had seen the whole frontier, the woods, the Indian country of the great plains, the frontier towns, the building of railroads in wild, unsettled country, homesteading and farmers coming in to take possession. I realized that I had seen and lived it all—all the successive phases of the frontier, first the frontiersman, then the pioneer, then the farmers, and the towns. Then I understood that in my own life I represented a whole period of American History.

Laura Ingalls Wilder

The Ingalls crossed into Dakota Territory in the late summer of 1879. When the family arrived, the railroad graders were already dismantling their flying camp and preparing to reestablish it at their next worksite several miles due west. Like traveling carnival workers, the men tore down shanties, dismantled the cookhouse and bunkhouses, loaded their equipment into wagons, and packed out. The departing railroad workers were leaving a string of towns in their wake; the city of Brookings, just east of the Big Sioux River, would be founded by the site of the railroad camp they had just torn down.

The Ingalls remained behind while Charles settled accounts. Twelve-year-old Laura was captivated by the fresh new country. She grew close to her cousins Lena and Gene, Docia's children by her first husband. Despite the resulting scandal and privation, Docia had divorced her first husband, August Waldvogel, after he was sentenced to eight years in prison for shooting and killing a man on their Big Woods property. Lena worked long hours in the camp cookhouse with her mother. In her limited free time, Lena taught Laura how to ride. Lena was a magnificent rider who could vault

Settling the West: The 1880s • 53

from the ground onto the bare back of one of her stepfather's black ponies and race her brother over the range. Laura found riding intimidating, but she learned.

Laura, mature beyond her years but small for her age, admired her fearless, free-spirited cousin. The girls hitched the Forbes's matching ponies to a wagon and raced over the open prairie, reveling in an unforgettable moment of pure exhilaration, youth, and freedom. It was an experience Laura loved to repeat in later years and may have sparked her enduring passion for horses. The cousins gave the ponies free rein as they lurched wildly over the prairie. Laughing and singing, they drove to a lonely farmstead where they had been instructed to collect a load of overdue laundry from the woman who took in their washing. As Laura and Lena bundled laundry into the cart, the laundress proudly explained the delay: her thirteen-year-old daughter had just been married. "She's got a good man," the woman told them. "It's just as well to be married young."[1] Slack-jawed with disbelief, the young cousins' ride back to camp was considerably less boisterous. They were in complete agreement—marriage at thirteen sounded less than ideal. Even in Dakota Territory, where single males greatly outnumbered available females, the average age of first-time brides was over twenty.

As soon as Charles had reconciled the company store accounts, the Ingalls set out for the new railroad campsite at Silver Lake. When they crossed the Big Sioux River, the landscape began to alter. The Dakota plains were higher and drier than western Minnesota. The untrammeled grasses grew coarse and tall. Cool winding creeks no longer laced the countryside; they were replaced by the ruts of old buffalo trails and abandoned wallows. Migrating to the pothole lakes and protective sloughs where they rested at night, flocks of shrieking wildfowl skimmed the Ingalls's heads as the family rode west.

When they reached the Silver Lake Camp, a surprise awaited. Caroline's brother, Henry Quiner, was there, along with two more Wisconsin cousins—Charley (the boy nearly killed by bees) and Louisa Quiner—whom Laura had not seen since her family left the Big Woods. Henry's farm in central Minnesota had also been consumed by locusts; like Charles he was seeking a new start.[2] Polly Ingalls Quiner remained back east, but Louisa was hard at work running the cook shanty and boarding workmen. Clearly, Docia Ingalls Forbes was doing her best to ensure that her entire family benefited from her husband's fortuitous connection with the Chicago & North Western Railroad. Even in later years when distance made frequent contact more difficult, the clan maintained their sense of solidarity and family bonds.

The Ingalls moved into a one-room shanty and quickly set up house. Caroline sewed calico curtains to partition the room and provide a modicum of privacy for the straw tick beds. Laura shared a bed with Mary and Carrie.

Grace slept in the trundle bed beside her parents. Even by pioneer standards, their temporary quarters were tight and conditions primitive. Dakota settlers often banked piles of dirt, straw, and manure around their tarpaper shanties to prevent them from blowing away in the relentless wind. Unlike Mary, Laura was able to spend much of her time outdoors caring for the cows with Lena, "in the great new country clean and fresh around us."[3] Laura saw no point in looking back. Like her father, she preferred Silver Lake and the raw, unbroken land surrounding it to established farming communities such as Walnut Grove, where the press of settlers was "too thick."

In *By the Shores of Silver Lake,* as in her memoir, the adult Wilder details daily life in the noisy, raucous railroad camp, which seems to be overrun with Western stock characters—Big Jerry the Half-Breed, Old Johnny the bandy little Irishman, Fred the befuddled clerk, and the despised East Coast railroad manager in his starched white collar and cuffs. These, however, were the individuals whose personal stories captured Laura's young imagination. But events took a far more serious turn when railroad workers at the Silver Lake Camp threatened to riot over what they considered a delay in payment of their wages. Charles was clearly in physical danger as the workers began massing outside the company store, shouting and firing shots into the air. There had already been one attempted lynching of a railroad paymaster and timekeeper at a nearby camp. Railroad riots were not isolated or uncommon events east or west of the Mississippi. In the crushing economic depression that followed the Panic of 1873 (which lasted from 1873 to 1879 and greatly compromised the ability of Western laborers and agrarian families such as the Ingalls to improve their circumstances), railroad strikes over wage cuts and unsafe working conditions had resulted in a virtual rebellion of American railroad workers. According to historian Howard Zinn, "When the great railroad strikes of 1877 were over, a hundred people were dead, a thousand people had gone to jail, 100,000 workers had gone on strike, and the strikes had roused into action countless unemployed in the cities. More than half the freight on the nation's 75,000 miles of track had stopped running at the height of the strikes."[4] In 1879, at the time the Ingalls were living and working at the Silver Lake Camp, railroad construction had only recently resumed after the depression of the mid 1870s, and the Great Railroad Strike of 1877 was a recent and ominous memory.

Although Charles quelled the angry railway workers, Laura's attempt to rush to his defense was forestalled by Caroline, who wrenched her headstrong daughter back inside the shanty with a sharp snap of Laura's thick, brown braid.[5] Despite their inherent drama and historical significance, the pay-day riots in *By the Shores of Silver Lake* are of secondary importance in Wilder's novel. Questions raised by the unsettling labor riots simply do not appear to be as compelling to Wilder as her true subjects—the

Settling the West: The 1880s • 55

living prairie, the families drawn to it, and the love of the land that bound them there.

As summer faded, mornings at the campsite turned hazy and cold. Huge flocks of egrets, pelicans, and cranes lifted off the glassy lake and departed with the railroad crews. Soon only the Ingalls remained. In Laura's words, "we were left with only the abandoned shanties and the wind."[6] Charles had struck a deal with the Chicago & North Western Railroad. In exchange for guarding the company's tools and equipment until spring, the Ingalls would move into the comfortable surveyor's house for the winter. Charles, like most Populist-leaning pioneers, resented the railroad companies for their acquisition of large tracts of public land, which they promptly resold to homesteaders at inflated prices. Wilder gleefully records how Charles and Hiram Forbes bilked the Chicago & North Western Railroad by double-dipping on Forbes's teaming contract so that Forbes could end the season with a profit—"beat[ing] the Chicago Northwestern railway at its own game," as Laura put it.[7] When they left the railroad camp in the fall, Docia, Lena, and Gene rode off in wagons overflowing with goods they had stolen from the company store. In "Pioneer Girl," when Hiram Forbes bids the Ingalls goodbye, he presses a fistful of bills into Mary's hand. In *By the Shores of Silver Lake*, Wilder will ascribe this event to Mr. Edwards, the most popular returning character in her novels. Like the death of Freddie, or the true cause of Mary's blindness, the generosity of kind Mr. Edwards is one of the concessions Wilder made to memory as she turned her personal history into art for young children. In the novel, Pa also takes Laura to watch the railroad graders lay track, an event Wilder later acknowledged did not take place—in real life, the protective Ingalls kept their daughters indoors and close at hand in the rowdy male railroad camp.

The Ingalls disdained complaining, crying, and lying, but duping the tightfisted, unpopular railroad company and forging government documents did not rank high on their list of offenses. Wilder retold the story of how her father and Robert Boast, who would soon become one of the Ingalls's closest friends, used Charles's old Justice of the Peace legal forms and an imitation sheriff's star to "arrest" a man who failed to pay for Boast's team of horses. Boast needed the money. He was leaving for Iowa, but planned to return with his new wife before the anticipated land grab in the spring. Wilder insisted on including these incidents in *By the Shores of Silver Lake*, despite repeated protests that the material reflected poorly on her father or did not belong in a morally uplifting children's book, simply because they were true to her experience of the West.

Winter brought rare days of leisure to the cozy surveyor's house. Laura read constantly, learned to play checkers, and listened to Charles's fiddle sing late into the night. In her novel covering the period, Wilder lavished detail on the riches Laura discovered in the pantry of the surveyor's house: soda crackers, pickles, salt fish, dried apples, canned peaches, white flour, and potatoes. In her memoir, however, it was Charles himself who "laid in a supply of provisions and simple medicines."[8] The family would be isolated for months; if anyone fell ill during this time, there would be no doctor to call. Any out-of-season addition to their grindingly monotonous diet—particularly canned fruits and vegetables—was significant to the Ingalls. Wilder preserved many traditional recipes in her work, from salt pork and beans to her mother's fried vanity cakes, but most of the food Wilder ate in childhood was prepared in a single cast-iron pot and depended on a few basic ingredients—usually lard, molasses, cornmeal, and salt. Game remained the staple of the Ingalls's diet. With the coming of winter, Charles scoured the countryside for antelope, jackrabbit, and deer. While he hunted and tended his trap lines, he kept one eye peeled for the best available homestead site. Caroline made a little extra money boarding Walter Ogden, a stubborn homesteader who had refused to leave Dakota for the winter and bunked in the stable. Christmas Eve—a magical night, the highpoint of every year in Wilder's novels—brought a spectacular surprise to the Ingalls's doorstep. Although forced to abandon his sleigh in a snowdrift, Robert Boast arrived like Santa with his merry bride Ella, tins of oysters, honey, home-dried fruit, new books, stacks of newspapers, and a bulging sack of candy.

By February, Charles had selected a choice homestead not far from Silver Lake. The land was well drained and well watered. It bordered the Big Slough, a shallow wetland that served as a magnet for game and wildfowl. There were valuable meadows in the upland, ideal for growing hay and grazing cattle. Charles hurried east to Brookings to file on his claim. The spring land rush had just begun. One sure sign was the arrival of the Reverend Edwin Alden at the Ingalls's door. At the first hint of a thaw, missionary societies sent preachers west to organize churches in the boomtowns. In *By the Shores of Silver Lake,* Wilder credits the Reverend Alden with telling Caroline about the existence of a college for the blind in faraway Vinton, Iowa. It was the type of institution a Congregational minister would be well aware of. Unable to read braille and without access to formal education, manual training, or rehabilitation, Mary's life was in stasis. She spent much of her day rocking in her chair by the fire, holding Grace, listening to Laura read aloud, or knitting. And no doubt attempting to reconcile her blindness with explanations, such as the one Wilder attributes to Brother Alden in *By the Shores of Silver Lake:* "We must remember that whom the Lord loveth, He chasteneth."[9] In the novel, Wilder describes Ma gripping the dirty dishpan and the "choked and hungry" sound of her voice as she asks Brother Alden about the college's cost.

The Dakota land rush was on. Nearly every day in the cold spring of 1880, bands of strange men began arriving at the Surveyor's House seeking food, shelter, and any advice on selecting the best available homestead claim. They showed up on foot, in lumber wagons, in buggies, and on horseback. When regular train service resumed, their numbers swelled. Laura and her mother charged the newcomers (as many as eighteen men a day) for meals and a spot to sleep on the crowded floor. Latecomers slept in the open or under their wagons. For the first time, Laura donned one of Mary's floor-length dresses. She also pinned up her hair, the outward sign of young womanhood. Although her previous hotel experience proved useful, even unflagging Laura found it impossible to keep up with the workload. When Caroline was confined to bed with a migraine one day, Laura assumed full responsibility for boarding the men. She worked to the point of exhaustion, finally collapsing on the floor. With Ella Boast's timely arrival and assistance, Laura got back on her feet. She washed the last towering stack of dishes, cleaned the kitchen, prepared to serve the next morning's breakfast, and helped Mary to bed.[10] Laura, who never quite reached five feet in height, had just turned thirteen. Her work ethic developed early, she had limited patience with those who did not share it, and she practiced what she preached.

As at Brookings, surveyors arrived to create an orderly plat map for the new town that was springing up alongside the railroad camp just west of Silver Lake. The town was named De Smet, for Jesuit missionary Father Pierre-Jean De Smet, friend of Sitting Bull. As soon as the surveyors' stakes were pounded in the ground, Charles bought two corner lots and began construction of a new frame building, which he hoped to turn for a quick profit. In April, the Ingalls left the Surveyor's House and moved into the hastily built storefront, where the snow penetrated the gaps in walls, drifted over them at night, and made a light insulating blanket atop their thin cotton quilts. Charles sold the first building and immediately began work on another. In the spring and summer of 1880, De Smet erupted from the prairie—a true frontier town replete with a bank, a hotel, grocery, drug and dry-goods stores, livery services, a saloon, bustling train depot, and lumber yard. Soon, the Chicago & North Western Railroad began hauling "emigrant cars" to De Smet. The famous British author, Robert Louis Stevenson, who actually traveled in one, described these cattle cars overflowing with hopeful farm families and everything they owned as "a Babel of bewildered men, women and children."[11] Early on, Dakota Territory attracted a large number of "Bohemian" settlers, along with Germans, Finns, and Poles. As in Kansas a decade earlier, the availability of arable homestead land failed to meet the overwhelming demand. Claim jumping and claim disputes were fairly common. After a local homesteader was shot and killed in a dispute over a claim he had vacated during the winter, Charles immediately moved

58 • Laura Ingalls Wilder: American Writer on the Prairie

his family out of the building in De Smet (which he most likely rented out for extra income) and into the shanty he had built as a place holder on his new homestead claim. Holding on to his prime homestead property was paramount. Laura, for one, was glad to go. The tiny one-room shanty was infested with mice, but it was located more than a mile from town "in the sweet prairie."[12] Laura soon acquired a newborn kitten. She fed it milk from a teaspoon until it grew large enough to hunt. Wilder's genuine love for animals struck a strong chord in her young readers. She was especially attached to dogs and horses, but she would write with the passion of John Muir on her love of wilderness and her sorrow at its passing.

> Laura thought how wild and beautiful it must have been when the twin lakes were one, when buffalo and antelope roamed the prairie around the great lake and came there to drink, when wolves and coyotes and foxes lived on the banks and wild geese, swans, herons, cranes, ducks, and gulls nested and fished and flew there in countless numbers.[13]

At thirteen, Laura was no longer simply performing chores for her father; she was actively farming by his side. When Charles tar-papered the shanty, she likely served as his lone assistant. She helped establish a cotton-wood windbreak on the farm, planted turnip seed, hauled water, and cared for two milk cows and the horses. She spent long days in the field loading and unloading the hay wagon for Charles while he cut slough grass, then helped him heave the hay into stacks for the winter. It was demanding physical labor, "heavy lifting," and generally regarded as work inappropriate for women. Although it is clear from Wilder's autobiographical memoir that Caroline did occasionally work beside her husband at planting and harvest time, Wilder minimized Ma's participation in her novels: "Ma did not like to see women working the fields. Only foreigners did that. Ma and her girls were Americans, above doing men's work."[14] It was a widely held sentiment at the time, especially by mothers who considered it their duty to uphold Victorian mores and social conventions. In the field or in the home, the hard physical labor of pioneer life took its toll. In a photograph of Charles and Caroline from this time, both husband and wife display the huge knobby knuckles, splayed fingers, and overworked, leathery hands of the pioneers. Laura clearly identified with her father and the freedom of a life lived outdoors. She also felt sense of solidarity with him in his struggle to provide for the family. Once again, startup farming expenses—a new mowing machine and hay rake—had taken a toll on the family's finances. When Laura noticed that her father was eating less to ensure sufficient food for the rest of the family, she cut back on meals as well. Laura and Charles weren't starving, but they were genuinely hungry; Wilder later recorded how she imitated her father and ate raw turnips—cattle fodder—to stave off hunger pangs between meals. Even so, she greatly preferred life on the farm to town life in De Smet. "Town was just a place where, for safety, we spent the winter," she wrote.[15]

Winter caught the Ingalls off-guard. One overcast October afternoon in 1880, while Laura was sitting outside the shanty plucking geese in the gray drizzle, Charles casually mentioned that the birds were racing south and that he did not like the look of the weather. By morning, the family woke to a howling blizzard. The tarpaper shanty was sheathed in ice and snow. Mary, Carrie, and Grace were told to remain in bed for warmth, but Laura insisted on rising. After three days, the gale force winds began to wane, and Laura peered out the small opaque window at a featureless landscape and a truly macabre sight. Driven by the storm, a herd of ghost cattle were standing in the yard, heads dangling, too exhausted to move. Charles bundled up and ventured out to investigate. Suddenly, he burst into a frenzy of activity. He tore at the cows' blind, ice-encrusted eyes and smashed the ice that had caked around their steaming mouths and had tethered them to the snow. Once released, the bawling cattle took shelter beside the Ingalls's haystacks. The haystacks also harbored a number of unfamiliar, half-dead birds, which the family gently gathered and brought inside the shanty until they recovered. The October Blizzard raged for three days and claimed scores of settlers and their livestock. It marked the coming of Wilder's Long Winter.

The Ingalls wasted no time moving back to their empty building in town. The severe and unseasonable weather had unnerved more than a few of the scattered settlers. As the weather grew colder, they fled their homesteads and packed into the thin-walled stores, stables, and newspaper-lined lean-tos of De Smet. Better insulated from the cold, a few sod house farmers decided to remain on their land, hunker down with their precious livestock, and take their chances. George Masters of Walnut Grove arrived on the Ingalls's doorstep seeking winter lodgings for his heavily pregnant bride Maggie while George sought employment farther west. Unwilling to turn her away (and probably still in debt to the Masters family in Walnut Grove), the Ingalls made room for Maggie in their crowded and inadequately stocked living quarters behind the store. Always popular with his peers, Charles again served as Justice of the Peace from the front office of the store. As a skilled carpenter, he would have found plenty of work in the boomtown, until dangerously low temperatures forced everyone indoors.[16]

The weather pattern that churned over the Dakotas in the brutal winter of 1880–1881 produced life-threatening conditions in De Smet: white-out blizzards, months of sub-zero temperatures, and, when nearly a hundred feet of snow buried the railbed at the deep grading cut at Tracy, the suspension of all train service. The Chicago & North Western Railroad was the only reliable means of transporting coal and food to De Smet. George Masters returned to De Smet from the west on one of the last trains of the season. With no money and nowhere else to go, he and his wife promptly moved into the Ingalls's store, creating an even greater drain on the family's limited food supply. The Masters's baby was delivered by Caroline and Margaret Frances Garland, a neighboring widow who ran a boarding house, in the frigid bedroom above the store. Every sound of labor and delivery would have reverberated through the paper-thin walls. Laura disliked George Masters from the start. George slept until noon. When he wasn't complaining, he ate like a horse. Worst of all, he didn't work. When the coal ran out, George didn't sit in the freezing lean-to as she did, laboriously twisting coarse slough hay into sticks of fuel. Instead, he elbowed his way to the stove and hogged the best place by the anemic fire. There was no escape from the relentless cold. When the last of the over brewed tea leaves ran out, Caroline revived an old recipe from her hardscrabble childhood. She roasted, ground, and brewed a bit of seed wheat to make a coffee substitute sometimes called *Sin and Misery* because it was a sin to burn the wheat and a misery to drink it.[17]

Charles was more fortunate. He could escape George Masters's company at Fuller's Hardware Store across the street, where a crowd of men, including two bachelor homesteaders, Almanzo Wilder and his older brother Royal, gathered almost daily to discuss the town's growing food and fuel crisis. Laura and Carrie found respite at school, but not for long. During the first week of December, out of the clear blue sky, a blizzard tore in from the west and slammed into the schoolhouse like "a mighty sledge."[18] Just nineteen years old, new teacher Florence Garland panicked at the violent rocking of the building, the screaming wind, and the total lack of visibility through the icy window. She ordered the children to bundle up, form a human chain, and follow her outside. They were going home. Nineteenth-century children were expected to obey teachers, parents, and their elders without hesitation, question, or protest. It was Charles's unwavering demand of his own children. Laura knew that leaving the comparative safety of the schoolhouse in dangerous white-out conditions made no sense, but she held her tongue and grasped Carrie's hand. Outside, Florence Garland and the students became instantly and hopelessly disoriented, unable to locate the main street just three blocks away or communicate with one another over the roar of the wind. Convinced they were wandering toward open prairie, Florence Garland's brother, Oscar Edmund "Cap" Garland, defied his sister and broke ranks. He left the group and took off running in the opposite direction. The children lowered their heads and staggered on. Just as they were about to stumble out of town, they rammed into the corner of De Smet's hotel. Having found a landmark, Laura and the other students stopped dead in their tracks. Cap Garland had managed to notify several men in town,

Settling the West: The 1880s • 61

who were already tethering themselves to long ropes and forming a rescue party. A few years later, on January 12, 1888, in the record-shattering storm known as "The Children's Blizzard," scores of reluctant if equally dutiful schoolchildren held hands, formed a line, and followed their teachers out of the schoolhouse and into brutal gale-force winds, having greatly underestimated the risk inherent in the dash for home. The regional death toll (estimated at between 250 and 500) included a sickening number of schoolchildren who died of hypothermia in South Dakota, Nebraska, and western Minnesota.[19]

Handsome and independent, blond Cap Garland had captured Laura's full attention, but she had no opportunity to indulge her interest. School shut down after the blizzard; few ventured outside unless absolutely necessary. De Smet was starving, cut off from resupply by rail, with spring still months away. Packed together in makeshift sheds, the settlers' cattle, hens, and horses began to succumb to the extreme cold. Hay was the Ingalls's only source of fuel for heating and cooking, and the only source of feed for their animals. Charles's hay supply was located on the homestead, over a mile from town through heavy drifting snow. Charles was forced to make regular sleigh trips back to the homestead to haul hay from his frozen stacks by the Big Slough. The unpredictable arrival of the blizzards made the timing of each trip a risky venture and was exhausting work for a hungry man with a hungry horse.

Farmers around De Smet had only begun to cultivate their land the previous season, so there were no root cellars larded with winter vegetables to supplement their dwindling supplies of cornmeal. Most homesteaders had produced little more than a few rows of turnips and sod potatoes. Even at wildly inflated prices, the last flour barrel and sugar loaf disappeared from the stores. The hungry, stressed cows went dry. A homesteader named French was somehow persuaded to slaughter his team of oxen and sell the meat, leaving him with no ability to farm his claim in the spring. Caroline improvised sourdough biscuits from water, salt, and a bit of ground seed wheat that Charles quietly purchased from the Wilder brothers' secret cache across the street. Mary spent hours balancing a coffee mill in her lap, laboriously grinding seed kernels into coarse, whole-wheat flour. Tempers began to flare in the close confines of the Ingalls's store. When George Masters complained about the cold, Laura told him to go sit in the freezing lean-to and twist hay for a while. For once, no one reprimanded her. Not long afterward, several men organized an antelope hunt despite the bitter cold. When Charles and the others finally managed to take down a single doe, butcher her, and divide out the meat, the kill brought Laura to the brink of tears. The death of the "little starved creature" whose struggle to survive winter proved futile hit too close to home.[20]

Laura's fourteenth birthday came and went amid rumors of an untouched store of seed wheat located on a homestead about twelve miles from town. Daniel Loftus, a local merchant, was willing to purchase the entire stock of seed for resale in town if anyone was willing to go after it. A twenty-four-mile round trip through deep snowdrifts pushed the edge of the possible, but Cap Garland and Almanzo Wilder agreed to try. Their lightning run to the remote homestead and eleventh-hour return to town with a sleigh full of wheat and a blizzard on their heels turned the two young men into local heroes. By the time the starving people of De Smet finally heard an engine whistle announce the long-awaited arrival of a train, even the new influx of seed wheat was nearly gone. Ironically, the train rolled in hauling plows, seeders, harvesters, mowing machines, and a thresher, all the equipment the townspeople needed to produce a bumper harvest in the fall. The people of De Smet tore through the cars in disbelief until they located an emigrant car full of food at the very end of the train. They broke into the car, seized the food, and immediately rationed it out to every household in town.[21] The arrival of the train, however, signaled the end of the unbearable Hard Winter.

A surviving photo of Laura, Mary, and Carrie dates to the end of the Hard Winter. It shows Mary and Laura in matching check-print dresses. Mary sits quietly in a chair, her face unreadable, her hands folded demurely in her lap; tiny Carrie hovers at her side. Laura towers over her sisters like a sentry. Her face is half turned from the camera, but the intense expression in her eyes and her confident, almost military bearing suggest a young woman who is considerably older than her years, someone who has already learned hard lessons in tenacity, endurance and resolve. Only on second glance does the viewer notice that the resolute young woman is strikingly pretty, with fine even features and a tumbling mass of dark wavy hair.

Single men in town were beginning to notice the Ingalls's second daughter. It wasn't long before Laura, now half-heartedly laced into a corset that she refused to cinch tight, began attracting suitors. Perhaps not surprisingly, given the disproportionate number of single men in town, Laura's many admirers were not drawn from the ranks of her snowballing schoolmates. In fact, nearly all of them were several years her senior. Laura reacted to their arrival with bemusement and disinterest. She was eager to leave town that summer and return to the shanty on the windy claim, the only place she considered home. "I did not care for so many people. I loved the empty prairie and the wild things that lived on it, much more."[22]

For all its attendant hardships and disappointments, Laura Ingalls loved farm life. In her memoir, she describes the blooming prairie in rich detail; she particularly loved the low tangled mats of wild roses that carpeted the prairie in June. She spent as much time as possible outdoors, caring for the garden, the weed-eating pig, and the cows and their calves. For Laura, daily chores like hauling water from the well provided a welcome opportunity to observe wildlife at the edge of the Big Slough, a pristine wetland teeming with meadowlarks, skittish jackrabbits, and the graceful garter snakes she refused to kill. Laura constantly marveled at nature, at just "how much variety and how much of interest" could be found in a quarter-section of land, from vigilant gophers racing underground at the shadow of a hawk to the summer corn growing "astonishingly tall and strong and a most vivid green" as it rocketed out of the virgin ground.[23] "I don't see how anyone could improve on your use of words. You are perfect in describing landscapes and things," Laura's daughter Rose Wilder Lane later admitted admiringly.[24] The "word pictures" to which Lane referred were invariably descriptions of the natural world and the "quiet prairie" her mother loved so well.

"But it seemed I could not stay there," Laura added sadly.[25] The family needed cash. Every morning, Charles walked into booming De Smet to find carpentry work. His conscientious daughter found employment in a dry-goods store, sewing shirts for twenty-five cents a day. Once again she was "living out," an arrangement she loathed. Laura sewed shirts at the back of the store, took her meals with the shopkeeper's family, and shared an attic bedroom with her employer, the merchant's elderly mother-in-law, who spent most of her time castigating the Roman Catholics she was convinced were coming to confiscate her Bible and waiting for the end of the world.[26] Laura plugged her ears, rolled her eyes, and soldiered on. Although she was relieved to return home when the sewing work ran out, Laura and her family were working with renewed purpose to reach a common goal—sending Mary to the College for the Blind in Vinton, Iowa.

While it is possible that the Reverend Alden was the first person to inform the Ingalls about the existence of the college, he probably did not need to make inquiries on their behalf. Because there was no school for the blind in Dakota Territory, the Territorial Legislature arranged for blind students who met specific requirements to receive their public education at the Iowa College for the Blind. Until a territorial school for the deaf was established, deaf students were also enrolled at schools in neighboring states. County commissioners were responsible for reporting qualified deaf, mute, and blind students to the governor for further action. Charles Ingalls was involved in local government and served as a county commissioner in fall of 1880;[27] over time, he would hold a number of public offices in De Smet and Kingsbury County, including Justice of the Peace, Deputy Sheriff, and Street Commissioner, positions of respect and influence, but rarely remunerative. In 1880–1881, when the Ingalls were cutoff and buried by De Smet's Hard Winter, three blind students from the Dakota Territory were already enrolled at Vinton.[28] Mary Ingalls was about to join them. Although the territory likely paid her full tuition, the Ingalls were responsible for all of Mary's travel and incidental expenses, a hefty sum for any homesteading family. College records, few of which survive from the period, indicate that the Ingalls were classified as a family of "moderate" means.[29]

By the time Mary left for Iowa, the Ingalls were eating blackbirds. Great clouds of blackbirds descended on their glorious cornfield and helped themselves to the crop. At first, Charles shot the birds and left them in the field where they dropped. Soon however, the blackbirds became breakfast, lunch, and dinner—day after day of pan-fried blackbird. The economizing continued as the Ingalls prepared for Mary's departure. In the fall, Charles and Caroline escorted Mary to stylish, well-established Vinton, with its tidy lawns and Painted Lady Victorian homes. The Iowa College for the Blind offered a rigorous and demanding academic curriculum, considerably more challenging than the typical prairie high school of the day. Core classes, including algebra, rhetoric, chemistry, political economics, botany, and history, were taught at a college level, along with vocal and instrumental music, braille, and a variety of manual and industrial courses. The campus was approached by a wide circular drive. Framed by white pillars, a grand portico, and sweeping verandas, Old Main was an impressive sight. Admission to the college was a remarkable turn of events for Mary and a source of profound relief and pride for her family. Mary had always been more compliant than Laura, more conventionally religious, and her Calvinism broached little questioning or complaint or second-guessing of God's will. Even so, Laura quickly recognized that Mary was far happier after she enrolled at Vinton than she had been rocking listlessly in the shanty on the homestead claim. "And I," Wilder later recorded, "who wanted a college education so much myself, was so very happy in thinking that Mary was getting one."[30] Although Laura was undoubtedly happy for her sister, her private feelings were probably more mixed. After all, she was the one who had worked interminable hours basting shirts and boarding with strangers to help defray the cost of Mary's college education. Throughout her life, even after her unprecedented literary success, Wilder expressed lingering regret and self-consciousness over the fact she had "never graduated from anything."[31] Soothing, watchful Caroline may have sensed her younger daughter's conflicted feelings. She bought a special gift for Laura in Vinton—a volume of Walter Scott's poems, sure to please—which she carefully hid until Christmas.

In the fall, after the heavy work of helping her father put up hay, Laura returned to school. De Smet had a new teacher, Eliza Jane Wilder, Almanzo Wilder's domineering older sister. The two young women had little in common other than their strong wills and mutual dislike. The term got off to a rough start. Laura deeply resented Eliza Jane's high-handed treatment of

Settling the West: The 1880s • 65

Carrie and felt Eliza Jane singled Carrie out for embarrassing reproof. Laura was the acknowledged leader of the classroom, but it was apparent to her that she was being secretly ridiculed for her family's lack of funds. There had been no new shoes, ribbons, and dresses for Laura and Carrie that fall; all the money had gone toward Mary's wardrobe, school, and traveling expenses. Geneva Masters, George Masters's sister and teacher's pet, made cutting comments about Laura's appearance, called her fat, and criticized her worn-out clothes. Laura was sick with rage at Geneva's dismissive treatment of her. In Wilder's novels, nasty composite character Nellie Oleson was based in part on Geneva Masters. Laura liked Eliza Jane Wilder even less than she did Geneva and lampooned her in *Little Town on the Prairie* as "lazy, lousy, Lizy Jane." Famously, Laura nearly rocked Carrie's school desk off its floor bolts in an attempt irritate Eliza Jane and undermine her authority. Much to Laura's satisfaction, Eliza Jane Wilder was replaced by a new teacher before the end of term.

The "big boys" returned to school after the harvest. The young men of De Smet who had seen little of Laura over the summer lined up when she returned to town for the winter. Cap Garland brought her candy (which Geneva Masters gobbled down). Young lawyer Alfred Thomas attempted to ask her to a Literary Society event, but his tongue-tied approach only baffled and annoyed her. Suddenly, Almanzo Wilder began quietly attending Literary Society meetings as well. Ernie Perry took her to country dances and parties, but Laura disliked "the kissing games" and Ernie's awkward attentions.[32] Still, a sleigh-ride and winter party for young people was considerably more entertaining than the Religious Revival or the Women's Christian Temperance Union meetings she would sometimes attend with her mother when she wasn't babysitting. One evening, as she was leaving church with her parents and sneaking a last admiring look at Cap Garland, Laura felt someone touch her arm. It was Almanzo Wilder, asking if he could escort her home. As Almanzo fell in beside his daughter, Charles placed his own hand firmly on the back of his astonished wife, propelled her out the door, and hustled her home.[33]

Almanzo Wilder, Laura's laconic Prince Charming, still eludes biographers. Even his birthday proved mysterious. Census records strongly suggest that he added a year to his age at the time he filed on his Dakota homestead claim.[34] Since he had not yet turned 21 at the time, he was legally ineligible to file. Apparently, he never felt the need to rectify the difference. Laura was just 15 when the couple met; Almanzo was probably 24. He had recently returned from the Chicago and North West Railroad camp near Huron, where he had worked for a season. A keen horseman, he probably worked as a teamster rather than as a general laborer.[35] His family's old New England roots and his own New York childhood were similar in many ways

66 • Laura Ingalls Wilder: American Writer on the Prairie

to that of Charles Ingalls, but the Wilder family had always been far more prosperous. Charles liked the young man with the strange name. He called him Wilder; others frequently referred to Almanzo as the "younger Wilder boy." Almanzo's background and interests would have qualified him as an acceptable suitor for his daughter, in Charles's mind.

Compact and handsome in his twenties, Almanzo was an experienced farmer, a successful homesteader, and an expert at handling and breeding Morgan horses. His matching team of elegant Morgans was instantly recognizable and admired throughout the county. Almanzo had grown up on a prosperous farm near Malone, New York, where he had received a private education at the Franklin Academy. In the 1870s, he left frigid upstate New York and moved west with his parents and several siblings to Spring Valley, Minnesota, not far from Burr Oak, Iowa. There, he farmed with his family until he, older brother Royal, and unconventional sister Eliza Jane threw themselves into the Dakota Boom and staked out individual homesteads near De Smet. Like Charles Ingalls, Almanzo Wilder was hardworking and versatile, a tenacious farmer who had already mastered the dizzying array of skills that made independent family farms possible, if not always profitable. He also possessed patience, loyalty, and persistence, all qualities he would need as his long courtship of Laura Ingalls slowly progressed.

Not yet sixteen, Laura was young to entertain a serious suitor, and Almanzo Wilder meant business from the start. "No old bachelor would go with a young girl like that, unless he did," the mother of one of Laura's friends stated categorically.[36] Sensitive to the discrepancy in their ages, Laura called him "Mr. Wilder" long after their first tongue-tied walk home from the Revival Meeting. In December, these introductory walks came to an abrupt halt. Twelve miles south of De Smet, on the Bouchie farm, local homesteaders had managed to raise a shanty schoolhouse and forty dollars for a teacher's salary. Qualified teachers were difficult to find, much less retain on the frontier. Married women were not allowed to teach school, a restriction that resulted in continual and disruptive teacher turnover. For bright young women, teaching provided respect, autonomy, and better wages than almost all other employment options. The Ingalls's old friend Robert Boast put forth Laura's name. Laura could not afford to refuse such a lucrative offer, even if it meant living far from home in the dead of winter. Although she was legally underage and uncertified, she passed the qualifying examination with flying colors, at which time the school examiner conveniently neglected to ask her age. Within days, Laura was on her way to her first classroom. She arrived determined, nervous, and completely unprepared—not only for her new position as teacher, but also for the challenges of daily life in the simmering, hostile, and unstable Bouchie household.

Delilah Olive Bouchie was the model for the disturbed and muttering "Mrs. Brewster" of *These Happy Golden Years*. Her struggle with depression, isolation, and grinding poverty was not uncommon among homesteaders, but Wilder's vivid depiction of Mrs. Brewster as a volatile, knife-wielding menace was almost unprecedented in contemporary children's literature. Laura shared their ominous shanty, slept on a small sofa behind a makeshift curtain, ate her meals in stony silence, spent as much time as possible in the rickety school building, and pined for home. On weekday mornings, muffled in every layer of clothing she owned, she trudged through knee-deep snow to the school shanty. Frontier schoolhouses were so cold in winter that students generally remained bundled and gloved throughout the day, but the school offered a brief respite from the Bouchie's house.

Laura was a conscientious teacher who quickly warmed to her duties and her students, but she was desperate to escape the Bouchie's threatening, claustrophobic household. She missed her family, who were spending the gloomy winter in town. And she was she missed as well, far more than she realized. Egged on by Cap Garland's inarguable assertion "God hates a coward," a smitten Almanzo began hitching his team of Morgan horses to his handmade cutter and driving all the way to the Bouchie school on Friday afternoons. Once there, he helped Laura collect a few belongings, bundled her under a buffalo robe, and whisked her home until Sunday afternoon, when he would return her to the Bouchie farm. It was an unassuming act of kindness and consideration on the part of a young man who clearly understood Laura quite well. Every Friday afternoon, as class dismissed in the early dusk, Laura listened for the sound of Almanzo's sleigh bells, a sound that carried for miles over the white featureless prairie and signaled to her that her rescue was at hand. Despite brutal subzero weather, Almanzo made the long trip every weekend without fail until Laura's teaching term expired.

Laura, however, remained unconvinced. She told Almanzo point blank that, while she appreciated the ride, she had no intention of "going with him" after she returned to De Smet. Almanzo let the comment slide and Laura's adamant declaration did not last for long. Soon she was seen riding through the snow-packed streets of De Smet in Almanzo's cutter and the two had settled on pet names for each other. She considered Almanzo's name "outrageous" and decided she would call him Manly. Almanzo claimed he preferred Laura's middle name, Elizabeth, to Laura. For the rest of the couple's long courtship and the remainder of their lives, to each other they were Manly and Bess.

Even though she was now certified to teach, Laura returned to school with Carrie for the winter term. She also accepted several different jobs to augment the family's income. Many women on the frontier sewed for extra cash. Laura worked for a seamstress in town and began to hone her

68 • Laura Ingalls Wilder: American Writer on the Prairie

excellent sewing skills and her abiding interest in hats, hoops, style, and fashion. Throughout her life, Laura followed fashion closely, dressed well, and consulted seasonal pattern books for the latest styles. She also assisted Mrs. McKee, the lumberyard owner's wife, when she had extra sewing projects. The older woman was moving with her ten-year-old daughter to the family's homestead claim near the town of Manchester. She invited Laura to join her, probably to sew, assist with housework, and provide companionship for her and her daughter. The McKees were a pleasant family and Laura did not object to living away from home on their farm, although she was concerned about leaving her father. Charles, she noted, looked thin and worn. Worse, for the first time Laura suspected that her cheerful, fiddle-playing father was not happy. The wild prairie surrounding De Smet had transformed dramatically in the first years of the Dakota Boom. An orderly grid of wheat fields replaced the sea of grass. Like his daughter, and unlike his wife, Charles clearly harbored conflicted feelings about the advantages of "civilizing" the West, the creation of towns, and the massive influx of settlers. Bonded by chance and disaster, Charles had maintained a correspondence with the devastated beekeeper he had met years earlier when the Ingalls fled the locust invasion. The beekeeper had moved on to Oregon—the end of the West—and he wrote to encourage Charles to join him. It would be several years before Charles could prove up on his homestead claim. Even if he owned the land, his farming operation was only marginally profitable. His daughters would marry; he had no sons to inherit the land. Charles approached Caroline with the idea of one final move—to Oregon.[37] Caroline flatly refused. She liked town, she liked church, and she liked the Women's Christian Temperance Union meetings. If he wanted to go, he could go without her.

Unable to afford a mechanical harvester, still swinging his old wooden cradle, Charles cut his entire wheat and oat crop by hand that season. Mary's education remained the family's first priority. In her painstaking longhand, Mary wrote regular letters from Vinton where she was learning to read and write braille. Mary was an exemplary student; she threw herself into the academic challenge of her coursework and thrived on the camaraderie of the college. She had discovered a latent talent for music and she excelled at the organ. Laura hung on every word of Mary's absorbing college adventures. She apparently did not question the fact that the money she earned was not her own or that so much of it went to Mary's education, even as she continued to live and work on the McKee homestead. The McKees were fervent Presbyterians, much to Laura's chagrin and occasional amusement. Laura rarely minced words. Sundays with the McKees were stultifying and "stupid"—long her favorite world of opprobrium.[38] On Sunday there was no work, no play, no laughter, no reading of anything except the Bible. Laura

Settling the West: The 1880s • 69

did enjoy her lively debate with Robert McKee about the doctrine of preordination. She dismissed this central point of McKee's theology as damned-if-you-do, damned-if-you-don't nonsense and asked him point-blank what difference it made if one chose good or evil if everyone's eternal fate was predetermined? As would many others, Robert McKee grew to appreciate the frank young woman and her bold, unvarnished opinions.

Mr. Owens, Laura's teacher that term, also recognized and acknowledged something unusual about his gifted student. He encouraged her, complimented her "wonderful mind and memory," and told Charles that his second daughter should have every opportunity for higher education.[39] Although Laura hated public speaking and spent hours rehearsing her lessons by repeating them to the corner of her bedroom wall, she discovered that she did like to write. Her first essay, "Ambition," with its nod to Shakespeare, was not especially skilled but Mr. Owens urged her to write more. Perhaps he was simply delighted to discover a Shakespeare-reading student. Laura was under no illusion that there would be any higher education in her future. The only expectation for Laura, as for almost all young women of the nineteenth century, was marriage and motherhood. The summer brought tornados, severe thunderstorms, and sleepless nights spent in the wet storm cellar. But even as the workload increased, Laura felt happiest working outside in the scrubbed air and the fields of the farm.

When Laura returned home, Almanzo wasted no time pressing his suit. He arrived at the homestead in a brand new buggy, ready to resume the couple's long treks around the scenic countryside. Almanzo was doing very well for a farmer in his twenties; he could afford to marry. He had filed for a 160-acre tree claim in addition to his homestead, thereby increasing his land holdings to 320 acres. By farming cooperatively with his brother Royal and his sister Eliza Jane, the Wilder siblings held an impressive amount of farm ground, nearly a section of land (one square mile or 640 acres), provided they could keep it. One evening after a long ramble in the buggy, while Laura sang some of the old ballads she loved, Almanzo asked her simply and sincerely if she would like an engagement ring. Laura claimed she was not expecting the proposal, but she accepted it. In fact, she sealed the deal. As the newly engaged couple returned to the Ingalls's shanty to deliver the news, she turned to Almanzo and nudged him, asking point-blank, "Aren't you going to kiss me good night?"[40]

Soon Laura was sporting a seed pearl and garnet engagement ring. Still a schoolgirl herself, she took the territorial teacher's examination for second-grade certification and passed with honors. Armed with her new credentials, she applied for an even-more-lucrative teaching position at the Wilkins School north of town: thirty dollars a month for a three-month term. It was a significant sum, perhaps her last chance to earn money before her impending marriage precluded employment, but it came at a price. In order to teach at the Wilkins School, Laura would have to interrupt her own education one last time. Since she planned to marry after teaching the spring term, she would not be able to graduate high school. This proved a lasting disappointment to Laura, who only recently had been encouraged to view herself as a bright and gifted scholar, a candidate for higher education. Mary returned home for the summer, full of exciting college tales.

When Laura returned from her teaching assignment, her wedding plans were in a state of flux. Almanzo reluctantly informed her that his mother and overbearing sister Eliza Jane were eagerly planning an elaborate wedding and reception, which the couple did not want and the Ingalls could not afford. Manly and Bess decided to take matters into their own hand. On August 25, 1885, they drove to the home of Congregational minister Reverend Brown—a fire and brimstone preacher Laura could barely tolerate—and were married in his parlor without any family in attendance and with only two close friends to stand as witnesses. Laura specifically requested that the word "obey" be removed from her wedding vows, a request honored by the Reverend Brown.[41] The eighteen-year-old wore her new "best dress," an elegant ensemble of fine black cashmere that she and her mother had made for Laura's trousseau. Caroline had also helped outfit her daughter's first home by sewing long strips of fabric into bed sheets and making feather pillows. Laura's black wedding dress was a sensible and common indulgence. Like almost all pioneer brides, she would expect to wear it many times after the wedding to church events, the baptism of her children, and other special occasions. After the brief ceremony, the newlyweds returned to the Ingalls's home for a festive wedding luncheon. Charles and Caroline's generous wedding gift to their daughter was a cow, likely one of the Ingalls's own, which no doubt pleased the practical bride who had spent so many happy hours wandering open sunny meadows in search of wayward cattle.

Late that afternoon, the Wilders waved goodbye to the Ingalls and drove back to De Smet. They passed the old familiar livery barn, crossed the railroad tracks, and continued north to Almanzo's tree claim, where Almanzo had just finished building a new farmhouse, a present of his own to welcome the bride. The little gray house on the tree claim was more substantial and impressive than all the other little houses Laura had ever known. She explored the sitting room, the unfamiliar bedroom with its one small bed, her bright new kitchen, and the ingenious pantry Almanzo had designed for her, stacked with cabinets and drawers. There was fresh bread in the pantry and a neighbor's pie graced their table. She made supper, washed the dishes, and then went to join her new husband on the stoop. Together, they watched the moon sail over their fine dark fields, so full of peace and

Settling the West: The 1880s • 71

plenty, and drank in the quiet sounds of a country evening. Almanzo's dog Shep stirred at their feet. Laura Ingalls Wilder was exactly where she was meant to be, her whole life lay ahead of her, and she had finally found the place called home.

For millions of readers, young and old, Wilder's seductive frontier fairytale had just come to its tremendously satisfying conclusion in *These Happy Golden Years*. Like any good fairytale or great Shakespearean comedy, the story had ended in the long-awaited wedding of the brave and happy couple and the promise of life lived happily ever after. In reality, what came next for Bess and Manly was a series of unmitigated disasters that would claim their home, their farm, their health, their livelihood, their life savings, their future in the Dakotas, and their only son.

Notes

1. LIW, "Pioneer Girl," 70.
2. Laura Ingalls Wilder Family Correspondence, 1861–1919, Wisconsin Historical Society manuscript collection Stout SC 142.
3. LIW, "Pioneer Girl," 73.
4. Howard Zinn, *A People's History of the United States* (New York: HarperCollins, 1980), 251.
5. LIW, "Pioneer Girl," 76.
6. Ibid., 82.
7. Ibid., 80.
8. Ibid, 82.
9. LIW, *By the Shores of Silver Lake* (New York: Harper & Bros., 1953), 217.
10. LIW, "Pioneer Girl," 87.
11. Robert Louis Stevenson, *Across the Plains* (New York: C. Scribner's Sons, 1892), 3.
12. LIW, "Pioneer Girl," 90.
13. LIW, *These Happy Golden Years,* 182.
14. LIW, *The Long Winter,* 4.
15. LIW, "Pioneer Girl," 110.
16. Ibid., 102.
17. Favell, Angela Haste. "A Girl Pioneer,"
18. LIW, "Pioneer Girl," 95.
19. David Laskin, *The Children's Blizzard* (New York: HarperCollins, 2004), 2.
20. LIW, "Pioneer Girl," 106.
21. Ibid., 107.
22. Ibid., 110.
23. Ibid., 113.
24. Lane Papers, RWL to LIW. Dec. 19, 1937.
25. LIW, "Pioneer Girl," 112.
26. Ibid., 113.
27. Ibid., 94.
28. *General Laws, and Memorials and Resolutions of the Territory of Dakota* (1885). Also, laws of 1879 concerning the blind, Chapter 13, Section 5.
29. Records of the Iowa Braille and Sight Saving School, "The Mary Ingalls Era," Vinton, Iowa.
30. LIW, "Pioneer Girl," 114.
31. "Let's Visit Mrs. Wilder" interview with John F. Case, *Ruralist* editor, February 1918.
32. LIW, "Pioneer Girl," 123.

72 • Laura Ingalls Wilder: American Writer on the Prairie

33. Ibid., 124.
34. Almanzo Wilder was enumerated in the 1880 census twice, in Kingsbury and Beadle counties. Both times, he has advanced his age by one year over all previous census records of his birth year as recorded by his parents in New York.
35. 1880 Federal Census of railroad camp near Huron, South Dakota.
36. LIW, "Pioneer Girl," 135.
37. Ibid., 138.
38. Ibid., 136.
39. Ibid., 140.
40. Ibid., 151.
41. Ibid., 159.

CHAPTER **4**

LEAVING THE WEST: THE 1890S

We joined long wagon trains moving south; we met hundreds of wagons going north; the roads east and west were crawling lines of families travel-ing under canvas, looking for work, for another foothold somewhere on the land . . . The country was ruined, the whole world was ruined; noth-ing like this had ever happened before. There was no hope, but everyone felt the courage of despair.

Rose Wilder Lane

They were intelligent, experienced, and adaptable, but the Wilders could hardly have chosen a worse time and place to farm. Their first most-pressing concern was debt. Like most Dakota farmers, Almanzo had plenty of it. Debt was the price of a modern wheat farming operation, but debt could be managed over time as long as the farm produced high yields and consistent crops. Almanzo Wilder was no novice. He came from a successful farming family and his methods and techniques were advanced for Kingsbury County at the time. He was confident in his own ability and, unlike many homesteaders, he was thoroughly committed to farming as his lifelong occupation, not just as a speculative side venture. At the time of his marriage, Almanzo Wilder doubled-down on his bet and purchased a fleet of new equipment: a new wagon, a ride-on sulky plough, a reaper-binder for harvesting wheat, a mechanical weeder, a seeder, a mowing machine, and hay rake. He paid for the machinery by mortgaging the new house on the tree claim, which increased his cash flow and paid for his wheat seed.

Almanzo Wilder had a secret advantage: the farmer's wife liked to farm. His Bess, who would not promise to obey, was more than ready to stand by and farm. Her frequently stated belief in marriage as an equal partnership extended to the business of farming which, although personally satisfying, often involved dangerous, dirty, and physically exhausting labor. Sharing the workload increased productivity, and Laura was a major asset from the first season. She shared Almanzo's passion for horses, especially Morgan horses, and learned how to drive the binder behind a restless team.[1] Early in the marriage, probably with Almanzo's expert instruction, she began to break and train bronco ponies. As always, she tended the cows and kept a large garden, which increased the self-sufficiency and profitability of the Wilder farm.

Still in her teens, Laura was pregnant within a few months of the wedding. The excitement of the new baby was tempered by a series of frustrations that shadowed the couple's honeymoon. The Wilder's first wheat crop, which grew beautifully all summer and should have redeemed their mortgage with cash to spare, was pounded to the ground in an August hailstorm. The crop was a total loss in 1886. The baby was due in December. The loss of the wheat crop was disappointing, but endurable. The underlying problem was the Wilders' need for cash, which was increasing even faster than their debt. Their most viable solution required them to assume yet another mortgage in order to finance the upcoming season on the farm. They decided to mortgage Almanzo's original homestead claim (which they finally owned free and clear), rent out the new house on the tree claim, move back into Almanzo's bare-bones bachelor shanty, and wait on the birth of their first child.

Baby Rose was born in the claim shanty on December 5, 1886. Laura chose to name her daughter not for a family member as was traditional, but for the riotous prairie wildflower she loved best. Caroline attended Laura during labor and delivery along with the mother of Laura's close friend, Mary Power. Dr. Ruggles Cushman arrived in time to deliver Laura's "rose in December," who was strong and healthy and looked very much like her father. Caroline stayed for a few days to care for Laura and the baby. When she left, Laura assumed full responsibility for Rose's care in the cold and comparatively primitive, but familiar, conditions of the claim shanty. Rose, however, was a sturdy child who thrived. Laura may have hoped to deliver the baby with only her mother and another matron in attendance. In later years, she remembered that "a hundred precious dollars had gone for doctor bills and medicine and help."[2] It was an expense the growing family could ill afford.

The birth of Rose was the one great and joyous event of the Wilder's fledgling marriage. In 1887, debt and frustration gave way to disaster. Although Laura did not specify the cause, the couple's barn caught fire that summer and burned to the ground, consuming the adjacent haystacks as well. Somehow, the couple managed to feed and stable their livestock through the winter and carry on farming in the spring. But 1888 (the year of The Children's Blizzard and an exceptionally hard winter) exacted an even greater toll on their overextended finances. In the spring, Almanzo and Laura both came down with diphtheria, one of the most dreaded diseases of the nineteenth century. At risk to his own life, Almanzo's bachelor brother Royal moved in to nurse the incapacitated couple. Rose was immediately dispatched to her grandparents in town, where Charles had built a comfortable home. Rose, less than two years old at the time, always claimed to remember the intense fear and uncertainty of her parents' illness. It is possible that she did retain some memory of the traumatic separation from her mother. "For a long time I had been living with Grandpa and Grandma and the Aunts in De Smet because nobody knew what would become of my father and mother. Only God knew. They had diff-theer-eeah; a hard word and dreadful. I did not know what it was exactly, only that is was big and black and it meant that I might never see my father and mother again."[3] Rose chose the word *black* with precision. Diphtheria typically causes a thick black membrane to form in the throat, obstructing the airway. Pioneers called diphtheria "the strangling angel of children." All across the West, lonely hilltop cemeteries were packed with infants who had died from the disease.

Initially, Almanzo appeared to recover more rapidly than Laura, who had been gravely ill. Anxious about the care of his livestock and determined to salvage what remained of the season, Almanzo went back to work before he had fully recovered. One morning as he rose from the bed, he collapsed; his legs would no longer support him. He had suffered a form of debilitating paralysis, possibly the result of a stroke. From that point on, the loss of the farm became inevitable. By the time Rose was finally reunited with her parents, her father had learned how to walk again, but not without the conspicuous limp and cane that would remain with him all his life. Almanzo and Laura scrambled to rescue what remained of their investment and property. They sold the homestead and moved back to the house on the tree claim, where the fragile trees they had so carefully nurtured were desiccating in the scorching heat. South Dakota, soon to be admitted as a state, was gripped by severe drought. The Wilders needed to prove several acres of living trees in order to gain title to the timber claim, which looked increasingly doubtful. In partnership with Peter Ingalls, Laura's cousin, the couple purchased a herd of Shropshire sheep. Although sheep farming was hugely unpopular in the West, where sheep were thought to overgraze the prairie, the Wilders' decision to attempt it demonstrated their shrewdness and their dogged determination to stay on the land. Even if the drought did not abate, with luck the Wilders could raise a herd of sheep on the baked grass of the timber claim, sell them for a profit, and finance another planting season.

Pregnant again in 1889, Laura was likely suffering from stress and exhaustion. She left no record of this period in her life except for her draft manuscript *The First Four Years,* originally entitled *The First Three Years and a Year of Grace,* written long after the fact. The novel was not published until after her death, the tone of the book is strangely staccato, almost dead-pan, and reveals little about Wilder's personal thoughts and feelings at the time. Just as Wilder's novels omit the birth and death of her infant brother Freddie, in *The First Four Years* Wilder chose to reveal little about what must have been the most private and heartbreaking experience of her life.

In the novel, Laura's second labor and delivery progressed more rapidly than her first. The doctor did not arrive until after the baby was born, a ten-pound boy this time. Perhaps Wilder suspected something was wrong with her son from the start; she did not name him immediately after his birth. Although delayed naming was not unusual in the late nineteenth century, it wasn't common practice for the Ingalls and Wilders. He was still unnamed three weeks later when the Wilders summoned the doctor back to the house on the tree claim. The baby had been convulsing ("taken by spasms") and once again the doctor arrived too late.[4] Grace Ingalls, who was keeping a schoolgirl diary at the time, wrote forlornly, "Laura's little baby boy only a month old died a little while ago, he looked just like Manly." Wilder was only twenty-two, but she would never bear another child.

In the very same entry, Grace continued:

> Last friday Manly's house caught fire and burned to the ground. The furniture in the front room and in the bedroom and pantry was saved but nothing in the kitchen where the fire started. Laura had just built a fire in their stove and went into the other room and shut the door so she could sweep when the noise of the fire startled her and on opening the door she saw the roof and side of the kitchen was on fire . . . they could not save the house.[5]

In later years, Rose Wilder Lane claimed that it was she who inadvertently started the fire while trying to "help" her grieving, weary mother by feeding straw into the kitchen stove.[6] Whatever the cause, the result was the same: the Wilders were wiped out. With nothing but a few old clothes they had saved from the conflagration, the Wilders went to live with Charles and Caroline in town for a time before moving on to "keep house" for Mr. Sheldon, a widowed neighbor.[7] When they weren't tending sheep, Almanzo and Peter Ingalls, Laura's cousin, erected a tarpaper shanty where the little gray house with its carefully crafted pantry once stood. As Laura, Almanzo, Peter, and Rose prepared to endure another Dakota winter in the shanty, the drought conditions intensified, killing everything green. Soon, there weren't enough surviving trees on the timber claim to prove up, which meant they lost access to 160 acres of their grazing land. Preempting the claim was a pipedream. They were landless farmers. In November, Laura rode into town to call on her parents and told them that she and Almanzo were quitting South Dakota. "They expect to go to Spring Valley next spring," Grace wrote simply. "I am so sorry."[8]

In the spring, the Wilders sold their flock of Shropshires to the butcher and packed out. They were not alone. Royal Wilder gave up on Dakota farming at about the same time. Although hindered by his limp, Almanzo drove what remained of his assets—the cows, the horses, and Laura's pony— before the wagon as the family trudged 300 miles back east. Since leaving upstate New York in the 1870s, Almanzo's parents James and Angeline Wilder had operated a prosperous farm in rolling, southeastern Minnesota. They opened their large stately home and, just as importantly, their massive horse barn to their beleaguered son, providing him with respite in Spring Valley. In return, the young Wilders assisted Almanzo's aging parents with the farm and house. They probably sought supplemental employment in town, where Royal Wilder opened a variety store. They prayed at the Methodist Church. They hunkered down and tried to formulate a new plan, any strategy that would put them back on the land. It could not have escaped Wilder's notice that her adventures in agriculture were beginning to mirror those of her father's. What she and Almanzo did next was as risky, as impulsive, and as unprofitable as any of the multiple moves Charles Ingalls had made. After a period of rest and recovery in Spring Valley, the Wilders moved once again—this time to a one-mule farm in the Florida panhandle.

Tired of failure and herding sheep on the drought-stricken plains, Peter Ingalls had decided to try homesteading in Westville, Florida, where rice, sugar cane, hogs, and small crops had been raised predictably for decades in the temperate climate. Almanzo's partial paralysis had not improved in Minnesota; the frigid winters only increased his discomfort. Encouraged by Peter Ingalls, who had claimed 160 acres, the Wilders left Spring Valley and followed Peter south by train. They may have rented a small farm of their own, but they could not adjust to the life, climate, and customs of the Deep South. While Almanzo may have found some relief for his stiff legs, Laura could not tolerate the sweltering heat and became ill. In a photograph taken at the time, she looks haggard and considerably older, her mouth turned down in an unmistakable scowl. Almanzo sits stiffly in a straight-back chair, which he grips tightly with both hands for stability; Laura stands beside him, her hand draped protectively over his shoulder.

It is difficult to gauge Laura's reaction to the racist and segregated South, where Confederate veterans and their wives determined social order and mobility. She apparently made few friends among the local white women, who deemed her a haughty "up-north gal."[9] Years later when she commented on her time in Florida, her languid description suggests what she found threatening, off-putting, and oddly compelling about their sojourn. "We went to live in the piney woods of Florida, where the trees always murmur, where the butterflies are enormous, where plants that eat insects grow in moist places, and alligators inhabit the slowly moving waters of the rivers. But at the time and in that place, a Yankee woman was more of a curiosity than any of these."[10] Family members preserved a story of "Bessie" awkwardly balancing a massive umbrella above her head as she struggled to plant a row of corn by hand. Laura, whose approach to personal safety was generally cavalier, bought a revolver. She, not Almanzo, made the decision to leave.[11]

Upon close personal inspection, mule-farming in Florida was not what the Wilders had in mind, but the price of fertile farmland in Minnesota or South Dakota was far beyond their reach—several thousand dollars for a quarter section—and the availability of homestead land further west was limited or located on marginal land. The Wilders packed a trunk and headed for home. They returned to De Smet in the summer of 1892, where their prospects were so poor that the Wilders, no doubt overwhelmed by frustration, considered immigrating to New Zealand.[12] It was, after all, good sheep country. In De Smet, they moved into a small, unfurnished house, bided their time, reviewed all their options, worked odd jobs, and saved every penny. They made no effort to set down roots this time, as if they had already decided against a future in South Dakota. Almanzo, the expert horse handler, found work as a drayman or teamster. He worked as a carpenter, probably alongside his father-in-law. He tended shop, filling in for clerks over the dinner hour. Laura went to work for a dressmaker in town where, as long as there was demand, she sewed twelve hours a day for a dollar a day. When she was not in kindergarten, the dynamic, extraordinarily precocious Rose stayed with her grandmother and her three doting aunts who fed her books and news journals—*Robinson Crusoe, Gulliver's Travels,* the *Chicago Inter Ocean*—and challenged her mind with their byzantine lacemaking, knitting, and needlework patterns. Rose taught herself to read before she started school, cracking the code of English with the same alacrity that she would later apply to several other languages. She rocked the foundations of her grandmother's conventional, hymn-singing household from the moment she returned. She was more high-strung, more verbal, more opinionated, and less manageable than her mother. Like her mother, she possessed a formidable memory and was a born raconteur:

> When I was five years old, sitting one day in my grandmother's parlor in De Smet on a footstool beside her rocking chair, and helping her sew carpet rags, after a meditative silence I said dreamily, "I wish I had been there when Christ

was crucified." My sincerely, deeply pious grandmother was (as I now recall) deeply touched by this tender, young piety; I can recall the tone of her voice saying softly, "Why, dear?" I replied, "So I could have cursed him and been the Wandering Jew."[13]

As it happened, Rose would see almost as much of the world as her fictional and eternally wandering counterpart, but the impression she made upon her grandmother at the time was typical of the impression she would make on nice respectable people, orthodox thinkers, and the unsuspecting throughout her life. "I'm sure I recall the incident because of the inexplicable effect, upon my grandmother, of these candidly innocent words. It was like an earthquake, a silent one. She *said* nothing. Somehow the air sort of crashed, terrifically."[14]

Meanwhile, as the Wilders continued doggedly planning and saving for their increasingly unlikely return to farming, the drought cycle that had devastated the Great Plains for several years segued directly into the Panic of 1893, a full-blown national depression. Bank failures, foreclosures, tax sales, and ten-percent unemployment rates sent rural residents fleeing farms and small towns to search for work in larger communities, looking for an alternative, any new provision for feeding, clothing, and housing their large families. The Wilders had chattel-mortgaged their furniture. They were living in an empty house between the town barns and the railroad tracks furnished with little more than crates; there was no room left for belt-tightening. To young Rose, "The blank windows seemed to stare at us, and through the empty rooms there were breathings and crawlings and creakings in the dark. And the wind had a different sound around that house, it sounded mean and jeering."[15] The diet of most pioneers had never been varied, plentiful, or nutritious, but Rose Wilder Lane would later refer to herself as "one of the malnutrition children" of the 1890s, of whom there were millions.[16] The Ingalls's finances were nearly as constrained. Charles had exited farming in 1887, but still supported a family of five. He operated a retail store for a time and later sold insurance. Mary Ingalls was absent from the Iowa College for the Blind in 1887, presumably due to illness, but in light of Laura's marriage and the fact that Laura no longer contributed to her sister's college fund, a change in family finances is equally likely. In 1892, Mary underwent surgery for neuralgia, which had caused her facial pain for years. Not long after her surgery, she wrote a letter to the school matron and asked if it would be possible for her to return to the college. "We would like to have you back with us again but I fear that would be impossible. Your state has appropriated no money for the education of the blind. There are just two students from South Dakota and their bills are paid by their respective counties," her friend Mrs. Robert Carothers gently

80 • Laura Ingalls Wilder: American Writer on the Prairie

informed her. "You will never be forgotten by us and we trust that you will always hold us in tender memory."[17] Mary's letter did not survive. Whether she wished to return to the college (where she had spent the happiest, most productive years of her life) for personal reasons or because she felt she was a financial burden on her family at home may never be known.

Despite persistent drought, more efficient farming methods and higher yields had resulted in overproduction on the vast checkerboard of wheat fields that defined the Great Plains, further depressing wheat prices and eroding farm incomes. The Wilders had already made that calculation; it was a cycle from which they could see no imminent escape, but it was the game-changing Panic of 1893 that forced their next move, even if they had been weighing their limited options from the time they left Florida and returned to De Smet. The Panic of 1893, triggered in large part by the burst of a national railroad investment bubble, resulted in a massive credit crisis, which in turn led to bank runs, business failures, mortgage foreclosures, and overwhelming job losses. At the same time, the repeal of the Sherman Silver Purchase Act, which linked the price of silver to the value of the gold-backed dollar, shut down silver mines all over the drought-stricken West. Farmers, ranchers, miners, bankers, and small-town business owners in mining states like South Dakota (where Black Hills mining operations were central to the economy in the western part of the state) were especially hard hit.

Even though the Wilders had rejected the uncomfortable heat and unfamiliar culture of the South, they had learned a great deal about small-scale agriculture in Florida. During their time in De Smet, Laura had managed to save $100 dollars sewing shirts and buttonholes. Taking a page from Charles Ingalls's book, the Wilders decided to leave South Dakota for Missouri, the extravagantly publicized "Land of the Big Red Apple," where they hoped to buy a small farm, diversify, and reenter farming on an entirely different scale.

They left De Smet on July 17, 1894. Almanzo slapped a coat of black paint on their old two-seater hack and tacked on oilcloth curtains. The wagon held a stockpile of fireproof asbestos mats Almanzo planned to sell or trade along the way. Laura loaded it with containers of hardtack she had baked, their few possessions, and several crates of frantic, shrieking chickens. Tellingly, her one luxury item was a writer's lap desk that Almanzo had made for her and lined with green felt. In it, she had carefully concealed her $100 bill. On the eve of their departure, Charles took down his fiddle and, at Laura's request, played her favorite songs one last time, the songs she had always associated with wagon travel and the search for home. As she rolled away from her parents' house on Third Street, Charles, Caroline, Mary, Carrie, and Grace stood in the yard and waved goodbye. Laura would not see her family again for nearly a decade, not until Charles was on his deathbed and her mother called her home.

They traveled with Frank and Emma Cooley, whose two sons were close to Rose in age. The rural roads south and east were clogged with emigrant wagons and displaced farmers. Refugees appeared to be pouring in and out of South Dakota in roughly equal proportion; some of them discouraged the Wilders and the Cooleys from continuing their precipitous journey to the Ozarks. Southwest Missouri was "the place to go if a man wants to bury himself from the world and live on hoecake and clabber," one disillusioned farmer informed them.[18] At night, at their campsites by the river, Laura settled down with her lap desk and logged her impressions of the day. On one level, her journal is a perfunctory account of the day's events, but it also reveals a wealth of detail about Wilder's personality, her likes and dislikes, her omnivorous curiosity, and the early development of her writing style. Even by Wilder's stoic standards, the trip was a hard slog in temperatures that regularly exceeded 100 degrees. The temperature rose even higher inside the black sweatbox where Wilder frequently checked her thermometer and her outraged chickens. The Wilders and Cooleys fished, foraged, and occasionally purchased food from local farmers along the way. "Mrs. Cooley and I went to a house to buy milk," Wilder recorded with a trace of her occasional acerbity. "It was swarming with children and pigs; they looked a great deal alike."[19] She is fascinated by the changing landscape as they rolled south, especially the crumbling banks and river bluffs, and wonders at their evolution over time: "What is it about water that always affects a person? I never see a great river or lake but I think how I would like to see a world made and watch it through all its changes."[20]

"We tend to forget that homesteaders were not a type," declared Western writer Mari Sandoz, reflecting on her own Great Plains childhood, "not as alike as biscuits cut out with a baking-powder can. They varied as much as their origins and their reasons for coming west. There were Daughters and Sons of the Revolution located next to the communal communities of the Mennonites, say, or the Hutterians. An illiterate from some other frontier might be neighboring with a Greek and Hebrew scholar from a colony of Russian Jews in the Dakotas. A nervous-fingered murderer who fled west under a new name might join fences with a non-violent River Baptist or a vegetarian who wouldn't kill a rabbit eating up his first sprouts of lettuce, no matter how hungry the settler might be."[21]

As New Western historians argue, America's frontier had always more closely resembled a tenuous meeting place of disparate cultures than the refining bowl of myth and legend. Successive waves of emigration had brought change and diversity to the Plains, which Wilder found intriguing. She describes in detail her encounter with a community of Russian farmers

82 • Laura Ingalls Wilder: American Writer on the Prairie

working in long blue tunics near the South Dakota border. She strikes up a conversation with an elderly Canadian woman who is leaving Nebraska and returning to the West Indies, where she says life is monotonous but far less arduous. In central Nebraska, long favored by German and Bohemian settlers, Wilder notes the surprising appearance of their Catholic churches where snow-white statues of the Virgin Mary hovered over massive arching doors.

When they reach the wide streets of Lincoln, Nebraska, the Wilder and Cooley wagons jockey for position amid a jaw-dropping fleet of motorized streetcars. To Laura's dismay, the clattering streetcars spook the weary, hard-working horses. By the time they roll into Kansas, her compassion for animals extends to "a little black-and-tan dog in the road, lost. He is skin and bones, must have been starving, and is afraid of us."[22] She picks him up, lets him ride in her lap until he stops trembling, and gives him a name, Fido ("I am faithful"), and a home for life. He would become devoted to her. The travel journal captures some of her earliest attempts to describe landscape and the natural world, the heart and soul of all her later work. When they finally entered the Ozarks, Wilder wrote: "The road goes up hill and down, and it is rutted and dusty and stony but every turn of the wheels changes our view of the woods and the hills. The sky seems lower here, and it is the softest blue. The distances and the valleys are blue whenever you can see them. It is a drowsy country that makes you feel wide awake and alive but somehow contented."[23]

Mansfield, Missouri, a small but thriving community near bustling Springfield, was their final destination. They rolled into town with ten other emigrant wagons and camped in a grove of shady trees on the edge of town. Mansfield offered nearly everything Laura required; all it lacked was a Congregational Church. The Methodists would have to do. With more wagons arriving daily, Almanzo wasted no time. Rose recalled how he immediately began limping over the countryside with land agents in search of a suitable piece of property. A few weeks later, with fall settling in, he thought he had found it: a forty-acre tract of land close to town. The property was ridge land—hilly, rocky, and covered in brush and timber—but it came with a dilapidated log cabin, a small orchard, and about a thousand apple saplings. Full partners in marriage and business, Almanzo valued Laura's opinion and wanted her approval for the purchase. According to Rose, after her mother walked the grounds she returned even more enthusiastic about the land's potential than Almanzo. She donned her black wedding dress, coiled her thick brown braid around her head like a basket, and prepared to accompany Almanzo to the bank to sign the purchase agreement. To Wilder's rage and disbelief, her carefully concealed $100 bill was missing from the writing desk. After relentlessly interrogating Rose (something Rose never forgave or forgot) and tearing apart the desk, Laura and Almanzo finally discovered the bill in the crack where it had fallen and pried it out. But the ensuing panic over the loss of the money illustrates the strain and sense of vulnerability the Wilders were experiencing at the time. Crisis averted, the Wilders assumed a relatively small mortgage to cover the remaining $300 of the sale. On paper at least, they were back in the business of farming.

Wilder named their new home Rocky Ridge. The primitive two-room log cabin was not uncommon for housing in the Ozarks at the turn of the century, but it had been standing empty and neglected for some time—as had the log barn, which lacked a roof. The cabin was dirty, littered with leaves and crumbling chinking. There was no window, but an open hole in the wall let in light and a shutter blocked the rain. The door hung askew. The fireplace doubled for heating and cooking, but the cabin was probably no more uncomfortable than the average claim shanty. It was a work in progress and Laura had grand plans for the place. The couple's first task was to settle in and somehow make enough money to carry them until spring and through the first critical year. Their only source of income derived from the land itself. Almanzo and Laura began the laborious process of clearing brush and timber from the property to create new fields and expand the orchard. The wood was cut, stacked, and hauled to town by Almanzo, where he sold it for fifty cents a load. Laura no longer owned a cow, so she could not churn and sell butter the first year, but her hens produced eggs: "Believe me," she later wrote, "I learned how to make them lay."[24] Rose foraged for nuts, wild berries and fat rabbits. What they didn't eat, they sold. Rose remembered hearing the ringing sound of her father chopping wood in the frosty morning as she left for school and hearing the same rhythmic sound when she returned home in the afternoon. Building Rocky Ridge was backbreaking work with no certainty of success, but Rose (very like her mother) painted cabin life as a winter's idyll, a domestic scene by Currier & Ives:

> Winter evenings were cozy in the cabin. The horses were warm in the little barn, the hens in the new wooden coop. Snow banked against the log walls and long icicles hung from the eaves. A fire of hickory logs burned in the fireplace. In its heat, over a newspaper spread on the hearth, my father worked oil into the harness straps between his oily-black hands. I sat on the floor, carefully building a house of corncobs, and my mother sat by the table, knitting needles flashing while she knitted warm woolen socks for my father and read to us from a book propped under the kerosene lamp. She read us Tennyson's poems and Scott's poems; those books were ours. And she read us *Prescot's Conquest of Mexico*, and *Conquest of Peru*, and *The Green Mountain Boys*, and *John Halifax, Gentleman*. She read us *The Leatherstocking Tales*, and another true book, the biggest

84 • Laura Ingalls Wilder: American Writer on the Prairie

of all: *Ancient, Medieval and Modern History*. I borrowed those from the shelf of lending-books in the Fourth Reader room at school. The teachers let me borrow them, though I wasn't in the *Fourth Reader* yet.[25]

Rose's exceptional intelligence, drive, and hypersensitivity were apparent from early childhood. Outspoken, bohemian by nature, terribly bored at school, and dismissed by her classmates as an insignificant country girl, Rose seethed with academic and social frustration. She once stormed out of class, shouting "stupid, stupid!" at her teacher.[26] "Stupid" was also her mother's favorite term of derision. But even Laura, who understood her daughter quite well and who had also been taunted at school for poverty, seemed to underestimate the depth of Rose's outrage and anxiety. Preoccupied with developing Rocky Ridge, self-confident, and unapologetic about their own circumstances (and no doubt convinced they were saving Rose time and effort), the Wilders sent Rose off to school each morning on a braying donkey, the evil and conspicuous Spookendyke, and hoped for the best. No matter how much Rose loved her parents and relied on their reassurance and approval at home, she was a fish out of water in Mansfield. She showed up at the brick schoolhouse if and when she felt like it. She spent much of her free time alone with her books, which increased the sophistication of her fiery intellect even as it fueled her feelings of rejection and isolation. Above all, she resented and rebelled against the hardships and obscurity of farm life.

"It was a hard, narrow relentless life," she later wrote—in second person, as if she still needed to distance herself from its raw reality.

> It was not comfortable. Nothing was made easy for us. We did not like work and we were not supposed to like it; we were supposed to work, and we did. We did not like discipline, so we suffered until we disciplined ourselves. We saw many things and many opportunities that we ardently wanted and could not pay for, so we did not get them, or got them only after stupendous, heartbreaking effort and self-denial, for debt was much harder to bear than deprivations.[27]

Although the Wilder's financial situation improved considerably within a few years of moving to Rocky Ridge, Rose never shed her thin skin. Although she was exceptionally self-aware, her letters and journals reveal a melodramatic aspect to her personality, an over-the-top reaction to criticism and a desperate desire to please, all of which were on display years later when she described her father's first sale of farm timber in Mansfield.

> The wagon box was empty and I almost shouted, "You sold it!"
>
> "Finally I did," my father said in triumph.

"How much did you get for it," I asked. He was beginning to unharness the horses. He bragged, "Fifty cents."

I set down the lantern and ran into the house to tell my mother, "Fifty cents! He sold it all for fifty cents!" Her whole face trembled and seemed to melt into softness, she sighed a long sigh. "Aren't you glad?" I exhulted.

"Glad? Of course I'm glad!" she snapped at me and to herself, "Oh, thanks be!"

I ran out again, I pranced out, to tell my father how glad she was. And he said, with a sound of crying in his voice, "Oh, why did you tell her? I wanted to surprise her."

You do such things, little things, horrible, cruel, without thinking, not meaning to. You have done it; nothing can undo it. This is a thing you can never forget.[28]

All her life, Rose's assessment of her childhood would swing between wild, sometimes histrionic, extremes. In her forties (when she had returned to live with her parents at Rocky Ridge), she declared her childhood had been "a nightmare." Her mother had made her so miserable that Rose had never gotten over it, had made her "morbid," a tortured bundle of "raw nerves."[29] Rose confided to a friend that her parents had no idea how much she had suffered in silence, of how her controlling and overprotective mother considered her incapable of executing even basic chores. But on other occasions, Rose applauded Wilder for her progressive childrearing practices, her rejection of corporal punishment, and her disavowal of "breaking a child's will."[30] Written in 1918, Rose's tender (if self-referential) tribute to both her parents probably provides a more balanced assessment.

My mother loves courage and beauty and books; my father loves nature, birds and trees and curious stones, and both of them love the land, the stubborn, grudging, beautiful earth that wears out human lives year by year. They gave me something of all these loves, and whenever I do something that I really can't help sitting down and admiring, I always come plump up against the fact that I never would have done it if I hadn't been wise enough to pick out these particular parents.[31]

For the next several years, Laura and Almanzo would work tirelessly and in tandem to convert their rock-encrusted ridge land into a small, sustainable family farm. "Our ideal home should be made by a man and a woman together," Wilder wrote.[32] They diversified their crops and livestock: potatoes, oats, corn, hogs, dairy cows. The crates of leghorn chickens Wilder hauled from South Dakota became the basis of her large, highly productive flock. In the process of establishing her brood, she became a regional

86 • Laura Ingalls Wilder: American Writer on the Prairie

expert on poultry and egg production. When they had cleared enough land to expand the orchard and plant their hundreds of apple seedlings, they grew sweet timothy grass between the tree rows, which produced hay for Almanzo's horses. The chickens ate insects and provided fertilizer for the trees. When Wilder could afford to keep a cow, she churned butter, which she sold in town for 25 cents per pound. Only a year after moving into the inadequate log cabin, they expanded it. Wilder, however, harbored day-dreams for another, not-so-little house on Rocky Ridge. In Rose's words:

> My mother stood under [a white-oak] in her brown-sprigged white lawn dress, her long braid hanging down her back. Below the curled bangs her eyes were as purple-blue as the violets. It would be a white house, she said, all built from our farm. Everything we needed to build it was on the land: good oak beams and boards, stone for the foundation and the fireplace. The house would have large windows looking west across the brook, over the gentle little valley and up the wooded hills that hid the town, to the sunset colors in the sky. There would be a nice big porch to the north, cool on hot summer afternoons. The kitchen would be big enough to hold a wood stove for winter and one of the new kerosene stoves that wouldn't heat up the place worse in summer. Every window would be screened with mosquito netting. There would be a well, with a pump, just outside the kitchen door; no more lugging water from the spring. And in the parlor there would be a bookcase, no two bookcases, big bookcases full of books, and a hanging lamp to read them by, on winter evenings by the fireplace.[33]

In the meantime, the Wilders rented a small house in town, where they relied on tried-and-true methods of making extra money to grow the farm. Mansfield was a railroad town. After Frank Cooley's untimely death, Almanzo purchased his hauling business and began delivering stock and merchandize from depot to destination with his own wagon and team. Laura cooked and served meals to men traveling through town. They were northern newcomers, but they quickly gained friends and acceptance and rose in social prominence. Almanzo became a Mason; Laura joined the Masonic women's auxiliary, The Order of the Eastern Star. They were active in the religious and social activities of the Methodist Church. Rose attended school, grudgingly. She no longer felt coldshouldered, but she would leave the Ozarks and strike out on her own at the first possible opportunity.

Wilder kept in touch with her immediate family and the far-flung Ingalls–Quiner clan by long letters which, once read, were circulated among her relatives. In 1902, she made an emergency trip to De Smet. Charles Ingalls, who suffered from heart disease, was dying. It's entirely possible that Wilder returned home at her father's request and that it was Charles who asked to see his favorite child, the one who most resembled him, one last time. Unlike many Victorian families, the Ingalls did not make a cult of death and mourning. If anything, they tended to meet death with resignation and silence, but with the consoling conviction that they would meet again in "The Sweet By and By," Charles's favorite hymn which was played at his funeral. Wilder arrived in De Smet in time to talk with her father before he died. On his deathbed, Charles bequeathed her his violin. This was more than a sentimental gesture. No mention was ever made of how or under what circumstances Charles acquired his violin, although he played the instrument by ear and probably taught himself as a boy. But both Charles and Laura (who ultimately had the violin appraised) were under the impression that the violin was an original Italian Amati worth tens of thousands of dollars.[34] In fact it was not, but Charles had always handled the instrument gingerly and treated it with the utmost care. With Charles's death, Caroline and Mary were plunged back into hard times. And yet Charles's violin, presumed priceless and the family's most salable asset, passed into Wilder's hands for preservation. In time, Wilder would donate it to the South Dakota Historical Society. Charles Ingalls's body was interred beside his unnamed grandson in De Smet's hilltop cemetery, with sweeping views over the rolling countryside.

Caroline would long outlive her limited savings and income. Mary crafted hammocks, tied fly-nets for horses, and created beadwork for sale. Literary Carrie, who had learned typesetting at the *De Smet Ledger,* helped support her mother and sister as a printer, publisher, and pioneer newspaper reporter. Eventually, she left De Smet and tried homesteading on her own in the Black Hills. The shanty she occupied looked like a rolling chicken coop, but Carrie would ultimately own the claim. Grace worked as a local teacher until she married farmer Nathan Dow the year before her father's death. Grace was often ill (like many of the women in her family, she developed diabetes) and farmed near Manchester with her asthmatic husband. At times, in order to save money and to assist Caroline and Mary, the Dows moved back into the Ingalls's home in De Smet. Caroline took in laundry. She also accepted boarders, who slept in two tiny bedrooms upstairs. An excellent cook, she served meals to workmen from the back door of her kitchen. The Ingalls women did everything in their power to keep up appearances. Discreet and well groomed, usually dressed in black, Caroline and Mary were often spotted walking arm-in-arm to the Congregational Church on Sunday mornings. Although Caroline owned the house in De Smet, the loss of Charles's income bit hard. "Does everyone bring food to the Ingalls?" a De Smet child innocently inquired.[35]

Almanzo's prosperous parents, James and Angeline Wilder, also faced financial difficulties in the new century. They survived the Panic of 1893 on their Spring Valley farm, only to lose most of their life savings in a Louisiana rice-farming venture promoted by their daughter Eliza Jane, or "EJ" as she called herself. En route to Louisiana, still feeling flush and no doubt concerned about the financial security of their disabled son and his family, the old New Yorkers stopped in Mansfield and presented Almanzo with enough money to purchase the house he had been renting in town. The windfall allowed Almanzo and Laura to invest more time and money in Rocky Ridge, where they carefully continued expanding and diversifying their business. Upon James Wilder's death in 1902, the couple received a small inheritance. They bought more unimproved land; over time, they would increase their holdings to 200 acres. They cleared enormous amounts of brush and rock to create green pastures for their Morgan horses and fields for oats, wheat, and corn. By the early years of the new century, their commercial apple orchard was heavy with fruit, and strawberry fields blossomed on the farm.

In 1903, another Wilder came calling at Rocky Ridge, iron-willed EJ herself. After working in Washington, D.C., for a time, she had married at forty and borne her only child. She arrived with her rock-throwing son, Wilder Thayer, and left with Rose. By the time EJ departed, the family had agreed that Rose would leave Mansfield and move to Crowley, Louisiana, to live with her aunt and complete her high school education. It was an unlikely decision, considering the longstanding antipathy between Laura and her sister-in-law EJ. Perhaps EJ recognized her own ferocious independence in her look-alike niece. It is also possible that Laura hoped her disgruntled daughter would experience some of the same dramatic transformation in happiness and outlook that Mary Ingalls had displayed after enrolling at the Iowa College for the Blind. Perhaps the plan was entirely Rose's idea, the first of many attempts to flee what she considered a stultifying life and dead-end future in the Ozarks. That there were inevitable pregnancy rumors was not surprising. Young unmarried pregnant women were often dispatched far from home on an "extended visit with relatives" for the duration of their pregnancies. Although Rose herself made a cryptic reference to the fact she had "gone further to smash in struggling with sex," perhaps involuntarily, at seventeen.[36]

Crowley did offer academic classes not available in Mansfield, including a demanding three-year course in Latin language and literature. When Rose turned her intellectual blowtorch on Latin, she mastered the entire curriculum in nine months and graduated at the top of her class. Rose had attracted an older suitor in Crowley, but upon graduation she did not marry or teach grade school or return to home and hearth to assist Mother, as was expected of a single girl her age. Instead, she returned to Mansfield with a new ambition and a thoroughly modern career plan. Rose stayed in Mansfield just long enough to learn Morse code, yet another language at which she excelled, at the local train station. Rose wanted to make and spend money, which she did. "My real desire was for money, clothes, social position (!), good times, admiration," she admitted frankly.[37] She set out for the big city, Kansas City, where the seventeen-year-old "bachelor girl" began supporting herself. In 1904, top telegraphers were paid as much as sixty dollars a month, which rivaled the average farm income. Laura, who had struggled with homesickness as a teenager, kept an eye on her head-strong daughter and visited Rose in Kansas City, despite her general reluc-tance to leave the daily demands of the farm to Almanzo. Telegraphy was just one of the new career opportunities available to clever single women at the turn of the century—nursing, secretarial work, clerking, and cashiering were among their expanding options.

Although Laura and Rose were separated by a mere nineteen years in age, they experienced a much greater generational gap in terms of their values, ideals, ambitions, and expectations for self-fulfillment. Rose occa-sionally displayed an aggravating tendency to underrate the sophistication of her mother's intellect; on occasion, she patronized her. For the most part, Laura appears to have allowed many of Rose's comments to slide off her back, seemingly adhering to a "less said, sooner mended" policy with her enormously gifted, but volatile, daughter.

As late as 1925, a frustrated Rose wrote to her lover, fellow writer Guy Moyston: "Where is perseverance, thrift, caution, industry—where are any of the necessary virtues? Simply not in me. It is, really, a sad thing for my parents. I mean this. I mean it quite gravely and sincerely. They would have had comfort and joy and pride from me, if I had married fairly well, had a good home, been steadily lifted a little in the world by my husband's efforts, become, say, a socially successful woman in Springfield, with a car and accounts in good stores, and friends visiting from Kansas City and St. Louis. This unaccountable daughter who roams around the world, borrow-ing money here and getting shot at there, learning strange languages and reading incomprehensible books even in her own language, is a pride in a way, but a ceaseless apprehension, too. We are all of us, after all, largely products of our environments, and thirty years on this Ozark farm . . . It's a marvelous thing, and a triumph of character and intelligence over environ-ment, that they go as far with me as they do, that they know as much of the world and its affairs as can be gained from St. Louis newspapers."[38]

Rose's intense, competitive, and at times conflicted relationship with "Mama Bess" was also, beyond question, the most influential and sustain-ing relationship of her life. Although Rose happily admitted that she had inherited none of her mother's frugality and caution, she and Wilder were very much alike in their interests, talents, and strong-willed personalities.

90 • Laura Ingalls Wilder: American Writer on the Prairie

These similarities, far more than their differences, fueled the fire of their mother–daughter conflicts—personal, literary, and financial. Paradoxically, their similarities would also provide a rock-solid foundation for a unique and powerful artistic partnership.

Only thirty-seven years old when her daughter left home, Laura threw herself into an ambitious creative project of her own—building her long-awaited dream house on Rocky Ridge. "I have a fancy that the farm home should seem to be a product of the soil where it is reared," Wilder wrote in 1920, still musing on architecture long after she had completed the house. "So far as possible, everything used in the building was to be a product of the farm, both for the sake of economy and because of the sentimental idea that we wanted the house actually to be part of the farm."[39] Wilder's belief in organic design, which she seems to have developed independently, resonates strongly with Frank Lloyd Wright's commitment to the "spiritual union" of form and function, a central principle of Prairie School architecture: "No house should ever be on a hill or on anything. It should be of the hill, belonging to it. Hill and house should live together, each the happier for the other," Wright wrote in his 1932 autobiography. By strange coincidence, Wilder and Wright, the two most famous natives of Wisconsin, born just weeks and miles apart, shared a remarkably similar design aesthetic. In building the farmhouse on Rocky Ridge, Wilder's use of these shared holistic and forward-thinking design principles resulted in one of her proudest and most satisfying achievements.

She harvested her building materials from the farm's ravines and hillsides: timber for framing, field rock for the chimney, oak for hand-hewn interior beams. When Almanzo balked at hauling the massive slab of stone Laura desperately wanted for her parlor mantelpiece, Laura was at her wit's end. Finally, she did the unthinkable—she cried. Almanzo, shocked in submission, let her have her way. The ten-room farmhouse at Rocky Ridge, unlike virtually all other contemporary Ozark homes, was the result of an intensely personal, well-executed, and harmonious plan. It was both the culmination and a renunciation of a lifetime spent winning and losing the place called home. It was a sign of the Wilders' hard-won success and a signal to the entire community that the couple had done more than just arrive, they were in Mansfield to stay.

As the house neared completion, the Wilders sold their home in town and moved back to the farm year-round. Tiring of Kansas City and the long hours she spent mechanically tapping out code, Rose was also on the move. In 1908, she left Kansas City for exotic San Francisco, a city ripe with opportunity and in a frenzy of reconstruction following the great earthquake of 1906. Rose probably had another reason for relocating. In Kansas City, she had met and fallen for aspiring journalist, advertising promoter, and part-time salesman Claire Gillette Lane (known by his middle name), whose writing career was based in San Francisco. Upon her arrival in California, Rose moved into the same apartment building as Gillette, although she roomed with Bessie Beatty, a reporter for the *San Francisco Bulletin*. Gillette was a writer for the *San Francisco Call,* but his side interests included Rose, selling patent medicine, promoting advertising schemes, and speculating in real estate. They married on March 24, 1909, with no family in attendance. A photograph of Rose taken at the time of her marriage reveals a radiantly happy and vital young woman. The photograph, likely taken by Gillette and meant to be viewed by no one but themselves, shows Rose standing in a sheer nightgown, her hair a disheveled mess, a rare and beaming smile on her face. She holds up her left hand, long fingers spread wide, to show off her new wedding ring.[40]

She became pregnant almost immediately. Soon after their marriage, the couple began travelling around the West, probably in connection with one of Gillette's advertising or real estate ventures. They were in Salt Lake City, living at the Colonial Hotel, when Rose went into premature labor. She was six months pregnant, but if labor could not be stopped the baby was beyond almost any hope of viability. Rose was admitted to the Catholic Hospital of the Holy Cross, where she delivered a premature son who died at birth on November 23, 1909.[41] The unnamed boy was buried in Mount Olivet cemetery as "Infant Lane." The death of her son seems to have triggered a severe depression for Rose, the first in a series of depressions that she would battle throughout her life. Her marriage deteriorated and Rose probably became dependent on opiate-laced patent medicine. "I wasn't physically normal between 1909 and 1911," she later confided wearily, "nor mentally normal until 1914."[42] When she summarized her disillusionment with her husband, her marriage, and herself, her analysis was typically direct, unflinching, and succinct. "When Gillette came along, I wanted him because (1) I wanted sex, (2) I took him at his own stated value, as representing success and money and the high cultural level of newspaper work. When I married him another reason was added; I was tired of being a working girl and wanted the freedom and fun of a home."[43] Domestic life quickly bored her, as did chasing after money with Gillette. Divorce at the turn of the twentieth century, even if uncontested, required the injured party to demonstrate just cause—usually adultery or mental cruelty. It was a messy and stigmatizing affair. The Lanes' troubled marriage would survive until 1918, but it never really recovered from Rose's postpartum depression and the death of the couple's premature son.

By 1910, Rose had returned to Rocky Ridge to recuperate at home.[44] It was a protracted recovery. She had to undergo a follow-up gynecological procedure in Kansas City that year, which apparently left her unable to bear children. Laura's reaction to Rose's deep depression is unknown. However, as Wilder spent time with her devastated daughter, her own suppressed memories of grief and loss may have begun to resurface, including the death of her infant brother, her infant son, and now her infant grandson. Only forty-three at the time of Rose's return, the year 1910 marked a turning point in the life of Laura Ingalls Wilder. She seems to have slowed down for a time, just long enough to cast a lingering look over her shoulder. Half of her life and all of her formative and self-defining frontier adventures lay behind her. She had left the West, buried a father, reared a child, created a home, preserved a loving equitable marriage, and wrested a farm from a pile of rocks. Wilder was grateful by nature, but like her daughter she was never still and rarely content. By December, Rose had left home to join her freewheeling husband at the Waldorf-Astoria in New York. Christmas came to Rocky Ridge. In winter, the farm rested and the house grew quiet. One evening instead of reading, Wilder set down her book. She picked up her pencil and a dime store tablet of lined paper and she began to write.

NOTES

1. "Let's Visit Mrs. Wilder" interview with John F. Case, *Ruralist* editor, February 1918.
2. LIW, *The First Four Years* (New York: Harper & Row, 1971), 72.
3. Rose Wilder Lane, "Introduction to On the Way Home," in *A Little House Traveler: Writings from Laura Ingalls Wilder's Journeys Across America* (New York: HarperCollins, 2006), 7.
4. LIW, *The First Four Years*, 127.
5. Lane Papers, Grace Ingalls Diary, File 257.
6. William V. Holtz, *The Ghost in the Little House* (Columbia, MO: University of Missouri Press, 1993), 121.
7. Lane Papers, Grace Ingalls Diary, File 257.
8. Ibid.
9. *Little House Sampler,* 41.
10. Ibid., 40.
11. Arlene Warnock, *Laura Ingalls Wilder: The Westville Florida Years* (Leonardtown, MD: Heritage Printing & Graphics, 1979), 8.
12. RWL, *Little House Traveler,* 230.
13. Holtz, 26.
14. Ibid.
15. *A Little House Sampler,* 66.
16. "A Fireside Chat with Rose Wilder Lane," *Women's World,* September 1939.
17. Lane Papers, letter from Mrs. Robert Carothers to Mary Ingalls, December 7, 1892.
18. RWL, *Little House Traveler,* 67.
19. Ibid., 23.
20. Ibid., 34.
21. Sandoz, *Sandhill Sundays,* 6.
22. RWL, *Little House Traveler,* 59.
23. Ibid., 77.
24. "Let's Visit Mrs. Wilder" interview with John F. Case, *Ruralist* editor, February 1918.
25. RWL, *Little House Traveler,* 108.
26. Holtz, 36.

Leaving the West: The 1890s · 93

27. Ibid., 39.
28. RLW, A *Little House Traveler,* 106–107.
29. Holtz, 245.
30. RLW, "Grandpa's Fiddle," in *A Little House Sampler,* 65.
31. RWL, "Rose Wilder Lane, by Herself," in *A Little House Sampler,* 12.
32. LIW, "Favors the Small Farm Home," in Stephen W. Hines, ed., *Laura Ingalls Wilder: Farm Journalist,* 14.
33. RLW, "On the Way Home," in *A Little House Traveler,* 112–113.
34. Lane Papers, LIW Correspondence. Hoover Presidential Library. Also, Laura Ingalls Wilder Historic Home and Museum exhibit.
35. Kirkpatrick, Patricia, "It Is Better Farther On," *Minnesota Historical Society Archives* 8, no. 9 (September 1974).
36. Holtz, 172.
37. Ibid.
38. Miller, *Becoming Laura Ingalls,* 166–67. (RLW to Guy Moyston, July 27, 1925, Lane Papers, Box 9).
39. Pamela Smith Hill, *Laura Ingalls Wilder: A Writer's Life* (Pierre: South Dakota State Historical Society Press, 2007), 94.
40. Lane Papers, Photo File.
41. *Holy Cross Hospital records, Accn 588.* Special Collections and Archives. University of Utah, J. Willard Marriott. Salt Lake City, Utah.
42. Holtz, 172.
43. Holtz, 50.
44. In the 1910 Federal Census, Rose is living at home with her parents in Mansfield, Missouri.

CHAPTER **5**

WRITING THE WEST: 1911 TO 1943

A pioneer should have imagination, the ability to enjoy the idea of things more than the things themselves.

Willa Cather

All I have told is true, but it is not the whole truth.

Laura Ingalls Wilder

An undated letter fragment from Rose to her mother strongly suggests that Wilder was already working on a series of stories for children, or possibly a collection of children's verse, around the time Rose left Rocky Ridge in 1910.[1] Two decades would pass before Wilder returned to children's literature, but her instincts as an aspiring writer were accurate. She had an early, intuitive sense that writing for children might best fit her interests, style, and talent. In the interim, she served her long apprenticeship in an entirely different field. Following the old adage "write what you know," Wilder first broke into print as a farm journalist. Dismissed by some later critics as an underwhelming achievement that could not possibly provide the training required for her astonishing future success, Wilder's contribution to regional papers like the *Kansas City Star* was, in fact, a significant and unusual accomplishment for a woman of her day, so much so that some of her earliest writing appeared under the byline "A. J. Wilder." Almanzo's name, not her own, leant credibility to her writing and was more likely to win initial approval from a rural audience unfamiliar with her work. Still occasionally employed by writers and journalists, the gender-neutral byline also provided Wilder with a degree of cover as she slowly acquired regular readers, both male and female.

Wilder did not actively seek what would become her breakthrough writing assignment. Instead, the job found her. But given the chance, Wilder chose to explore her latent talent and make the most of an unexpected opportunity. An acknowledged expert on poultry farming, Wilder was asked to speak to a local agricultural group about the methods and techniques she employed in raising her prize chickens. Wilder, who disliked public speaking, wrote a speech summarizing her approach to chicken and egg production, but did not attend the meeting herself. However, the editor of the *Missouri Ruralist* who was in the audience that day was favorably impressed. The *Missouri Ruralist's* circulation was expanding and he was actively scouting for contributors who could write about farm life with enthusiasm and conviction. He invited Wilder to submit some material for consideration. Her first article, "Favors the Small Farm," appeared in February 1911, a week after Wilder's forty-fourth birthday. Although she had begun writing for publication comparatively late in life, Wilder was hardly Grandma Moses. A born storyteller and a voracious reader, Wilder's first article for the *Missouri Ruralist* was not a "how-to" article on the proper ratio of corn to cowpeas in leghorn chicken feed; it was a startling love song to "green slopes, wooded hills, pure running water and health giving breezes of the country." Her voice was refreshingly direct and confidential, "I am an advocate of the small farm and I want to tell you how an ideal home can be made, and a good living made from, five acres of land." She concluded her column with a bit of unsolicited and revealing advice for her readers. "I must say if there are any country women who are wasting their time envying their sisters in the city—don't do it. Such an attitude is out of date. Wake up to your opportunities . . . the real cultured, social and intellectual life will be in the country."[2]

In July, she expanded on her theme. "The Story of Rocky Ridge Farm" (subtitled "How Mother Nature in the Ozarks Rewarded Well Directed Efforts after a Fruitless Struggle on the Plains of the Dakotas. The Blessings of Living Water and a Gentle Climate") narrates a personal account of her farm's history. Wilder's strengths as a descriptive writer, her tendency to moralize, her touch of wry humor, even her hint of triumphalism are all clearly in place. "When I look around the farm now and see the smooth, green, rolling meadows and pastures, the good fields of corn and wheat and oats; when I see the orchard and strawberry field like huge bouquets in the spring or full of fruit later in the season; when I see the grape vines hanging full of luscious grapes, I can hardly bring back to my mind the rough, rocky, brushy, ugly place that we first called Rocky Ridge Farm. The name given it then serves to remind us of the battles we have fought and won and gives a touch of sentiment and an added value to the place."[3]

The *Ruralist's* readers wanted more. While Wilder continued drafting farm articles, Rose roamed New England with her husband. They travelled as far north as Maine, working a variety of jobs. Rose sold patent medicine and advertising space. She promoted Del Monte canned fruits and waited on Gillette's next big strike-it-rich scheme. In Maine, their chief source of income turned out to be the cash settlement they negotiated for a dubious "slip and fall" claim involving Gillette.[4] Not long afterward, the couple returned to San Francisco, where Rose tapped Gillette's newspaper connections and those of well-known *San Francisco Bulletin* correspondent Bessie Beatty to jumpstart her own writing career. She began as Beatty's assistant, but would soon become a regular writer for the *Bulletin*. At the same time, she and Gillette found work as commissioned agents for Stine and Kendrick, a land development company. Their outworn, uncomfortable marriage was headed for divorce, a fact Wilder must have discerned as Rose's letters home became increasingly vague on the subject of Gillette Lane. To add to their worry and discomfort over Rose's failing marriage, the Wilders had made a substantial personal loan to Rose and Gillette, as yet unpaid.

By 1915, Wilder had written ten columns for the *Missouri Ruralist* and a number of articles for other periodicals. Meticulous in her bookkeeping, Wilder was no saver when it came to preserving rough drafts or printed copies of her newspaper work. Some of her writing may not even have carried her byline. When Wilder replied to a Minnesota Writers' Survey about 1940, she provided a list of her publication credits and outlined the plan for the remainder of the *Little House* series. She stated that she was also the author of numerous farm and poultry articles, but "of these I have no record."[5] Anonymous, irregular, and/or ill-paid newspaper writing was anathema to Rose, whose writer's resume had increased exponentially after her return to California and who was preoccupied with new strategies for raising her professional profile. She was brimming with ideas about how to launch a similar career for her mother and was certain she could teach Wilder how to write for the national market. Mother and daughter had not seen each other in over four years, at which time Rose had been profoundly depressed and physically ill. Their complicated relationship was marked at times by conflict, competition, and misunderstanding, but the tender bond that bound them was unbreakable. "Muvver dear," Rose wrote from San Francisco, probably around 1914. "I am awfully lonesome for you—I wish you were out here in this little apartment with me, writing for the papers out here. You would make such a good feature writer, and we would have heaps of fun."[6] She even tried bribing her mother with an airplane ride; Rose had already strapped herself to the wing of a biplane and soared over the Golden Gate in pursuit of a story. Mama Bess melted. Despite her misgivings about leaving Almanzo with the yeoman's work, Wilder left by train for San Francisco in August 1915. Twenty years after fleeing the Dakotas, Wilder was heading west again—the direction of all good things—rolling over the Kansas plains, the Rocky Mountains, the red rock landscape of Utah, and the Great Basin Desert of Nevada, all the way to the Pacific on a new horizon-expanding adventure of her own.

Laura sent long letters from San Francisco to Almanzo; she was impatient to share the excitement of her discoveries with him ("I'll go see some more to write you").[7] Wilder's letters offer a rare glimpse into her private thoughts and her ongoing development as a writer. Despite constant pressure from Rose to step up her game and try writing stories for major national magazines like *The Country Gentleman,* Wilder remained non-committal about her future writing plans. She was willing to learn what she could from Rose, but she simply did not share her daughter's primary motives for writing—an unquenchable thirst for money and recognition. Rose, who had taught herself touch typing in Kansas City, could bang away on her manual typewriter for up to twelve hours a day. "The more I see of how Rose works," Laura confided to Almanzo, "the better satisfied I am to raise chickens. I intend to try to do some writing that will count, but I would not be driven by the work as she is and I do not see how she can stand it."[8]

Exotic San Francisco made an indelible impression. Rose's apartment crowned Russian Hill, offering panoramic views over the sparkling bay. Wilder rode the cable cars up and down the foggy streets, wandered red and gold Chinatown, and dined in Little Italy, where she was fascinated by the waiters speaking rapid-fire Italian. She insisted on wading in the Pacific and splashed about with the same childlike glee she had once displayed on the banks of Plum Creek. She spent several days covering the Panama-Pacific International Exhibition, San Francisco World's Fair, for the *Ruralist,* where her feature story on Missouri's agricultural prizes and exhibits landed on page one. "It gives a stay-at-home Middle Westerner something of a shock to meet a group of turbaned Hindoos on the street, or a Samoan, a Filipino or even a Mexican," she reported.[9] But she adjusted quickly. Wilder furiously scribbled down the recipes she liked best in order to share them with her readers back home: tamales, tagliarini, matzos, Chinese almond cakes, and Indian poori.

Her front page feature story for the *Ruralist* was a coup for Wilder, but the writing she did in San Francisco was significant for another reason. No doubt thanks to Rose and her connections, several of Wilder's poems for children appeared in the *Bulletin's* "Tuck 'em In Corner." It was standard bedtime fare, and not particularly accomplished verse, but the fact of their publication indicates that Wilder was continuing to pursue her interest in children's writing over the loud objections of Rose, who considered it a colossal waste of her mother's time and talent. "I have not had time to go over the children's stories. I glanced through them, and think them good. But they are not so important as the articles, for there is no opportunity

98 • Laura Ingalls Wilder: American Writer on the Prairie

to make a name with children's stories."[10] It was an objection Rose would often repeat, as if there were no other motivation for her mother's self-expression. By 1914, Rose was rapidly making a name for herself, writing columns and feature stories for the *San Francisco Bulletin*. She would go on to sell serialized biographies of Charlie Chaplin, Herbert Hoover, and Jack London to *Sunset* magazine by 1920, then switch to novels and highly lucrative serialized fiction in the 1920s and 30s. Rose insisted on blocking out an Ozark-themed story for Wilder to finish when she returned to Rocky Ridge, a return that was delayed when Wilder fell from a moving streetcar and was briefly hospitalized. Rose worried constantly about her mother's welfare in San Francisco and her ability to navigate the big city. On one occasion before her mother's fall, Rose raced home in a blind panic when her mother failed to answer the telephone, only to find Wilder happily typing away in the back bedroom. Rose also viewed her vigorous, forty-eight-year-old mother as an object of concern and a candidate for immediate retirement, even though Wilder had no difficulty actively farming Rocky Ridge, while simultaneously writing for the *Ruralist* and managing her blistering social schedule. Rose lobbied strenuously for her parents to sell the farm and move to California, a plea Laura politely considered and utterly ignored. Over the years, it became increasingly clear that Wilder had no intention of giving up Rocky Ridge for the rocking chair—not ever. But Rose, usually so perceptive, often failed to recognize the difference between what she wanted for her mother and what her mother wanted, a source of recurring friction between the two strong-willed women.

Wilder's experiences in California did seem to stimulate her writing and her sense of the possible. After she returned to Rocky Ridge from San Francisco in 1915, she began increasing her output for the *Ruralist* and soon was contributing a regular column to the journal, best known by the title "As a Farm Woman Thinks." Wilder's eclectic interests, unflinching opinions, and wide-ranging imagination were well suited to column writing and allowed her to tackle a kaleidoscope of subjects: "When Is a Settler an Old Settler?" "Mrs. Jones Takes the Rest Cure," "Santa Claus at the Front," "New Day for Women," "Swearing Is a Foolish Habit," and "Make Your Dreams Come True." She discussed time management, dispensed beauty tips, boosted the sale of war bonds, and mused on her love of dogs. By 1918, the *Ruralist's* circulation had increased to almost 90,000. Wilder's supportive editor John F. Case realized that subscribers were curious about his star columnist so he ran a profile of Wilder that year:

> Missouri farm folks need little introduction before getting acquainted with Mrs. A. J. Wilder of Rocky Ridge Farm. During the years she has been connected with this paper—a greater number of years than any other person on the

editorial staff—she has taken strong hold upon the esteem and affections of our great family. Mrs. Wilder has lived her life upon a farm. She knows farm folks and their problems as few women who write know them. And having sympathy with the folks whom she serves she writes well.[11]

At midlife, Wilder had never been busier—a fact also mentioned in Case's interview. During World War I, she volunteered with the Red Cross. She served as an officer in the Masonic Order of the Eastern Star. In time, she would serve as a member or founding member of several area women's clubs and organizations, most notably her literary study group The Athenians, the Justamere Club (a sororal society), and the Methodist Church. In 1917, she helped found and eventually accepted a position as secretary-treasurer of the National Farm Loan Association in Mansfield, an organization in which she remained actively involved for over a decade.[12] She judged poultry at the fair. She kept an immaculate house, loved to entertain guests, farmed alongside Almanzo, grew and preserved the majority of their food, and helped run the dairy operation. Twice a month, Wilder sat down at her tiny desk and composed her *Ruralist* column. In 1925, she ran (and lost) in her only bid for public office, as collector for Pleasant Valley Township. Much to Rose's bewilderment, Wilder showed no sign of retiring from Rocky Ridge and seemed to relish every minute of the Ozark farm life her daughter found so backward and uninspiring.

In 1918, Rose divorced Gillette Lane with a parting yawn. Reveling in her new freedom, she was writing for major national magazines, serializing and syndicating her stories, commanding large fees, and working on a new biography of Herbert Hoover, who was destined to become a close friend. Rose soon traded San Francisco for New York. She lived in Greenwich Village for a time, meeting and charming many of the leading literary luminaries of her day, before she latched onto her dream assignment as correspondent and spokeswoman for the Red Cross in still-smoldering postwar Europe. Rose was a wicked writer with a rollicking sense of humor. She stopped in Mansfield on her way to Europe and dispatched a letter to her friend the artist Berta Hader in New York:

Dear Comrades—

Having come so far on my journey back to the people, I am at this moment sitting on the second floor of a plain but comfortable peasant's hut in the Ozark wilderness . . . In such humble surroundings, with what longing my heart turns to those dear comrades whom I have left in that beloved New York . . . But I have given it up willingly, even gladly, in order to go to the people. No doubt the people will give a tea-party for me soon, and then heaven knows I shall suffer for my convictions![13]

Like her daughter, Wilder knew good material when she saw it. During Rose's stint with the Red Cross in Europe and the Middle East, Wilder mined Rose's mesmerizing letters home for her *Ruralist* columns, which sported exotic captions in 1920–1921: "We Visit Arabia," "We Visit Bohemia," "We Visit Paris Now," "We Visit Poland." Rose's gritty and sometimes hazardous work for the Red Cross took her as far as Egypt, Russia, and Azerbaijan. For her part, Rose alternated between the exhilaration of foreign travel (she began a lifelong love affair with Muslim Albania) and homesickness. From Jerusalem, the would-be Wandering Jew sent picture postcards of the Holy Land to her devout grandmother in South Dakota.[14]

When Caroline Ingalls died in 1924, Laura did not return to De Smet for the funeral. Her writing from the period, however, indicates that Wilder had been spending a considerable amount of time reflecting on her childhood, her parents, and her past. Anecdotes from her prairie years began showing up in her columns, just as they would later work their way into her novels for children. Not long before her mother's death, Wilder wrote,

> A letter from my mother, who is 76 years old, lies on my desk beside a letter from my daughter, far away in Europe. Reading the message from my mother, I am a child again and a longing unutterable fills my heart for mother's counsel, for the safe haven of her protection and the relief from responsibility which trusting her judgment always gave me. But when I turn to the letter written by my daughter, who will always be a little girl to me, no matter how big she grows, then I understand and appreciate my mother's position and her feelings toward me."[15]

Wilder had just anticipated the major source of the disagreements and power struggles she and Rose would wrestle with in the decade to come, as the two women held hands and knocked heads over Wilder's work.

In 1924, Rose had recently returned to Mansfield and was living with her parents at Rocky Ridge. Having tired of global travel and frustrating love affairs, she tired of hearth and home even faster. "This life is almost intolerable," she wrote, just weeks after her return.[16] So, apparently, was the thought of leaving. Rose's struggle with clinical depression compounded her dissatisfaction with life at home and abroad. For the next fifteen years, she would divide her time between Mansfield and the wider world. Although she would complain bitterly of financial and emotional entrapment at Rocky Ridge, she would never really leave the farm. Wilder's reaction to her daughter's dependency (and to Rose's compulsive, sometimes misguided, gestures of generosity) is much harder to assess. Rose ultimately diagnosed herself as suffering from manic depression, known today as bipolar personality disorder. The massive highs and lows she experienced in her forties, while living at home, could not have been lost on her sharp-eyed mother. Wilder who, by temperament and upbringing, admitted she "always hated

Writing the West: 1911–1943 · 101

a fuss," is silent on the subject of Rose's emotional difficulties. Whenever she does refer to Rose in her letters, columns, or interviews, she reveals her pride in Rose's accomplishments, and little more.

Although the farm was hardly conducive to Rose's frenetic flapper lifestyle, it did provide a peaceful place to write. Throughout the 1920s, when she felt well enough to write, Rose commanded thousands of dollars for her work, which was prominently featured in *McCall's, Sunset, The Saturday Evening Post, Harper's,* and numerous other national women's publications. She spent money freely and lavished gifts on her skeptical parents: a Victrola, a luxury Buick touring sedan, a six-week road trip to California, and eventually a new house. The house, a faux English Rock Cottage, was a head-turner. Modern, electrified, spectacularly situated with long views over the green velvet countryside near the Wilders' farmhouse, the rock cottage was a generous, overreaching disaster on Rose's part. Laura had nothing to do with the planning, furnishing, or design of the house, much less the decision to build it at all. Rose, who like her mother tended to spend a great deal of time thinking about architecture and the design of little houses, did not draft a unique plan for the cottage. Instead, she made modifications to a standard Sears-type house kit, which nearly tripled the cost of construction. Rose presented her parents with the keys for Christmas in 1928, and then promptly booted them out of the old farmhouse, which she took over with her dogs and her close friend, fellow writer Helen "Troub" Boylston. Rose and Boylston had just spent a year in Europe together, smoking, drinking, and laughing their way through Albania in a black Model T they nicknamed "Zenobia." Perhaps because Laura did not want to appear ungrateful or because she did not want to agitate her volatile daughter, she packed up her dignity with her belongings and removed with Almanzo to the Rock Cottage—where for years she apparently suffered loudly in silence. The instant Rose left Missouri for good, Wilder moved back to her beloved handcrafted farmhouse.

The year 1928 was the last good year for some time to come. Rose had persuaded her parents to invest a large portion of their savings, as she had, with the Palmer Company in New York. When the stock market crashed, Rose lost her substantial investment and the income it generated. The Wilders' retirement fund was another casualty. Rose was overextended before the crash. She provided varying amounts of financial assistance to family, friends, and Albanian Rexh Meta, the first of several surrogate sons whose education she helped underwrite. Consumed with financial uncertainties and the thought of death, she poured her misery and her soul into her diaries:

> The characteristics weakest in me: self-confidence, prudence, forethought, industry, will, unity of purpose, discrimination, presence of mind. Strongest

102 • Laura Ingalls Wilder: American Writer on the Prairie

characteristics: restlessness, tenacity, imagination (fancy), impulsiveness, generosity with money or things, desire to acquire (things, experience, information), nervous irritability, morbid sympathy, vanity, recklessness. I most like my intelligence. I most dislike my appearance . . . I look forward to a mediocre old age.[17]

and

Woke this morning, remembering my realization of some time ago. "I shall never have what I want." And thinking, "I shall never have more than I have now." But I do not want to believe that this is the end, though contentment would be a relief, restful.[18]

For both women, however, the need to make money took on a greater sense of urgency. For Wilder, advancing age, the death of her sister Mary in 1928 at Carrie Ingalls Swansey's home in the Black Hills, and bittersweet childhood memories triggered by the hardships of the Great Depression may have also propelled her to act.

By 1930, Wilder had written her autobiography. She called it "Pioneer Girl," and hoped to place the story with a major magazine as a non-fiction serial. Nostalgic, heartwarming, packed with fascinating detail about daily life on the Western frontier, the manuscript was unsalable. Rose resubmitted the material to her new agent, George Bye, whose initial reaction to the manuscript was echoed by a second round of editors. "A fine old lady was sitting in a rocking chair and telling a story chronologically but with no benefit of perspective or theatre," was Bye's blunt assessment.[19] In many ways, Wilder's first-person narrative read like an extended column for the *Ruralist,* more didactic and declarative than dramatic. Rose knew just how to fix that. Although Rose had typed and probably line-edited her mother's manuscript before submitting it to her agent on Wilder's behalf, the tone of the work is distinctly Wilder's and suggests that Rose did not play a large editorial role in the preparation of "Pioneer Girl." But that hands-off approach to her mother's work was about to change.

By the late 1920s when she began her memoir, Wilder was an experienced writer and columnist. She was neither particularly dejected by her manuscript's failure to sell, nor did she give up on the project. "She says she wants prestige rather than money," Rose recorded in her diary, incredulously.[20] Ultimately, the first two rounds of rejection allowed Wilder to pursue the idea of rewriting the manuscript—fictionalizing it—with the intention of selling it to a children's publisher, a market she had long found intriguing. The manuscript, much of which covered the period of Wilder's early childhood, provided a host of anecdotes suitable for individual picture or chapter books. Wilder's original opening line of "Pioneer Girl," altered in subsequent drafts, read "Once upon a time . . ."[21] Through close friend Berta Hader, Rose approached children's editor Marion Fiery at Alfred A. Knopf. This time, Rose had a newly edited version of her mother's material. But this "edit" had resulted in an entirely new genre, a chapter-book manuscript entitled "When Grandma Was a Little Girl." A letter from Rose in New York to Wilder suggests that Rose may have created the new manuscript with limited, if any, input from Wilder. It appears that Rose, using her copy editor's skills and her own discretion, had judiciously selected scenes from "Pioneer Girl," recast them in third-person—*I will never sell*"—and strung them together in standard chapter-book format. Marion Fiery (who knew little or nothing of Rose's creative involvement in the project) warmed to the subject matter, recognized its potential, and noted the fact "it covers a period in American history about which very little has been written, and almost nothing for boys and girls."[22] Within weeks, Wilder was revising "When Grandma Was a Little Girl" and preparing to sign her first book contract, at which point the story became hers. But the ensuing mother–daughter battle over the issues of authorship, autonomy, and artistry would last for years.

When Fiery asked for more specific detail on domestic frontier life, Wilder knew exactly what to supply. Wilder was a painstaking writer and a careful fact-checker; she filled her novels with authentic and telling period detail. Not long after Caroline Ingalls's death, Wilder had written to her aged aunt Martha Carpenter requesting old recipes, reminiscences, and family apocrypha from their days in the Wisconsin woods. Wilder used Martha's letters and her own formidable memory to resurrect primitive cabin life for young readers: how to make cheese, mold bullets, build a log smoker to cure ham, tap maple trees, dangle dead deer from stout branches to protect the meat from bears, eat roasted pig's tail on a stick, and make candy in the snow. Although the "Grandma" of the manuscript disappeared with the title, Wilder rejected Fiery's request that she change the words "Pa" and "Ma" to something less "colloquial."[23] As frequently happens in publishing, there were several alternative titles for the work: "Trundle-bed Tales," "The Little Girl in the West," and "Little Pioneer Girl" among them. Fiery picked the title; the book would be called *Little House in the Woods*. Wilder provided the compelling new heroine, a feisty four-year-old named Laura Ingalls.

Wilder's final draft was sitting on Fiery's desk when Knopf killed the book, along with its entire children's division.

Then, in a fortunate turn of events, departing editor Fiery encouraged Rose and Wilder to resubmit the manuscript to another publisher. Fiery

104 • Laura Ingalls Wilder: American Writer on the Prairie

then proceeded to lobby her colleagues and rivals for its acquisition. Ultimately, Wilder's manuscript was picked up by legendary children's editor Virginia Kirkus at Harper & Brothers, who recognized the newly retitled *Little House in the Big Woods* as "a book no Depression could stop."[24]

In the summer of 1931, after completing her revised version of *Little House in the Big Woods,* Wilder did something unexpected. She went home. De Smet was celebrating Old Settlers' Days, fifty years after the end of the Long Winter. Leaving Rose at Rocky Ridge to mind the farm, Laura and Almanzo, now aged 64 and 73, respectively, set out for South Dakota by car, slowly reversing the route they had taken to Mansfield by wagon almost four decades earlier. Dog Nero came along for the ride, eagerly lapping the ice cream cones Wilder bought for him. As in 1894, Wilder kept a travel diary of the journey. In it, she carefully recorded her impressions of the drought-stricken farms and rural communities she passed along the way. "And my God it is a ruined country," she wrote. "Being sold out on taxes. Fifty of these wonderful farms now advertised for (property) tax sale."[25] As she watched the changing scenery from the bench seat of her chugging Buick, Wilder noted the elements of her lost world that still survived. In Nebraska, farmers still plowed their fields with teams of draught horses. Hand-churned butter was served in the roadside cafes. Small towns continued to be characterized by their emigrant roots and traditions; some towns were "German Catholic" with wonderful cakes. The rest were indistinguishable and hot.

Laura and Almanzo drove to Manchester to see Grace Ingalls Dow on her dustbowl farm. "Grace seems like a stranger only now and then something familiar about her face. I suppose it is the same with me," Wilder mused.[26] She visited old friends in town. Most were long gone, like Cap Garland, who had died in his twenties, the victim of a boiler explosion. His sister, Wilder's teacher Florence Garland, was delighted to see her again. Wilder stopped at her parent's old home on Third Street to inventory what remained of Caroline and Mary's personal belongings. She drove out to her father's homestead; the dirt lane had become a highway. She recognized the small sand hill that once stood near the farmhouse and little more. A few of the cottonwood trees she had carefully planted and watered were still alive. Then, probably with mixed emotions, she and Almanzo drove north of town to view their own former farm and tree claim. Nothing remained of the couple's time there. The buildings were gone and the tree claim had been reclaimed by grass. A grain field spread over the hill where the little gray farmhouse had stood before the fire.

The Wilders left De Smet and drove as far west as Keystone, where they visited Carrie Ingalls Swanzey and where Gutzon Borglum was in the process of blasting George Washington's profile out of Mount Rushmore. After

Writing the West: 1911–1943 • 105

touring the Black Hills, the tired couple returned to Mansfield. Wilder's retrospective homecoming served several purposes. Intentionally or not, the trip back to the place she called "The Land of Used to Be" had whetted her memory and her desire to write, both of which were necessary if she planned to capitalize on her new writing opportunities. *Little House in the Big Woods* had barely scratched the surface of Wilder's "Pioneer Girl" memoir. She could expect to be offered a standard three-book contract from her publisher. Wilder was about to turn sixty-five, but appeared younger. With her carefully coiffed white hair and expressive blue eyes, she remained attractive, vital, and alert. She had ceased writing her farm column for the *Ruralist* in 1923, had reduced some of her strenuous daily farm chores, and, despite the gloom and financial uncertainty of the Depression, was enjoying semi-retirement at Rocky Ridge. Would she write another children's story for Harper & Brothers? And if so, what would she write?

All of these questions became far more pressing when *Little House in the Big Woods* was released in April 1932 to glowing reviews and—even more importantly—strong sales. As a recommended selection of the Junior Literary Guild, the book gained instant visibility and critical acclaim. Wilder needed a follow-up fast and made the decision not to change what had been a successful formula. She decided to write a story based on Almanzo's childhood this time, following his adventures over the course of a single farming year in Malone, New York. Having a male protagonist increased Wilder's readership with boys, but the story was not grounded in Wilder's own experiences and she knew nothing about farming in upstate New York. Despite Wilder's strong debut novel, her new project was initially rejected and is still regarded as her least satisfying work. The project floundered until Rose made a scouting trip to Malone to research the area and dig up some local color for her mother's book. *Farmer Boy* was published in 1933. Reviews were positive, sales brisk, and Harper's began to express a growing interest in acquiring more of Wilder's work.

Rose understood the allure of frontier mythology, even if she had no interest in the subject herself. She considered her own serial novels set in the Ozarks, *Cindy* and *Hillbilly*, as nothing more than dreadful, if highly lucrative, hackwork. Unfortunately, Rose's need for money, which had never been greater, coincided with her total lack of new ideas for work, which in turn magnified her personal insecurities, professional doubts, and her profound depression. In 1932, she made a furtive and strictly commercial decision that understandably upset and infuriated her mother: Rose stole her mother's material. Just as she had initially reworked segments of "Pioneer Girl" into chapter-book format for "When Grandma Was a Little Girl," Rose helped herself to the manuscript for a second time. Rose's serial novel, *Let the Hurricane Roar*, was published in *The Saturday Evening Post* to great acclaim and quickly repackaged in book form. *Let the Hurricane Roar* tells the pioneer adventure story of Charles and Caroline, newlywed homesteaders who live in a railroad camp before moving to their dugout on Wild Plum Creek, where they fight grasshoppers, howling blizzards, and wolves with the help of their Swedish neighbors, the Svensons. Rose had dusted off her copy of "Pioneer Girl" and surgically extracted her mother's childhood memories, the biographical material Wilder would use as the basis for the entire *Little House* series. Wilder had no trouble recognizing blatant (and emotional) plagiarism when she saw it. Rose had displayed a sweeping disregard for her mother's talent and personal feelings. Worse, she feigned not to understand the fuss and complained that Wilder's natural reaction of betrayal and disgust had ruined "the simple perfection of my pleasure."[27] The damage done to their relationship seems to have been partly assuaged by the time Rose returned from her scouting trip to Malone for *Farmer Boy*, but the territorial battle would continue as the two women fought over their respective rights to the Wilders' past. Rose would rewrite additional scenes from "Pioneer Girl" as successful short stories for the adult market.

Over the next five years, Laura and Rose wore out a path between the two houses on Rocky Ridge. Rose's diary records their day-to-day interaction, although she provides limited detail on precisely how or what she is contributing to her mother's "goddam juvenile(s)" other than the retyping of them.[28] Almanzo is also largely absent from Rose's diaries. A quiet peace-loving man, perhaps he took refuge in the barn. It was not long, however, before mother and daughter had effectively blocked out something unprecedented in children's publishing—a series of novels, each covering a single year in the life of the heroine, taking her from early childhood, through adolescence, and up to the time of her marriage. J. K. Rowling would apply the same formula to her *Harry Potter* novels, but Rowling's novels take place in a magical wizarding world, the realm of pure imagination that delineates much of children's literature. Wilder latched on to an even more potent myth for young readers growing up in America in the 1930s. She was writing an epic Western for children, as seen through the eyes of a child, the first of its kind in a country fearing for its future, looking to its past for hope and glory, and yearning for what it perceived as its long-lost Golden Frontier, the place where hard work met opportunity and reaped success.

For more than a decade, Wilder's highly anticipated novels appeared at regular intervals: *Little House in the Big Woods, Farmer Boy, Little House on the Prairie, On the Banks of Plum Creek, By the Shores of Silver Lake, The Long Winter, Little Town on the Prairie,* and *These Happy Golden Years.*

Rose left Rocky Ridge for good in 1935. She spent much of her time in New York, eventually relocating in Danbury, Connecticut. By 1938, she stopped writing fiction entirely and embarked on her ninth or tenth career as a political theorist, essayist, and founding mother of the Libertarian Movement, along with friends Ayn Rand and Isabel Paterson. Laura and Rose continued a long and affectionate correspondence, even as they butted heads over the content and direction of the *Little House* series. Wilder, who had previously tended to defer to her daughter's superior writing and marketing credentials, had no trouble pushing back as she gained skill and confidence. Wilder was emotionally invested in her characters and her subject, in ways that doctrinaire Rose failed to comprehend. Wilder's own instincts for the material were sharper than her daughter's. When Rose suggested that Wilder add George and Maggie Masters to the cast of characters in *The Long Winter* (the couple had in fact lived with the Ingalls in De Smet), Wilder flatly refused, viewing their inclusion as distracting to the plot. Rose thought it unwise to include Mary's blindness in the novels, advice Wilder dismissed out of hand. At one point, Rose even advocated changing the protagonist of the series from Laura to Carrie. Editors also weighed in and Wilder did not win every contest. Wilder's historically accurate title "The Hard Winter" was deemed inappropriate for children; the book was published as *The Long Winter.*

In 1937, Wilder was invited to make a high-profile speech at the Detroit Book Fair, to a national trade audience packed with top editors, publishers, acquisition librarians, reviewers, agents, and teachers. Wilder, who white-knuckled her way through the address, was warmly received by the crowd and her literary star was on the rise. The year 1938 was even better and more noteworthy. *On the Banks of Plum Creek*—heavily edited by *both* Wilder and Rose, but written well after Rose's final departure from Mansfield—was named a Newberry Honor Book, the first of five for Wilder. Rose was hard at work on a second pioneer serial, *Free Land.* Like *Let the Hurricane Roar,* the new serial was also based on Laura's (and Almanzo's) frontier experiences in the Dakotas, but this time Rose was writing with her mother's full awareness and approval. The serial produced another critical and money-making hit for Rose. In the process of writing *Free Land,* Rose prepared a long questionnaire for her father, in which she solicited specific information on everything from Western dialect to farm machinery. Almanzo's monosyllabic written responses probably provided far less information than Rose had hoped to glean, but when she asked her father to describe a single moment of personal triumph in the Dakotas, one moment of transcendent happiness, Almanzo's reply was startling. He could think of nothing. "My life," he said, "has been mostly disappointments."[29]

A decade after she began reimagining her childhood for generations of children yet to come, Wilder submitted her eighth and final manuscript in the *Little House* series to agent George Bye. The year was 1942. Europe was in flames, World War II raged in the Pacific, scrap drives and rationing preoccupied the home front, and Wilder's new novel went to press. She called it *These Happy Golden Years*. It read like a wistful antidote to modern madness, something many of her readers desperately desired. By 1942, many of Wilder's original readers were long grown and far from home, serving as nurses and soldiers in the war effort.

Wilder had written herself out. She set down her pencil and resumed her life as a respected citizen of Mansfield. Letters, awards, and accolades poured in to Rocky Ridge. Wilder had an oversized mailbox installed at the end of the drive. On her eighty-sixth birthday, she received more than 1,000 pieces of mail. With her nineteenth-century sense of propriety, duty, and obligation, Wilder replied individually to her legion of fans well into her eighties. Fame, on the other hand, was another matter. Wilder may have written largely "for the prestige," which she had earned and in which she took pride, but she clearly had little interest in celebrity. In town, at church, at Eastern Star meetings, and at the library where she sometimes read to school children or checked out the latest novel by Zane Grey, her growing celebrity was burdensome, a nuisance and a hindrance. It had the potential to distance her from the very people whose company she genuinely valued and enjoyed; her growing reputation as a national treasure and the upsurge in her financial status was something to be downplayed at home. Late in life, when Wilder had to hire a chauffeur to drive her over the Ozark hills in order to participate in her favorite clubs and social activities, she made sure that her new Oldsmobile was well hidden from view. As in any small town, this strategy was hopelessly unsuccessful. As she aged, Wilder retained a core of close friends, including Irene Lichty and Neta and Silas Seal, who checked on Mrs. Wilder and helped her with chores, errands, and housework.

With her cool head for business, Wilder had negotiated hard for better contracts and greater artistic control over the design of her work. The original series of Wilder's work featured illustrations by Helen Sewell and Mildred Boyle, whose art echoed a distinctive woodblock print style popular in children's book design throughout the 1920s and 1930s. In 1947, young, newly commissioned artist Garth Williams arrived at Rocky Ridge. Wilder had argued for years with Ursula Nordstrom, her long-term editor at Harpers, that the entire series of novels should be available for purchase as a single set and needed a consistent, cohesive design. Garth Williams did exactly that for the new edition of the *Little House* books, which was finally released in 1953. He spent time with the Wilders before setting out to tour the sites where the novels took place. Williams was quite taken with Wilder. "She was small and nimble. Her eyes sparkled with good humor and she seemed a good twenty years younger than her age."[30] Wilder, for her part, was delighted with Williams's artwork. "Mary, Laura and the folks live again in these illustrations," she telegraphed the artist.[31]

Because Rose had no interest in farming or returning to Rocky Ridge, the Wilders began selling off land soon after the war. They retained their rights to the farmhouse, where ninety-year-old Almanzo collapsed and died of a heart attack on October 23, 1949. Friends found Laura in the bedroom, cradling Almanzo's body in her arms. "I am so lonely," she acknowledged to a friend. "My heart is too sore to write more."[32] After a twelve-year absence, Rose returned to Missouri for her father's funeral, but when she went home to Danbury, Connecticut, she left her eighty-two-year-old mother alone on Rocky Ridge. Wilder would not budge. Even after her head was badly lacerated in a fall, she refused to leave the farm. "I wish she did not like to live alone but there isn't much I can say about that when I am doing the same thing myself because I like to," Rose wrote in a letter to Neta Seal, thanking Neta for watching over her mother.[33]

For Wilder, the losses piled up even as the accolades rolled in. Sisters Grace and Carrie both died before Almanzo, although they lived long enough to witness the apex of Wilder's literary success, unlike their mother and sister Mary, who both died before the publication of the *Little House* books. Most if not all the Ingalls women appear to have suffered from diabetes and its complications, Wilder included. Wilder's diabetes went undiagnosed and untreated until her final illness. But even as Wilder grew physically frail, her mind remained sharp and focused, and she resolved to stay on Rocky Ridge where, at eighty-eight, she kept a handgun by the screen door and a shotgun in her bedroom, just in case. Fame, not chicken thieves, seems to have been the motivating factor. In fact, curious fans and gawkers had begun cruising by or stopping at the farmhouse, some of whom had to be shooed off the property by protective neighbors or the Seals.

Due to Almanzo's last illness, Wilder was unable to travel to Detroit in 1949 when the city dedicated one of its branch libraries to her. Not to be outdone, Mansfield soon followed suit. In 1954, the American Library Association created the Wilder Medal. Along with the coveted Newberry and Caldecott awards, the Laura Ingalls Wilder Award ranks as children's literature's highest honor—its lifetime achievement award—and acknowledges "a substantial and lasting contribution to literature for children." Winners include Wilder herself, along with list of legendary children's writers: E. B. White, Theodor S. Geisel (Dr. Seuss), Beverly Cleary, Maurice Sendak, Eric Carle and Tomie DePaola, to name only a few.

By the winter of 1956, the old pioneer was clearly failing. A few years earlier, for one of Wilder's last Christmases, a group of local children made an impromptu decision to go caroling at Rocky Ridge, where they gathered under the trees and sang to her in the falling snow. Wilder remained inside the farmhouse, her delicate figure framed and backlit by the broad picture windows of her living room. As she listened to the children serenade her, tears streamed down her face.[34] She died on February 10, 1957, three days after her ninetieth birthday, in her own bed at Rocky Ridge. Rose came home to be with her at the end.

NOTES

1. Miller, *Becoming Laura Ingalls*, 139.
2. LIW, "Favors the Small Farm Home," *Laura Ingalls Wilder, Farm Journalist: Writings from the Ozarks,* 16.
3. LIW "The Story of Rocky Ridge Farm," ibid., 19.
4. Holtz, 53.
5. Materials Relating to Minnesota Authors: Laura Ingalls. Minnesota Historical Society Library.
6. Lane Papers, RWL to LIW, Box 13, c. 1914.
7. RWL, *A Little House Traveler,* "West From Home," 169.
8. Ibid., 242.
9. LIW, *Laura Ingalls Wilder, Farm Journalist: Writings from the Ozarks*, 39–41.
10. Holtz, 86.
11. "Let's Visit Mrs. Wilder" interview with John F. Case, *Ruralist* editor, February 1918.
12. Miller, *Becoming Laura Ingalls*, 136.
13. Holtz, 90.
14. Lane Papers, RWL to LIW, September 10, 1923.
15. LIW, *Laura Ingalls Wilder, Farm Journalist: Writings from the Ozarks,* 260.
16. Holtz, 142.
17. Ibid., 201.
18. Ibid., 219.
19. Lane Papers, George Bye to RWL, April 6, 1931, Box 13.
20. Holtz, 374.
21. Hill, *Laura Ingalls Wilder,* 131.
22. Ibid., 135.
23. Ibid., 136.
24. Virginia Kirkus, "The Discovery of Laura Ingalls Wilder," *The Horn Book Magazine,* December 1953, reprinted in William Anderson, ed., *The Horn Book's Laura Ingalls Wilder: Articles about and by Laura Ingalls Wilder, Garth Williams, and the Little House Books* (Boston. MA: Horn Book, 1987), 38.
25. *LIW, Little House Traveler,* "The Road Back," 301.
26. *LIW, Little House Traveler,* "The Road Back," 307.
27. Lane Papers, RWL Journal, January 25, 1933, Box 23.
28. Lane Papers, RWL Diary, May 10, 1936, Box 23.
29. *A Little House Sampler*, 213.
30. *The Horn Book,* December 1953, reprinted in Anderson.
31. Anderson, 7.
32. Miller, *Becoming Laura Ingalls Wilder*, 251.
33. Hill, 186.
34. Private tour of Rock Cottage, Laura Ingalls Wilder Historic Home and Museum, November 2, 2012.

CHAPTER **6**

I Am Your Laura: 1943 and Forward

It is with the greatest pleasure that The Horn Book *here honors one of the most beloved of all children's authors and joins in the tribute paid to her by all the contributors to this Christmas issue. It is a tribute that will grow with every reader of the magazine; so that Christmas wishes will be flying to Mansfield, Missouri, from all over America and from countries beyond the sea. It is fitting that this should be so, for seldom have there been any children's books so universally loved . . . It was the people like Pa and Ma with their high ideals and their practical industry and courage that made this country. If they were still alive they would feel deeply the responsibilities their America must now take in the wider world; and Laura and Mary would be taught to share all that they had.*

The Horn Book, 1953

I honestly cannot read Little House on the Prairie *as other than apology for the "ethnic cleansing" of the Great Plains. That her thought was unremarkable, perhaps even progressive, for the time in which she lived and wrote should not exempt her books from sending up red flags for contemporary critics who believe in diversity, multiculturalism, and human rights . . . Laura Ingalls Wilder and Rose Wilder Lane wrote in and for their time, and their political philosophy, particularly Lane's growing libertarianism, made stereotyping Native peoples and refusing to see the communitarian virtues of tribal societies a valid strategy for expressing their version of truth. That we should continue to accept their stereotyping without question, and even to profess to find it liberating, is our shame and not theirs.*

Frances W. Kaye

In 1953, Wilder was interviewed for a radio broadcast by Wright County librarian and personal friend Docia Holland. It is the only known recording of her voice. In the crackling broadcast, Wilder sends her thanks and greetings to a group of children and librarians in California who have given her a set of Ingalls family figurines for her eighty-sixth birthday. Wilder's voice has acquired a hint of a drawl over the course of sixty years in the Ozarks, although she retains her formal diction and the long-obsolete pioneer pronunciation of the word Iowa, which she enunciates as "I-oh-way." She praises the craftsmanship of the figures and then signs off. "I am," she says, "your Laura." There is the slightest hesitation in her voice before she adds, "of the *Little House* books."[1]

And so she remains. Whatever Wilder's private thoughts about the conflation of her own identity with that of her doppelganger, she could not have anticipated the fiery debate and unanswered questions generated by her work: "Which Laura?" "Whose history?" "What frontier?"

For years after her death, Laura Ingalls Wilder and Laura the Heroine were indistinguishable in the eyes of the majority of her readers, young and old. The assertion that they were one and the same was passionately advocated by Rose Wilder Lane, even as curious readers and educators began discovering and questioning the biographical differences between the two. "They [the *Little House* books] are the truth, and only the truth; every detail in them is written as my mother remembered it," Rose insisted. "These books are entirely the 'true stories' that they claim to be."[2]

Upon Wilder's death Rose inherited her mother's estate and her royalties, which increased exponentially in the 1950s and 1960s as Garth Williams' newly illustrated set of *Little House* books went through repeat printings. Rose lived modestly, almost eccentrically, with her beloved Maltese dogs in the home she remodeled in Danbury. In a 1960 feature article on her Danbury house that ran in *Woman's Day,* Rose was photographed in her newly remodeled kitchen—clearly sporting a shower cap. She was a ferocious guardian of her mother's mystique and literary legacy, summarily dismissing any suggestion that the significance and appeal of Wilder's work depended on artistic embellishment as well as autobiographical fact. To Rose, Wilder's novels hardly qualified as novels. At the time, Rose was preoccupied with nonfiction writing, political journalism, and existential theory. She may have thought that any attempt to separate her mother's life from Laura's adventures would somehow undermine the historical integrity of the books (which were read and taught in elementary schools all over the country with the gravitas of supplemental history texts). When Rose died in her sleep in 1968, having just covered the Viet Nam War for *Woman's Day,* and just days before she prepared to leave on yet another grueling round-the-world trip, Wilder's estate and legacy passed from Rose to Rose's heir and political protégé, Roger Lea McBride.

There is no disputing Wilder's profound impact on twentieth-century elementary education. In 1948, she was voted the nation's most popular living writer by students in Chicago, hardly rural readers. Her books were a staple of "reading time" in classrooms around the country, and her interpretation of historical events like the removal of the Osages from Kansas heavily influenced the way in which children viewed the past. *Little House on the Prairie*, Wilder's most controversial book, inculcated the concept of the "Noble Savage" for millions of children more effectively than "The Lone Ranger" and genre Westerns of the time, but with the heightened moral authority of the classroom. In his provocative study of the depiction of Indians in white culture, *The White Man's Indian*, author Robert Berkhofer, examines the "Western" in popular art and literature:

> What distinguishes a Western from other types of adventure literature is the setting and the costumes. Originally set in the forest like Cooper's conception, the Western quickly moved to the plains, deserts and mountains of the trans-Mississippi United States. More significant than its actual locale is its timing in the history of the westward expansion of White society. It must be set at the moment when social order and anarchy meet, when civilization encounters savagery, on the frontier of White expansion, in order to give rise to the conflict that is the heart of the genre. In the Western formula, lawlessness and savagery must recede before the vanguard of White Society.[3]

Certainly, Wilder's depiction of the misidentified Osage warrior Soldat du Chene—"that's one Good Indian!"—who single-handedly saved the encroaching white settlers from massacre in *Little House on the Prairie* was typical of another Indian motif. In Berkhofer's words:

> On the other hand, the good Indian was the typical Noble Savage acting as a friend to the Whites fighting the bad White or Red outlaws. Regardless of which guise the Western presented the Indian in, he was the master of the wilderness and the possessor of physical prowess and/or crafty wisdom. In short, the Western perpetuated the traditional White images of the Indian.[4]

This does not mean that the historical events Wilder narrated in *Little House on the Prairie* did not actually occur (although it is less likely that Wilder, who was three at the time, could have retained such vivid memories of the Osages and their forced removal). In general, historians and researchers have corroborated Wilder's account. Even small details, such as the location of the Ingalls hand-dug well and the cabin's proximity to an

Osage campsite, have been authenticated. But Wilder's interpretation of the larger events, and the ways in which she molded them for her readers—including Laura's emotional ambiguity over the Osages removal—is entirely consistent with Berkhofer's observation of Indians in twentieth-century popular art.

> What the captivity narrative started, the Western novel and movie continued to finish long past the actual events of conquest—as if the American conscience still needed to be reassured about the rightness of past actions and the resulting present times. That the basic conflict over land and lifestyles should be so indelibly engraved upon the White mind so long after the actual events took place would seem to suggest the destruction of Native American cultures and the expropriation of Native American lands still demand justification in White American eyes.[5]

For English professor Frances W. Kaye, Wilder's inaccurate, inexpert, naïve, and overtly racist attempt at "justification" should disqualify her novels, particularly *Little House on the Prairie,* from being read, taught, or considered in the classroom. Although it is difficult to imagine any instructor today failing to point out the obvious Euro-American biases and contradictions in Wilder's work, it is almost as difficult to find many children's books of the period (and even later) that are not riddled with many of the same racial stereotypes and controversial assumptions regarding Manifest Destiny, Indian Rights, women, and minorities in the West and the role of government. Wilder's work is historical fiction, not fact. It is a snapshot in time, a fading photo of Wilder's childhood, superimposed on the backdrop of 1930s and 1940s culture when it was written, as reinterpreted by readers today. Like *The Adventures of Huckleberry Finn* (albeit without Mark Twain's sardonic social commentary) or the characterization of Injun Joe in *The Adventures of Tom Sawyer,* the *Little House* books raise uncomfortable questions about America's past, but for many Wilder readers and researchers, discomfort or dislike is not a disqualifier. It is simply an incentive to learn more.

In 1893, the year of the Panic, the year the Wilders prepared to quit the West for good, Frederick Jackson Turner delivered his famous paper "The Significance of the Frontier in American History" at a meeting of the American Historical Association. Known to successive generations as the "Turner Thesis" or the "Frontier Thesis," Turner's theory of Western history was simple, concise, and groundbreaking. American history was not the history of the American Revolution, the Founding Fathers, their legal documents, and disputes over civil, state, and property rights. The history of America was the growth and settlement of the West; the frontier was her reason to be. The organizing theme of American history was "the existence of an area of free land, its continuous recession, and the advance of American settlement westward." The frontier itself was responsible for American democracy, freedom, and individualism. It had determined the character of the nation. Turner described a series of successive frontiers, each defined by a process of expansion:

> Each type of industry was on the march toward the West, impelled by an irresistible attraction. Each passed in successive waves across the continent. Stand at Cumberland Gap and watch the procession of civilization, marching single file—the buffalo following the trail to the salt springs, the Indian, the fur trader and hunter, the cattle-raiser, the pioneer farmer—and the frontier has passed by. Stand at South Pass in the Rockies a century later and see the same procession with wider intervals between.[6]

Although Wilder never mentions Turner by name, she may have been familiar with his Frontier Thesis. Even if not, many of her own ideas about the march of Western history coincide with Turner's. Despite Wilder's assertion, "I did not know that I was writing history," her 1937 Detroit Book Fair speech demonstrates how significantly Turner's theory of "successive frontiers" had impacted her thinking and her work. "I began to think what a wonderful childhood I had had," Wilder said in 1937, when she addressed the Detroit Book Fair. "I had seen the whole frontier, the woods, the Indian country of the great plains, the frontier towns, the building of railroads in wild, unsettled country, homesteading and farmers coming in to take possession. I realized that I had seen and lived it all—all the successive phases of the frontier, first the frontiersman, then the pioneer, then the farmers, and the towns. Then I understood that in my own life I represented a whole period of American History."[7]

Turner's thesis was the dominant model of Western historiography for nearly half a century. In effect, Wilder condensed and dramatized Turner's theory for young readers. New Western historians such as Patricia Nelson Limerick ushered in a change in perception and viewpoint.

> If we give up a preoccupation with the frontier and look instead at the continuous sweep of Western American history, new organizing ideas await our attention, but no simple, unitary model. Turner's frontier rested on a single point of view; it required that the observer stand in the East and look to the West. Now, like many scholars in other fields, Western historians have had to learn to live with relativism . . . Turner's frontier was a process, not a place . . . Reorganized, the history of the West is a study of a place undergoing conquest and never fully escaping its consequences.[8]

If Turner's frontier was a process and Limerick's a place, then Wilder's West was both and neither. Wilder's West was a family. Hers was a domestic history of the American frontier as experienced by the Ingalls, in which the point of view resided firmly with an observant and engaging adolescent girl. Turner's frontier process, his march of "civilization" was an important aspect of Wilder's writing but ultimately incidental to Wilder's main subject: family and the search for home, arguably the two most resonant and psychologically potent concepts for young, developing minds. Wilder's West was also a place of conquest and fateful consequences for its victims, a theme she addresses with obvious discomfort and ambiguity in regard to the Osage Indians in *Little House on the Prairie,* and to which she rarely returns. In her art, Wilder draws a tight protective circle around home and hearth. It is not primarily the people of the West who are threatened and fighting for survival—it is the virgin West herself. Wilder's (and "Laura's") sense of the West as a "place" is more pastoral than communal. Wilder's ideal West is largely uninhabited; it is a "place" of pristine wilderness, with little reference to the people who move through it. It is the antidote to town. What is changing irrevocably, terribly, and decidedly for the worse is the West itself—the woods, the plains, the wilderness. As Caroline Fraser noted in her essay "Laura Ingalls Wilder and the Wolves":

> The Little House books have always been stranger, deeper and darker than any ideology. While celebrating family life and domesticity, they undercut those cozy values at every turn, contrasting the pleasures of home (firelight, companionship, song) with the immensity of the wilderness, its nobility and its power to resist cultivation and civilization. In her hymn to the American west, Wilder treasures forest, grasslands, wetlands and wildlife in terms that verge of the transcendental. Alive in Laura Ingalls Wilder's memory of it, the wilderness she knew—now lost—continues to reflect her longing for a vanishing world, a rough paradise from which we are excluded by a helpless devotion to our own survival.[9]

In 1974, Wilder's work was introduced to a new generation of diehard fans with the debut of Michael Landon's television series "Little House on the Prairie." The episodes, many of which were written by former *Bonanza* and other Hollywood Western screenwriters, took Wilder's work in an entirely different and contemporary direction. Many fans of the television series are still shocked to discover that Mary Ingalls never married, never ran a school for the blind, or lost her baby in a tragic fire; that the Ingalls never adopted a son; that the family actually lived in South Dakota; that Nellie Oleson's husband wasn't a New York Jew; and that Laura and Almanzo did not, in fact, strategically place dynamite and detonators in and around

Walnut Grove, then blow the entire town to smithereens rather than submit to having the town taken over by land swindlers and railroad tycoons.

Just as Wilder's work became increasingly commercialized and popularized in the 1970s and early 1980s, it has recently become more politicized. William Holtz's biography of Rose Wilder Lane, *The Ghost in the Little House*, makes the case for Lane as her mother's ghostwriter, the true shining artist behind the books. While there is no doubt that Lane played a pivotal role in shaping her mother's material in the early stages of Wilder's first *Little House* books, their mother–daughter collaboration ran both ways. Wilder was a writer in search of structure; Lane was a writer in search of a subject. Each influenced the other, but their writing styles remain distinctively and convincingly their own. In *Little House, Long Shadow: Laura Ingalls Wilder's Impact on American Culture,* feminist critic Anita Clair Fellman argues that Wilder's ubiquity in the American classroom and popular culture encourages negative attitudes toward government, regulation, and social welfare programs, serves up covert conservative messages to young impressionable readers, and ultimately paved the way for the resurgence of cultural conservatism in American society from the Reagan revolutionaries to the Tea Party. Although Wilder's traditional beliefs and values, including her faith in individualism and self-reliance, are hardly a matter of debate, neither is America's own recent history of political mood swings, ideological realignment and philosophical shifts. Wilder's work clearly mirrors her personal beliefs and her Calvinistic upbringing, but it is far from a manifesto.

Wilder was a lyrical and self-consciously uplifting writer, not a polemicist. But as in all fairytales and virtually all children's books, there is a moral to the story or, at a minimum, there is a point of instruction. Wilder's continuing relevance depends in large part on whether young readers still embrace the underlying premise of her books, whether her story engages their curiosity and holds their interest. And her message to her young readers remains redemptive: that every child is the hero of his or her own story, that life is an adventure into the unknown and the unknowable, but that love, family, work, home, and nature endow it with meaning, hope, and purpose.

Every summer, literally tens of thousands of tourists descend on the towns associated with the life of Laura Ingalls Wilder. They drive the scenic Laura Ingalls Wilder Memorial Highway through Wisconsin en route to picnic beside the Ingalls's replica cabin in the Big Woods. They marvel at the well Pa dug near Independence, Kansas, and learn how to work the windlass. The tiny Burr Oak hotel where Laura lived and worked is now a museum and open for visitors. In Spring Valley, tourists flock to the grueling Almanzo 100-mile gravel bike race. Many of them will drive on to attend

118 • Laura Ingalls Wilder: American Writer on the Prairie

the annual Laura Ingalls Wilder Pageant held at dusk on the edge of a scorched bean field near the banks of Plum Creek. Old Norwegian farmers squeeze into folding chairs while balancing tubs of popcorn on their laps. Mennonite girls in long sweltering skirts and starched white caps hurry to take their seats beside a group of girls from Los Angeles sporting cut-off shorts and tank-tops as they casually flip through a signed copy of Alison Arngrim's *Confessions of a Prairie Bitch: How I Survived Nellie Oleson and Learned to Love Being Hated.* At twilight when the fireflies appear, children begin rolling down the long hill.

In De Smet, children and their parents will tour the Surveyor's House and the house Charles built in town when he quit farming. Countless adults make the trip on their own and late in life. The site of the Ingalls former homestead hosts another museum with wagon rides, live animals, activities, and a swath of undisturbed prairie to explore. These places are more than living history sites or tourist attractions: to many, they are shrines. As psychologist Bruno Bettelheim explains:

> Today children no longer grow up within the security of an extended family, or of a well-integrated community. Therefore, even more than at the times fairy tales were invented, it is important to provide the modern child with images of heroes who have to go out into the world all by themselves and who, although originally ignorant of the ultimate things, find secure places in the world by following their right way with deep inner confidence.
>
> The fairy-tale hero proceeds for a time in isolation, as the modern child often feels isolated. The hero is helped by being in touch with primitive things—a tree, an animal, nature—as the child feels more in touch with those things than most adults do. The fate of these heroes convinces the child, that like them, he may feel outcast and abandoned in the world, groping in the dark, but, like them, in the course of his life he will be guided step by step, and given help when it is needed. Today, even more than in past times, the child needs the reassurance offered by the image of the isolated man [or Pioneer Girl] who nevertheless is capable of achieving meaningful and rewarding relations with the world around him.[10]

The vestiges of Wilder's lost world still remain, but the people who come to see and experience them all have one thing in common—they come for the love of Laura.

"It is a long story, filled with sunshine and shadow, that we have lived since *These Happy Golden Years,*" Wilder wrote near the end of her life.[11] That her long story commands the lingering affection and attention of so many, so long after the events have passed, is a testament to the power of her memory, her love of the living prairie, and her quiet art.

NOTES

1. *Laura Speaks* CD, script by William Anderson, narration by Erik Spyres, produced and distributed in conjunction with the Laura Ingalls Wilder Memorial Society, Mansfield, MO. Available at Wilder homesites.
2. Hill, 188.
3. Robert Berkhofer, *The White Man's Indian: Images of the American Indian from Columbus to the Present* (New York: Knopf, 1978), 97.
4. Ibid., 98.
5. Ibid., 104.
6. Frederick Jackson Turner, *The Frontier in American History* (New York: Holt, Rinehart and Winston, 1962).
7. LIW, Detroit Book Fair Speech, 1937, in *A Little House Sampler,* 217.
8. Limerick, 26.
9. Caroline Fraser, "Laura Ingalls Wilder and the Wolves," *Los Angeles Review of Books,* Oct. 10, 2012.
10. Bruno Bettelheim, *The Uses of Enchantment: The Meaning and Importance of Fairy Tales* (New York: Knopf, 1976), 11.
11. LIW's letter to all children and readers, 1947.

PART **II**

DOCUMENTS

1	*Missouri Ruralist* Interview, 1918	123
2	"Pioneer Girl" manuscript, Carl Brandt version, pages 111–15	126
3	An Autobiographical Sketch of Rose Wilder Lane	131
4	"As a Farm Woman Thinks"	136
5	Letter from San Francisco	140
6	Mountain Grove Sorosis Club Speech, 1936	145
7	Travel Diary Excerpt, 1931	149
8	*Wilson Library Bulletin*, Vol. 22, No. 8: April 1948	156
9	Letters to Laura: "I Am Always Dreaming About You . . ."	159

DOCUMENT 1

MISSOURI RURALIST INTERVIEW, 1918

In 1911, Wilder began her writing career as a farm journalist for the *Missouri Ruralist*. Her breezy, wide-ranging column "As a Farm Woman Thinks" ran until 1924. Editor John F. Case decided to profile Wilder in the February 20, 1918, edition of the journal. Case's interview provides a rare and revealing glimpse of Wilder at fifty. Although a well-known regional writer, successful farmer, and community leader, it would be another two decades before the series of "Little House" books established Wilder as a national figure.

LET'S VISIT MRS. WILDER

Missouri farm folks need little introduction before getting acquainted with Mrs. A. J. Wilder of Rocky Ridge Farm. During the years that she has been connected with this paper—a greater number of years than any other person on the editorial staff—she has taken strong hold upon the esteem and affection of our great family. Mrs. Wilder has lived her life upon a farm. She knows farm folks and their problems as few women who write know them. And having sympathy with the folks whom she serves, she writes well.

"Mrs. Wilder is a woman of delightful personality," a neighbor tells me, "and she is a combination of energy and determination. She always is cheery, looking on the bright side. She is her husband's partner in every sense and is fully capable of managing the farm. No woman can make you feel more at home than can Mrs. Wilder, and yet, when the occasion demands, she can be dignity personified. Mrs. Wilder has held high rank in the Eastern Star. Then when a Farm Loan Association was formed at Mansfield, she was made secretary-treasurer. When her report was sent to the Land Bank

124 • Documents

officials, they told her the papers were perfect and the best sent in." As a final tribute Mrs. Wilder's friend said this: "She gets eggs in the winter when none of her neighbors gets any."

Born in Wisconsin

"I was born in a log house within 4 miles of the legend-haunted Lake Pepin in Wisconsin," Mrs. Wilder wrote when I asked for information "about" her. "I remember seeing deer that father had killed hanging in the trees about our forest home. When I was 4 years old, we traveled to the Indian Territory—Fort Scott, Kansas, being our nearest town. My childish memories hold the sound of the war whoop, and I see pictures of painted Indians."

Looking at the picture of Mrs. Wilder, which was recently taken, we find it difficult to believe that she is old enough to be the pioneer described. But having confided her age to the editor (not for publication), we must be convinced that it is true. Surely Mrs. Wilder—who is the mother of Rose Wilder Lane, talented author and writer—has found the fountain of youth in the Ozark hills. We may well believe that she has a "cheerful disposition" as her friend asserts.

"I was a regular little tomboy," Mrs. Wilder confesses, "and it was fun to walk the two miles to school." The folks were living in Minnesota then, but it was not long until Father Ingalls, who seems to have had a penchant for moving about, had located in Dakota. It was at De Smet, South Dakota, that Laura Ingalls, then eighteen years old, married A. J. Wilder, a farmer boy.

"Our daughter, Rose Wilder Lane, was born on the farm," Mrs. Wilder informs us. "And it was there I learned to do all kinds of farm work with machinery. I have ridden the binder, driving six horses. And I could ride. I do not wish to appear conceited, but I broke my own ponies to ride. Of course, they were not bad, but they were broncos." Mrs. Wilder had the spirit that brought success to the pioneers.

Mrs. Wilder's health failed and the Wilders went to Florida. "I was something of a curiosity, being the only 'Yankee girl' the inhabitants ever had seen," Mrs. Wilder relates. The low altitude did not agree with Mrs. Wilder, though, and she became ill. It was then they came to Rocky Ridge Farm near Mansfield, Wright County, and there they have lived for twenty-five years.

Only forty acres were purchased, and the land was all timber except for a four-acre, worn-out field. "Illness and traveling expenses had taken our surplus cash, and we lacked $150 of paying for the forty acres," Mrs. Wilder writes. "Mr. Wilder was unable to do a full day's work. The garden, my hens, and the wood I helped saw and which we sold in town took us through the first year. It was then I became an expert at the end of a cross-cut saw, and I still can 'make a hand' in an emergency. Mr. Wilder says he would rather have me help than any man he ever sawed with. And, believe me, I learned how to take care of hens and to make them lay."

Missouri Ruralist Interview, 1918 • 125

Intelligent industry brings its own reward. Mr. and Mrs. Wilder not only paid for the forty acres, but they have added sixty acres more, stocked the farm to capacity, and improved it and built a beautiful modern home. "Everything sold by the Wilders brings a good price," their neighbor tells me, "because it is standard goods. It was by following strict business methods that they were enabled to build their beautiful home. Most of the material used was found on the farm. Fortunate indeed are those who are entertained at Rocky Ridge."

One may wonder that so busy a person, as Mrs. Wilder has proved to be, can find time to write. "I always have been a busy person," she says, "doing my own housekeeping, helping the Man of the Place when help could not be obtained, but I love to work. And it is a pleasure to write for the *Missouri Ruralist*. And, oh, I do just love to play! They days never have been long enough to do the things I would like to do. Every year has held more of interest than the year before." Folks who possess that kind of spirit get a lot of joy out of life as they travel the long road.

Joined the family in 1911

Mrs. Wilder has held numerous important offices, and her stories about farm life and farm folks have appeared in the best farm papers. Her first article printed in the *Missouri Ruralist* appeared in February 1911. It was a copy of an address prepared for *Farmer's Week*. So for seven years she has been talking to Missouri women through these columns; talk that always has carried inspiration and incentive for worthwhile work.

Reading Mrs. Wilder's contributions, most folks doubtless have decided that she is a college graduate. But "my education has been what a girl would get on the frontier," she informs us. "I never graduated from anything and only attended high school two terms." Folks who know Mrs. Wilder, tho, know that she is a cultured, well-educated gentlewoman. Combined with inherent ability, unceasing study of books has provided the necessary education, and greater things have been learned from the study of life itself.

As has been asserted before, Mrs. Wilder writes well for farm folks because she knows them. The Wilders can be found ready to enter wholeheartedly into any movement for community betterment, and the home folks are proud of the reputation that Mrs. Wilder has established. They know that she has won recognition as a writer and state leader because of ability alone.

SOURCE

"Let's Visit Mrs. Wilder" interview with John F. Case, *Missouri Ruralist* editor, February 1918. Stephen W. Hines, ed., *Laura Ingalls Wilder, Farm Journalist: Writings from the Ozarks* (Columbia, MO: University of Missouri Press, 2007).

DOCUMENT **2**

"PIONEER GIRL" MANUSCRIPT, CARL BRANDT VERSION, PAGES 111–15

When Wilder's autobiographical memoir "Pioneer Girl" failed to sell, she decided to rewrite the material for the children's market. Ultimately, she mined the entire manuscript for the *Little House* series. The excerpt below corresponds to the events covered at the end of Wilder's sixth novel, *The Long Winter*. Readers familiar with the novel will immediately notice the similarity of language and material (as well as the difference in pacing and tone) between Wilder's original first-person narrative and the polished, dramatized version she wrote for young readers.

Pa had rented our house [in De Smet] to a new-comer, and as soon as we learned that there was no further danger from the Indians* we gave the renters possession, and went home again, for the farm was home to us. Town was only a place in which, for safety, we spent the winter.

We now had several neighbors near the farm . . . I did not care so much for so many people. I loved the empty prairie and the wild things that lived on it, much more.

In the early morning I was always on my way to the well at the edge of the slough, for a bucket of fresh water. The meadow larks were singing in the dew-wet grass, and jack-rabbits hopped here and there, their bright black eyes watching and long ears twitching while they nibbled the tender grass that pleased them best for breakfast. And the sun was rising in a glory of colors, throwing streamers of light around the horizon and up the sky.

Later in the day the little reddish brown and black striped gophers would pop out of their holes in the ground and sit straight up on their hind legs, with their front paws close at their sides, so motionless that they could be mistaken for sticks. With their bright eyes they looked, with their sharp ears

"Pioneer Girl" manuscript, Carl Brandt version, pages 111–15 • 127

they listened, for danger. At a sound, a motion, the shadow of a large bird overhead, they slipped like a flash into their holes. But if all seemed safe to them they scurried away through the grass, about their business.

When the corn was planted these striped gophers would follow the row and dig with their little paws till they got the kernels. The never made the mistake of digging anywhere except exactly in the corn-hill, though how they could tell where the kernels were, when all the ground was soft plowed earth, was a mystery.

The little garter snakes come out in the warm sunshine too, and slithered across the path. They were quite harmless, not poisonous at all, and lived on grasshoppers and bugs. I thought them very pretty and graceful and we never killed them.

It was surprising how much variety and how much of interest could be found on 160 acres which at a careless glance looked just like all the rest of the prairie.

Pa had built an addition to the little slant-roofed shanty, so that the roof had its other half and we had two very small bedrooms. The cottonwoods we had planted around it were growing splendidly, and all summer long we carried water to keep them alive.

Again I was caring for the cows. We kept them on long picket ropes— there were of course no fences—and morning and night after milking I pulled the picket pins and drove them into the ground in a new place, so the cows had fresh pasture. Their calves were on short picket ropes nearby.

Ma and I milked, carried the milk to the house, strained it and set it in pans in the cellar. Then while Ma got breakfast I took the skimmed milk and fed the calves and changed their picket pins.

After breakfast Pa went to his carpenter work in town, and Ma and I and Carrie washed dishes, made beds, swept, scrubbed, washed or ironed or baked and churned, following the old rule for housework; "Wash on Monday, iron on Tuesday, mend on Wednesday, churn on Thursday, clean on Friday, bake on Saturday, and rest on Sunday." Mending, sewing, knitting were scattered along through the week, with the care of the chickens, working in the garden and feeding the pig. The pig, being kept in a pen, always got all the weeds we pulled or hoed from the garden. And sometime during the day we led the cows and calves to water at the well.

So much water in the sloughs made an excellent breeding ground for mosquitoes, and at night we had to build a smudge for the cows, a heavily smoking fire so placed that the smoke would envelop cows and calves. Our doors and windows were covered with mosquito bar to keep them out of the house, but anyone crossing the slough after sundown was very badly bitten.

In June, the wild roses bloomed. They were a low-growing bush and when in bloom their blossoms covered the prairie with masses of color, every shade of pink. And they were the sweetest roses that ever bloomed.

There were grass flowers, may flowers, thimble flowers, wild Sweet William, squaw pinks, buffalo beans and wild sunflowers, each in its season. There were many kinds of grass. Slough grass grew in all the low places. On the uplands blue-joint, or blue-stem, a tall grass, and the buffalo grass which never grew tall. The buffalo grass, short and thick and curly, did not lose its goodness when it ripened, but cured standing and retained its food values, making the best of pasture for stock or wild game through the winter. It got its name because the buffalo wintered on it.

An ugly grass that ripened early in the fall was called Spanish needles. The seeds had a fine, very hard, needle-like point an eighth of an inch long, and the seed itself was an inch long, covered with stiff hair all pointing toward a strong, tough, twisting beard about four inches long. When these seeds were ripe the needle-like point would stick into anyone brushing against the grass, and once started the stiff hairs and the screw-like beard would drive it farther in.

These needles worked though our clothing like a sewing needle. In the mouths of stock they made painful sores and had to be cut out. They often worked through the wool of sheep into the body, killing the sheep.

The early farmers killed out the Spanish needles by burning over the land at the right time.

That summer there was a 4th of July celebration in town, with speeches, singing and the reading of the Declaration of Independence in the morning, and in the afternoon foot-races and horse-races. Pa and Carrie and I took our dinner in a basket and walked in for the day. Ma stayed with Mary and Grace at home.

It was a tiresome day, I thought. I did not enjoy a crowd and would much rather have been at home on the quiet prairie.

But it seemed that I could not stay there. At one of the drygoods stores the merchant's mother-in-law made shirts from goods ordered in the store, and she needed help. As we needed money, I sewed for her for twenty-five cents a day, slept with her in the attic above the store, and ate with them all in the kitchen behind the store.

The merchant's wife and her mother were very much excited at the time for fear the Catholics would gain control of the country. There were rumors of the terrible things they would do to Protestants, of which massacre was not the more horrible. The younger woman would pace the floor and wring her hands, declaring that the Catholics would never, never take her Bible from her. Then a comet appeared in the sky and both women thought this meant the end of the world and were terrified about that.

But I did not see how I could be afraid of both the Catholics and the end of the world at the same time, so I worried about neither. Still, in spite of the need for my wages, I was glad when there was less work and I could go home again.

"Pioneer Girl" manuscript, Carl Brandt version, pages 111–15 • 129

Pa had planted corn on the newly broken land, and it grew astonishingly tall and strong and a most vivid green. Now that the ears were large enough to roast, great flocks of blackbirds settled in clouds upon the fields. There were thousands upon thousands of them, the common blackbirds and yellow-headed blackbirds and red-headed blackbirds with a spot of red on each wing. The yellow-headed and red-headed birds were much larger than the others.

They were destroying the whole field. Pa shot them and drove them off, but they only rose, whirled in great clouds, then came drifting back and settled down again.

At first Pa shot them by dozens and let them lie where they fell. Our kitten, now grown up, brought some of them to her kittens, but they were so stuffed with mice and gophers they had no appetite for blackbirds.

Then Pa brought several to the house and asked us to cook them. He said he had never heard of anyone's eating blackbirds, but they looked good. So Ma and I dressed a frying pan full, splitting them down the back and frying the halves. They were so fat that they fried themselves, and were tender and delicious.

After that we ate them at every meal every day, and we understood why four and twenty blackbirds made a dish fit for a king. By much shooting Pa managed to save the greater part of the corn.

When haying time came, Pa stopped work in town long enough to put up our hay with Ma's help and mine.

All summer we had been hoping to be able to send Mary to the Iowa College for the Blind at Vinton, Iowa. And now after the haying was done, Ma and I got Mary's clothes ready, for she was really going.

Jennie and Gaylord Ross stayed with us while Ma and Pa went with Mary to get her settled. They were gone a week, and then one night they came walking out from town. We were all so happy that Mary was where she would be warm and comfortable, with good food and good company, and that she could go on with her studies. She had always loved to study, had been the bright one of the family. Now she would have a college education and a manual training besides. She would learn music and sewing, even cooking and housework.

We were never tired of hearing from Ma every detail of the things she had seen at the college for the blind. It was wonderful, what they would learn to do without seeing. And I, who wanted a college education so much myself, was so very happy in thinking that Mary was getting one.

A few days after Ma and Pa came home, while I was hunting for something, I found a beautiful, red-cloth-bound volume of Scott's poems. Because it had been hidden, I knew that I was not expected to know about it, and so said nothing. The temptation to look at the book, to read a little

130 • Documents

in it when Pa and Ma had gone to town, was almost irresistible, but I did resist it.

The next Christmas Ma gave me the book for my Christmas present. She had brought it from Vinton, Iowa, for me.

Our school opened again that fall and Carrie and I walked in. The teacher was Eliza Wilder, an older sister of the Wilder boys.

We enjoyed walking the mile to school except that on the way we had to pass several cows and a pure-bred Jersey bull belonging to the banker, Mr. Ruth. They were allowed to range the prairies and in the morning and at night would be beside our road, just out of town.

The bull would lower his head, bellow at us and paw the dirt. His horns looked fearfully sharp and I was afraid to pass him—not for myself, I had the feeling that I could out-run him, but for Carrie. She had never been strong, was very thin and spindly, yet too large for me to carry, and I feared that I could not take her with me fast enough to escape the bull.

One night when we were going home we saw him beside the road and went far to one side and into the Big Slough. We followed a path until the tall grass was high above our heads and we could not be sure where we were coming out. We knew the road went through the Slough still farther over and that if we kept on we must come to it. So we went on until we came out of the grass into a mowed place. There we saw a team hitched to a load of hay.

A tall man on the ground was pitching more hay up into the load. On top of the load a big boy, almost a young man, lay on his stomach, kicking up his heels. Just as we saw them, the man on the ground pitched a great forkful of hay square on top of this boy, burying him under it. He scrambled out, laughing, and looked at me.

Carrie and I passed on, saying good afternoon, and when we were past I said to Carrie, "The man on the ground was Wilder. The other must be the younger Wilder boy." Though we had heard so much about him, I had not seen him before.

NOTE

* Wilder earlier recorded the violation of an Indian burial site by a traveling Chicago doctor, who had stolen the corpse of an Indian baby and shipped the body east for examination as a curiosity. Outraged tribe members demanded the immediate return of the body and threatened violence until the body was finally recovered. She probably learned of the story from Almanzo Wilder, who had witnessed the event while working at a Chicago & North West Railroad camp in 1880.

SOURCE

Rose Wilder Lane Papers, Herbert Hoover Presidential Library, West Branch, Iowa. Reprinted by permission of Little House Heritage Trust, the copyright holder. All rights reserved.

DOCUMENT **3**

AN AUTOBIOGRAPHICAL SKETCH OF ROSE WILDER LANE

In 1934, when Rose Wilder Lane composed this autobiographical sketch for her ardent *Saturday Evening Post* fans and readers, she was one of the best-known, best-paid writers in the country. Interestingly—and very like her mother—Lane spends the greater part of her autobiography expanding on events that took place in her early childhood or reflecting upon the significance of her parents' pioneering life and times. She treats her own extraordinary achievements and adventures in post-World War I Europe and Eurasia with casual nonchalance and gives little indication of the intellectual circles she frequented in New York, where she counted artists and literati such as Sinclair Lewis, Dorothy Thompson, and Upton Sinclair among her close friends and correspondents.

AN AUTOBIOGRAPHICAL SKETCH OF ROSE WILDER LANE

I was born in Dakota Territory, in a claim shanty, forty-nine years ago come next December. It doesn't seem possible. My father's people were English county family; his ancestors came to America in 1630 and, farming progressively westward, reached Minnesota during my father's boyhood. Naturally, he took a homestead farther west. My mother's ancestors were Scotch and French; her father's cousin was John J. Ingalls, who, "like a lonely crane, swore and swore and stalked the Kansas plain." She is Laura Ingalls Wilder, writer of books for children.

Conditions had changed when I was born; there was no more free land. Of course, there never had been free land. It was a saying in the Dakotas that the Government bet a quarter section against fifteen dollars and five

132 • Documents

years' hard work that the land would starve a man out in less than five years. My father won the bet. It took seven successive years of complete crop failure, with work, weather and sickness that wrecked his heath permanently, and interest rates of 36 per cent on money borrowed to buy food, to dislodge us from that land. I was then seven years old.

We reached the Missouri at Yankton, in a string of other covered wagons. The ferryman took them, one by one, across the wide yellow river. I sat between my parents in the wagon on the river bank, anxiously hoping to get across before dark. Suddenly the rear end of the wagon jumped into the air and came down with a terrific crash. My mother seized the lines; my father leaped over the wheel and in desperate haste tied the wagon to the ground with ropes to picket pins deeply driven in. The loaded wagon kept lifting off the ground, straining at the ropes; they creaked and stretched, but held. They kept wagon and horses from being blown into the river.

Looking around the edge of the wagon cover, I saw the whole earth behind us billowing to the sky. There was something savage and terrifying in that howling yellow swallowing the sky. The color came, I now suppose, from the sunset.

"Well, that's our last sight of Dakota," my mother said.

"We're getting out with a team and wagon; that's more than a lot can say," my father answered cheerfully.

This was during the panic of '93. The whole Middle West was shaken loose and moving. We joined long wagon trains moving south; we met hundreds of wagons going north; the roads east and west were crawling lines of families traveling under canvas, looking for work, for another foothold somewhere on the land. By the fires in the camps I heard talk about Coxey's army, 60,000 men, marching on Washington; Federal troops had been called out. The country was ruined, the whole world was ruined, nothing like this had ever happened before. There was no hope, but everyone felt the courage of despair. Next morning wagons went on to the north, from which we had been driven, and we went on toward the south, where those families had not been able to live.

We were not starving. My mother had baked quantities of hardtack for the journey; we had salt meat and beans. My father tried to sell the new—and incredible—asbestos mats that would keep wood from burning; no one had ten cents to pay for one, but often he traded for eggs or milk. In Nebraska we found an astoundingly prosperous colony of Russians; we could not talk to them. The Russian women gave us—outright gave us— milk and cream and butter from the abundance of their dairies, and a pan of biscuits. My mouth watered at the sight. And because my mother could not talk to them, and so could not politely refuse these gifts, we had to take them and she had to give in exchange some cherished trinket of hers. She had to, because it would have been like taking charity not to make some return. That night we had buttered biscuits.

These Russians had brought from Russia a new kind of wheat—winter wheat, the foundation of future prosperity from the Dakotas to Texas.

Three months after we had ferried across the Missouri, we reached the Ozark hills. It was strange not to hear the wind any more. My parents had great good fortune; with their last hoarded dollar, they were able to buy a piece of poor ridge land, uncleared, with a log cabin and a heavy mortgage on it. My father was an invalid, my mother was a girl in her twenties, I was seven years old.

Good fortune continued. We had hardly moved into the cabin, when a stranger came pleading for work. His wife and children, camped by the road, were starving. We still had a piece of salt pork. The terrible question was, "Dare we risk any of it?" My father did; he offered half of it for a day's work. The stranger was overjoyed. Together they worked from dawn to sunset, cutting down trees, sawing and splitting wood, piling into the wagon all it would hold. Next day my father drove to town with the wood.

It was dark before we heard the wagon coming back. I ran to meet it. It was empty. My father had sold that wood for fifty cents in cash. Delirious, I rushed into the house shouting the news. Fifty cents! My mother cried for joy.

That was the turning point. We lived all winter and kept the camper's family alive till he got a job; he was a hard worker. He and my father cleared land, sold wood, built a log barn. When he moved on, my mother took his place at the cross-cut saw. Next spring a crop was planted; I helped put in the corn, and on the hills I picked green huckleberries to make a pie. I picked ripe huckleberries, walked a mile and a half to town, and sold them for ten cents a gallon. Blackberries too. Once I chased a rabbit into a hollow log and barricaded it there with rocks; we had rabbit stew. We were prospering and cheerful. The second summer, my father bought a cow. Then we had milk and I helped churn; my mother's good butter sold for ten cents a pound. We were paying 8 per cent interest on the mortgage and a yearly bonus for renewal.

That was forty years ago. Rocky Ridge Farm is now 200 acres, in meadow, pasture and field; there are wood lots, but otherwise the land is cleared, and it is clear. The three houses on it have central heating, modern plumbing, electric ranges and refrigerators, garages for three cars. This submarginal farm, in a largely submarginal but comfortably prosperous county, helps support some seven hundred families on relief. They live in miserably small houses and many lack bedsteads on which to put the mattresses, sheets and bedding issued to them. The men on work relief get only twenty cents an hour, only sixteen hours a week. No one bothers now to pick wild berries;

134 • Documents

it horrifies anybody to think of a child's working three or four hours for ten cents. No farmer's wife sells butter; trucks call for the cream cans, and butterfat brings twenty-six cents. Forty years ago I lived through a world-wide depression; once more I am living through a depression popularly believed to be the worst in history because it is world-wide; this is the ultimate disaster, the depression to end all depressions. On every side I hear that conditions have changed, and that is true. They have.

Meanwhile I have done several things. I have been an office clerk, telegrapher, newspaper reporter, feature writer, advertising writer, farmland salesman. I have seen all the United States and something of Canada and the Caribbean; all of Europe except Spain; Turkey, Egypt, Palestine, Syria, Iraq as far east as Bagdad, Georgia, Armenia, Azerbaijan. California, the Ozarks and the Balkans are my home towns.

Politically, I cast my first vote—on a sample ballot—for Cleveland, at the age of three. I was an ardent if uncomprehending Populist; I saw America ruined forever when the soulless corporations in 1896 defeated Bryan and Free Silver. I was a Christian Socialist with Debs, and distributed untold numbers of The Appeal to Reason. From 1914 to 1920—when I first went to Europe—I was a pacifist; innocently, if criminally, I thought war stupid, cruel, wasteful and unnecessary. I voted for Wilson because he kept us out of it.

In 1917 I became a convinced, though not practicing, communist. In Russia, for some reason, I wasn't, and I said so, but my understanding of Bolshevism made everything pleasant when the Cheka arrested me a few times.

I am now a fundamentalist American; give me time and I will tell you why individualism, laissez faire and the slightly restrained anarchy of capitalism offer the best opportunities for the development of the human spirit. Also I will tell you why the relative freedom of the human spirit is better—and more productive, even in material ways—than the communist, Fascist, or any other rigidity organized for material ends.

Personally, I'm a plump, Middle-Western, middle-class, middle-aged woman, with white hair and simple tastes. I like buttered popcorn, salted peanuts and bread-and-milk. I am, however, a marvelous cook of foods for others to eat. I like to see people eat my cooking. I love mountains, the sea—all the seas except the Atlantic, a rather dull ocean—and Tschaikovsky [sic] and Epstein and the Italian primitives. I like Arabic architecture and the Moslem way of life. I am mad about Kansas skies, Cedar Rapids by night, Iowa City any time, Miami Beach, San Francisco, and all American boys about fifteen years old playing basketball. At the moment I don't think of anything I heartily dislike, but I can't understand sports pages, nor what makes radio work, nor why people like to look at people who write fiction.

An Autobiographical Sketch of Rose Wilder Lane • 135

"But aren't you frightfully disappointed?" I asked a stranger who was recently looking at me.

"Oh, no," she said. "No, indeed. We value people for what they do, not for what they look like."

Source

Rose Wilder Lane, "An Autobiographical Sketch of Rose Wilder Lane," Federal Writers Project, 1940, http://www.loc.gov/resource/wpalh1.15100107/seq-1#seq-1.

DOCUMENT **4**

"AS A FARM WOMAN THINKS"

From 1911 until 1924, Wilder was a regular contributor to the *Missouri Ruralist*. Her popular column "As a Farm Woman Thinks" covered a kaleidoscope of rural issues, human interest stories, farm management advice, beauty tips, and Ozark lore. Wilder never hesitated to speak her mind; the column honed both her writing skills and her distinctive voice. Three of her columns appear below. [Wilder's mother, Caroline Quiner Ingalls, died on Easter Sunday 1924, just a few months after Wilder wrote the tender, raw, and unusually revealing tribute to her family dated August 1, 1923.]

AS A FARM WOMAN THINKS

March 15, 1922
Reading of an agricultural conference in Washington, D.C., I was very much interested in the address of Mrs. Sewell of Indiana on the place of the farmer's wife in agriculture. She drew a pathetic picture, so much so as to bring tears to the eyes of the audience.

Now, I don't want any tears shed over my position, but I've since been doing some thinking on the farm woman's place and wondering if she knows and has taken the place that rightfully belongs to her.

Every good farm woman is interested as much in the business part of farm life as she is in the housework, and there comes a time, after we have kept house for years, when the housekeeping is mostly mechanical, while the outside affairs are forever changing, adding variety and interest to life.

As soon as we can manage our household to give us the time, I think we should step out into this wider field, taking our place beside our husbands in the larger business of the farm. Cooperation and mutual help and understanding are the things that will make farm life what it should be.

And so, in these days of women's clubs from which men are excluded, and men's clubs that permit women to be honorary members only, I'm glad to know of a different plan whereby farm men and women work together on equal terms and with equal privileges. To a woman who has been an "auxiliary" until she is tired of the word, it seems like a start toward the promised land.

Nowhere in the constitution or by-laws of this club is any distinction made between men and women members. Meetings are held once a month at the homes of members and are all day sessions. The morning is devoted to the business of the club and a program. After dinner comes an inspection of farm, garden and stock and the day ends with music and discussion.

The men are interested and take part in the indoor program and the women assist in the inspection of the farm.

August 1, 1923

Out in the meadow, I picked a wild sunflower and, as I looked into its golden heart such a wave of homesickness came over me that I almost wept. I wanted Mother, with her gentle voice and quiet firmness; I longed to hear Father's jolly songs and to see his twinkling blue eyes; I was lonesome for the sister with whom I used to play in the meadow picking daisies and wild sunflowers.

Across the years, the old home and its love called to me and memories of sweet words of counsel came flooding back. I realized that all my life the teachings of those early days have influenced me and the example set by Father and Mother has been something I have tried to follow, with failures here and there, with rebellion at times, but always coming back to it as the compass needle to the star.

So much depends upon the homemakers. I sometimes wonder if they are so busy now, with other things, that they are forgetting the importance of this special work. Especially did I wonder when reading recently that there were a great many child suicides in the United States during the last year. Not long ago we never had heard of such a thing in our own country and I am sure that there must be something wrong with the home of a child who commits suicide.

Because of their importance, we must not neglect our homes in the rapid changes of the present day. For when tests of character come in later years, strength to the good will not come from the modern improvements or amusements few may have enjoyed, but from the quiet moments and the "still small voices" of the old home.

Nothing ever can take the place of this early home influence and, as it does not depend upon externals, it may be the possession of the poor as well as the rich, a heritage from all fathers and mothers to their children.

The real things of life that are the common possession of us all are of the greatest value; worth far more than motor cars or radio outfits; more than lands or money; and our whole store of these wonderful riches may be revealed to us by such a common, beautiful thing as a wild sunflower.

November 1, 1923

While driving one day, I passed a wornout farm. Deep gullies were cut thru the fields where the dirt had been washed away by the rains. The creek had been allowed to change its course, in the bottom field, and cut out a new channel ruining the good land in its way. Tall weeds and brambles were taking more strength from the soil already so poor that grass would scarcely grow.

A Stranger's Opinion

With me, as I viewed the place, was a friend from Switzerland and as he looked over the neglected farm he exclaimed, "Oh, it is a crime! It is a crime to treat good land like that!" The more I think about it the more sure I am that he used the exact word to suit the case. It is a crime to wear out and ruin a farm and the farmer who does so is a thief, stealing from posterity.

We are the heirs of the ages, but the estate is entailed as large estates frequently are, so that while we inherit the earth the great round world which is God's Footstool, we have only the use of it while we live and must pass it on to those who come after us. We hold the property in trust and have no right to injure it nor to lessen its value. To do so is dishonest, stealing from our heirs their inheritance.

The world is the beautiful estate of the human family passing down from generation to generation, marked by each holder while in his possession according to his character.

Did you think how a bit of land shows the character of the owner? As dishonest greed is shown by robbing the soil; the traits of a spendthrift are shown in wasting the resources of the farm by destroying its woods and waters, while carelessness and laziness are plainly to be seen in deep scars on the hillsides and washes in the lower fields.

It should be a matter of pride to keep up our own farm, that little bit of the earth's surface for which we are responsible, in good condition, passing

"As a Farm Woman Thinks" • 139

it on to our successor better than we found it. Trees should be growing where otherwise would be waste places, with the waters protected as much as possible from the hot sun and drying winds, with fields free from gullies and the soil fertile.

SOURCE

Laura Ingalls Wilder, columns from *The Missouri Ruralist,* reproduced in Stephen W. Hines, ed., *Laura Ingalls Wilder, Farm Journalist: Writings from the Ozarks* (Columbia, MO: University of Missouri Press, 2007).

DOCUMENT **5**

LETTER FROM SAN FRANCISCO

In 1915, Rose Wilder Lane was living in San Francisco, working as a freelance writer, selling real estate, and rapidly tiring of her husband, Gillette Lane. Lane begged her mother to visit her in California. Wilder agreed and used the trip as an opportunity to cover the Panama-Pacific International Exposition for the *Missouri Ruralist*. She made the long solo journey by train, but wrote almost daily to Almanzo at Rocky Ridge, describing the heady excitement of her discoveries as she waded in the Pacific, sampled dim sum in Chinatown, and explored the exotic, newly rebuilt city by cable car.

San Francisco
Sunday August 29, 1915

Manly Dear,

As you of course know I arrived safely in San Francisco. As I walked down the walk from the train toward the ferry, Rose stepped out from the crowd and seized me.

On the ferry we sat out on the upper deck and well in front, but a fog covered the water so I did not see much of the bay except the lights around it. I was so tired anyway and I could not realize I was really here. Gillette met us as we stepped off the ferry and we took a streetcar nearly home and climbed a hill the rest of the way. I went to bed soon and have been resting most of the time since.

It took all the first day to get the motion of the cars out of my head. Yesterday afternoon I went with Rose and Gillette down to the beach. We walked down the hill—all paved streets and walks and lovely buildings—to the car line and took a car to Land's End, from six to ten miles all the way through the city except for a few blocks at the last.

At Land's End I had my first view of the Pacific Ocean. To say it is beautiful does not half express it. It is simply beyond words. The water is such deep wonderful blue and the sound of the waves breaking on the beach and their whisper as they flow back is something to dream about. I saw a lumber schooner coming in and another going out as they passed each other in the Golden Gate. They sail between here and Seattle, Washington. We walked from Land's End around the point of land and came to the Cliff House and Seal Rocks but the seals would not show themselves.

We took a side path into the parks of the Sutro Estate, which has been turned over to the city as a public park under certain conditions as to its use. The lodge near the gates and the old mansion itself were built with materials brought around the Horn in sailing ships about a hundred years ago. We went through the massive arched gateway made of stone with a life-sized lion crouched at each side and through a beautiful park of about forty acres. I don't mean we walked over it all, but we walked miles of it. The soil in these grounds was all brought to them, for originally the surface was just sand. The forest trees were all planted by this first Sutro. At every turn in the paths we came upon statues of stone, figures of men and women and animals, and birds, half hidden among the foliage of flowering plants, or peeping out from among the trees.

The house itself is built at the top of the hill. The whole front and side of the house is glass so that one would have the view from every point. The pillars of the balcony have [Delft] porcelains inset, as do the posts of the stone fence around the house. They are small squares as smooth and glossy as my china. With quaint old-fashioned pictures of children and animals, instead of the flowers on my dishes. Just think, they have stood there for a hundred years exposed to the sun and wind and weather without a stain or a crackle. Close beside the house is a very tall slender building, an observatory with a glass room at the top where the family used to go to watch the ships come in through the Golden Gate. The building is so old that it is considered unsafe and no one is allowed to go in it now.

We went from there out on the edge of the cliff where there were seats and statues around the edge and one can sit or stand and look over the ramparts across the blue Pacific. An American eagle at one side. Two cannon were in place pointing out to sea and there were several piles of cannon balls. I kicked one to be sure it was real—and it was. The winds off the ocean are delightful.

We went down on the beach where the waves were breaking. There were crowds of people there and some of them were wading. I wanted to wade. Rose said she never had but would, so we took off our shoes and stockings

142 • Documents

and left them on the warm sand with Gillette to guard them and went out to meet the waves. A little one rolled in and covered our feet, the next one came and reached our ankles, and just as I was saying how delightful, the big one came and went above our knees. I just had time to snatch my skirts up and save them and the wave went back with a pull. We went nearer the shore and dug holes in the sand with our toes. Went out to meet the waves and ran back before the big one caught us and had such a good time.

The salt water tingled my feet and made them feel so good all the rest of the day, and just to think, the same water that bathes the shores of China and Japan came clear across the ocean and bathed my feet. In other words, I have washed my feet in the Pacific Ocean.

The ocean is not ugly. It is beautiful and wonderful.

We went from the beach to the Coast Guard or life-saving station and saw the lifeboat. Then we went to see the *Gjoa*, the only boat that has ever gone around the continent through the Northwest Passage. It is battered and worn but strong-looking still. The ship was made in Norway in 1878 and with a crew of six men and the captain was three years and four months making the journey from Norway though the Northwest Passage to San Francisco. The government of Norway and the Norwegians of California gave the ship to the city and left it here.

By this time I was tired, very tired, so we took a car back to the city and stopped for dinner at a restaurant. The waiter was an Alsatian, which is a cross between a Frenchman and a German. The dinner was delicious. French bread and salmon steak and tenderloin of sole, delicious fish. I could hardly tell which was the best. Then there was some kind of an Italian dish which I liked very much, and a French strawberry pie or "tarte" which was fresh berries in a pastry shell with some kind of rich syrup poured over. There was music in the restaurant and I heard "It's a Long, Long Way to Tipperary" for the first time.

Believe me, I was tired after seeing all this in one afternoon and we have been loafing all today. We went out on the walk before the house and saw Niles [an exhibition aviator] fly this afternoon. The Tower of Jewels is in sight from there too. Giles flew up and up, then dropped like an autumn leaf, floating and drifting and falling. He turned over, end over end, he turned over sideways both ways, then righted himself and sailed gracefully down.

Christopherson was flying at the beach yesterday and Rose says I shall have a flight before I go home. Gee, if it can beat wading in the ocean it will be some feat, believe me.

You know I have never cared for cities but San Francisco is simply the most beautiful thing. Set on the hills as it is with the glimpses of the bay here and there and at night with the lights shining up and down the hills and the lights of ships on the water, it is like fairyland. I have not seen any of the Exposition yet. San Francisco itself would be wonderful enough for

Letter from San Francisco · 143

a year, but we will begin this week to go the Fair. You must not expect me to see it all for it has been figured out that it would cost $500 just to see the five-cent, ten-cent and twenty-five-cent attractions.

Rose and Gillette have a dandy little place to live with a fine view from the windows. It is at the very top of a hill, with the bay in sight.

Just here Rose called to come quick and go see the fireworks at the Fair. We put on our heavy coats and went out to the walk before the house and just a little way along it and sat down on a stone curb. The white Tower of Jewels is in sight from there. The jewels strung around it glitter and shine in beautiful colors. The jewels are from Austria and cost ninety cents each and they decorate all the cornices on the high, fancifully built tower. A searchlight is directed on the tower at night to show it off and it is wonderful.

As we looked, the aeroscope rose above the tops of the buildings. It is a car that can hold five hundred people. Its outlines are marked by electric lights. It is on the top of a more slender part and is lowered for the people to fill the car, then raised high so they can look down on the whole Exposition at once. They have that instead of the Ferris Wheel. As it rises, it looks like some giant with a square head, craning his long neck up and down. I don't suppose it looks like that to anyone else, but that is the way it makes me feel.

Well, we sat and watched and soon a long finger of white light swept across the sky, then another and another of different colors, and then there was flashing and fading across the whole sky in that direction, the most beautiful northern-lights effect you can imagine. I think you have seen them. Well, this was more brilliant, more colors and *very* much higher on the sky. All the colors of the rainbow and some shades that I never saw the rainbow have. I have used the word "beautiful" until it has no meaning, but what other word can I use? There are forty searchlights producing this effect. Forty men handle them, producing the flashes in a sort of drill, under direction and orders as a drill march is done. It costs $40 a minute to show these northern lights, in salary alone. What the lights themselves cost is not for common mortals to know.

After a little of this, rockets went shooting up the beams of light, burst and fell in showers of colored stars and strings of jewels. The different colors of the searchlights were played upon the [artificially generated] steam making most beautiful and fantastic cloud shapes of different colors after the shower of stars had fallen. I do not know how long it lasted, but at last the flashes stopped and there was left the wonderful Tower of Jewels shining and glowing in the light thrown on it, with the aeroscope craning its long neck for a look down on the grounds.

I will meet some of Rose's friends this week and begin to get a line on things. Rose gets $30 a week now and she says she is saving ten percent of it, absolutely salting it down. She says it is not much but it is making a start.

144 • Documents

Gillette has worked on extra jobs for the *Call* since he came to the city, which leaves him at times without work but he has a promise of a good job as soon as a vacancy occurs, which is expected soon. Rose says they have $4,000 due them from their real estate work and that Gillette has made an assignment to us of what he owes us, but they do not know when they, or we, will get this money as the men who bought the land are unable to pay it now. The real estate business went all to smash and Stine & Kendrick are resting till things turn.

I am so glad Mr. Nell came so soon and to get your letter. I do hope you and Inky are getting along comfortably. Take care of yourself and him, and I will look for us both as much as possible.

What a time you must have had with those chickens and that milk. I'm glad the pie was good and the thing to do was to put it in the oven. I hope you did not burn it.

Rose says tell you those fireworks are the best the world has ever known. It costs hundreds of dollars to produce them and they had experts from all over the world at work on them. She says there never was anything like them in the world except those Roman candles you got for her the last Fourth of July we were in De Smet. They surpassed them, she says.

Well, goodbye for this time. I'll go see some to write you.

Lovingly,
Bessie

SOURCE

West from Home: Letters of Laura Ingalls Wilder to Almanzo Wilder, San Francisco, 1915. New York: Harper & Row, 1974. Used with permission of Little House Heritage Trust, the copyright holder. All rights reserved.

DOCUMENT **6**

Mountain Grove Sorosis Club Speech, 1936

Wilder was an active or founding member of several women's organizations in and around Mansfield. Women's clubs flourished in rural communities, expanding opportunities for social interaction, community service, and personal development. In 1936, Wilder gave a speech to the Mountain Grove Sorosis Club—a women's club dedicated to professional development—in which she directly addressed her motivation for writing, her personal values, her writing process, and the satisfaction she derived from her work.

My Work

I hope you will pardon me for making my work the subject of this talk, for I had no choice. The children's story I am writing completely filled my mind.

And again I must ask your indulgence for reading it. Since ten years have passed without my speaking to a crowd, I am some like one of the boys in the recent speaking contest. He said to me, "I was scared plum to death and it was actually pitiful how my knees shook."

When I began writing children's stories I had in mind only one book.

For years I had thought that the stories my father once told me should be passed on to other children. I felt they were much too good to be lost.

And so I wrote *Little House in the Big Woods.*

That book was a labor of love and is really a memorial to my father. A line drawing of an old tintype of father and mother is the first illustration.

I did not expect much from the book but hoped that a few children might enjoy the stories I had loved.

146 • Documents

To my surprise it was the choice of the Junior Literary Guild for the year 1932. In addition to this it ran into the seventh edition in its third year and is still going strong.

Immediately after its publication I began getting letters from children, individually and in school classes, asking for another book. They wanted to hear more stories. It was the same plea multiplied many times that I used to hear from Rose: "Oh tell another, Mama Bess! Please tell me another story!"

So then I wrote *Farmer Boy,* a true story of Mr. Wilder's childhood. This was a few years farther back than my own in a greatly different setting. Little House in the Big Woods was on the frontier of Wisconsin, while the Farmer Boy worked and played in Northern New York State.

Again my mail was full of letters begging for still another book. The children were still crying, "Please tell me another story!"

My answer was *Little House on the Prairie,* being some more adventures of Pa and Ma, Mary, Laura and Baby Carrie who had lived in the Little House in the Big Woods.

Again the story was all true but it happened in a vastly different setting than either of the others. The Little House on the Prairie was on the plains of Indian Territory when Kansas was just that.

Here instead of woods and bears and deer as in the Big Woods, or horses and cows and pigs and school, so many years ago, as in *Farmer Boy,* were wild Indians and wolves, prairie fires, rivers in flood and U. S. soldiers. And again I am hearing the old refrain, "Please tell another!" Where did they go from there?"

After being crowded on from one book to another I have gotten the idea that children like old-fashioned stories. And so I have been working in my spare time this winter writing another for them, which will likely be published within the year. It will tell of pioneer times in western Minnesota, of blizzards, of the 1873 [sic] plague of grasshoppers, of Laura's first school days, of hardships and work and play. With the consent of publishers, I shall call the story *On the Banks of Plum Creek.*

The writing of these books has been a pleasant experience and they have made me many friends scattered far and wide.

Teachers write me that their classes read *Little House in the Big Woods* and went on to the next grade but came back into their old room to the reading of *Farmer Boy* and that the next class was as interested as the first had been.

A teacher in Minneapolis writes me that *Little House in the Big Woods* and *Farmer Boy* are in every third grade classroom in the state.

There is a fascination in writing. The use of words is of itself an interesting study. You will hardly believe the difference the use of one word rather than another will make until you begin to hunt for a word with just the right

Mountain Grove Sorosis Club Speech, 1936 · 147

shade of meaning, just the right color for the picture you are painting with words. Have you thought that words have color?

The only stupid thing about words is the spelling of them.

There is so much one learns in the hours of writing, for instance in the writing of the grasshopper plague. My childish memory was of very hot weather. In making sure of my facts, I learned that the temperature must be at 68 degrees to 70 degrees for grasshoppers to eat well and it must be above 78 degrees before the swarms will take to the air. If the temperature is below 70 degrees the female grasshopper doesn't lay well, but above that she may lay 20 or more "settings of eggs."

In writing *Little House on the Prairie* I could not remember the name of the Indian chief who saved the whites from massacre. It took weeks of research before I found it. In writing books that will be used in schools such things must be right and the manuscript is submitted to experts before publication.

I have learned in this work that when I went as far back in my memory as I could and left my mind there awhile it would go farther back and still farther, bringing out of the dimness of the past things that were beyond my ordinary remembrance.

I have learned that if the mind is allowed to dwell on a circumstance, more and more details will present themselves and the memory becomes much more distinct.

Perhaps you already know all this, but I venture to say that unless you have worked at it, you do not realize what a storehouse your memory is, nor how your mind can dig among its stores if it is given the job. We should be careful, don't you think, about the things we give ourselves to remember.

Also, to my surprise, I have discovered that I have led a very interesting life. Perhaps none of us realize how interesting life is until we begin to look at it from that point of view. Try it! I am sure you will be delighted.

There is still one thing more the writing of these books has shown me.

Running through all the stories, like a golden thread, is the same thought of the values of life. They were courage, self-reliance, independence, integrity and helpfulness. Cheerfulness and humor were handmaids to courage.

In the depression years following the Civil War my parents, as so many others, lost all their savings in a bank failure. They farmed the rough land on the edge of the Big Woods in Wisconsin. They struggled with the climate and fear of Indians in the Indian Territory. For two years in succession they lost their crops to the grasshoppers on the Banks of Plum Creek. They suffered cold and heat, hard work and privation, as did others of their time. When possible they turned the bad into good. If not possible, they endured it. Neither they nor their neighbors begged for help. No other person, nor

148 • Documents

the government, owed them a living. They owed that to themselves and in some way they paid the debt. And they found their own way.

Their old-fashioned character values are worth as much today as they ever were to help us over the rough places. We need today courage, self-reliance and integrity.

When we remember that our hardest times would have been easy times for our forefathers it should help us to be of good courage, as they were, even if things are not all as we would like them to be.

And now I will say just this: If ever you are becoming a little bored with life, as it is, try a new line of work as a hobby. You will be surprised what it will do for you.

SOURCE

Excerpt from Laura Ingalls Wilder and Rose Wilder Lane, edited by William T. Anderson, *A Little House Sampler* (Lincoln, NE: University of Nebraska Press, 1988), pp. 176–80. Copyright © 1988 by HarperCollins Publishers, Inc. Reprinted by permission of HarperCollins Publishers.

DOCUMENT **7**

Travel Diary Excerpt, 1931

The year 1931 proved pivotal for Wilder. Although her "Pioneer Girl" manuscript had been rejected, Wilder sold *Little House in the Big Woods* to Harper & Brothers for release the following year. As Wilder revisited her childhood in her mind, she decided to return to De Smet—her fading "Land of Used to Be." In June, she retraced the steps of her make-or-break journey to Mansfield, Missouri, in 1893. Wilder had not returned to South Dakota since the death of her father in 1902; she planned to see her youngest sister Grace Ingalls Dow and then continue on to visit Carrie Ingalls Swanzey in the Black Hills. Wilder, Almanzo, and shaggy dog Nero chugged over the sweltering Plains in their cavernous 1923 Buick Touring Sedan, an extravagant gift from Rose to her parents. Distraught, nearly bankrupt, and struggling with depression, Rose remained at Rocky Ridge. Wilder kept a rare diary of the trip. Although the catastrophic Dust Bowl days still lay ahead, Wilder's travel diary provides a grainy snapshot of small Midwestern towns and farms in the throes of the Great Depression. Wilder, like any good farm journalist, notices even minor details. She is writing for herself, but her descriptive ability and her puckish, self-deprecating sense of humor shine through the text.

June 10

Left the ugly camp at 4:30 A.M. Nero tickled pink to get started. Drove through Columbus at 6 A.M. Beautiful German city. Rain last night. The air fresh and cool. No dust. Roads, these wonderful roads. Crossed Platte river flats and river on a long bridge, a short bridge, and another long bridge just before we entered Columbus. Each bridge a quarter of a mile long. One narrow and one wide enough to pass if each car drove on lengthwise planks. Manly is spoiled by the wide smooth roads, so he could not stay on the planks. Says he don't believe he will be able to drive when he gets home.

Fine farming country, both sides of Columbus level and rich. Great, beautiful farm homes set in groves of large trees. Simply stunning, large houses, great hay and horse barns, hog houses, chicken houses, granaries. Each farm place looks like a small village. Big, round corncribs without the crib! Corn right outdoors all alone in the fields in those crib-shaped piles. Every building—even the pig creeps—painted.

German Catholic country—Catholic churches now and then. Meadow-larks singing beside the road.

Stopped at Humphrey, 40 miles from last night's camp, for breakfast. Ate at a German bakery restaurant. Delicious coffee and Manly ate German cakes. I had the good German bread toasted with a great chunk of home-made butter, the best ever. Both breakfast and a pint of milk for Nero 35 cents. A quaint little German place and town.

A field of peonies by the road. Peonies for sale. Saw a snow fence by the R.R.

Through Madison, a county seat, and headed for Yankton 90 miles north at 8:20 A.M. Passed a rabbit farm and a licensed fur farm all fenced, dog and cat tight. North from Madison about 20 miles 2 nice clean camps on a river, boats and fishing. Nicest kind of people, kind, cheerful and jolly.

Norfolk is a nice town, with a fine, clean, large camp, filling station, place to eat, etc. (like the one on the way to St. Louis), just north of town. Meridian Cottage Camp north of Norfolk on Highway 81. All farming done by horses, 4-horse teams. Often 8 horses working in the field. Very few cars on the roads even near the cities. Gosh, I'd forgotten there was such a farming country in the U.S. And my God it is a ruined country. Being sold out on taxes. Fifty of these wonderful farms now advertised for tax sale. Many already have been sold and the rest just hanging on. Will not be able to last much longer. Haven't made any profit on their farms for 10 ten years now.

The young man we were talking to at the filling station is very intelligent. He looked at our license plate and asked about the conditions in Missouri. Said he saw people from everywhere and that was all they talked about—conditions—and they seemed to be the same everywhere.

The filling station man lost his 200-acre farm just recently, taxes and interest. His father has a 400-acre farm and his taxes amount to $100 a month.

Eastern loan companies are taking in the farms on their mortgages. People with federal loans are hanging on yet, but will not be able to make their payments unless there is a change in the prices of their produce. He said the places were not being kept up now. They were beginning to run down. Here is a home market for industry—steel, paint, R.R. and all if it could be used.

Pheasants—tame kinds but running wild—run across the road from one covert to the other.

Making hay all along the way. Alfalfa thick and high. Plowing corn, beautiful fields of corn, but late because of cold spring. Fields reaching from the road so far back that the great big horses look small. Eight and ten horses working on a field. Roads well marked. Every help given to keep one safe and the finest roads ever.

The man at the filling station said they were just beginning on cement in Nebraska and the taxes would be even higher. Well, I suppose there must be a good road for the farmers to walk out of the country on.

Eleven A.M. Getting into the breaks of the Missouri River, nearing Yankton.

Looking over the softly rolling countryside the colors are wonderful. The different shades of greens and yellows of the grasses, the soft, bright green of the new spring wheat. All shades of black and brown of the newly plowed soil with corn in straight green rows across it. Yellow alfalfa in bloom on each side of the road, a soft blue sky and clouds floating over all.

12 NOON, YANKTON, S.D.

Traffic was bad, Manly was tired and Nero and I nervous. Thought we would leave Nero in the car in a garage and eat, get postcards, etc. But trying to find a garage we drove through the traffic twice.

I thought if I could only get out of the traffic alive, I could die happily of fright and asked Manly to drive on and eat at the next town. We drove through the traffic again and at the next filling station were told that the next town was 70 miles away. Looks like the joke was on me.

We could only drive on, hoping that what he said was not true, eating some of the fruit we bought in Columbus.

Drove 20 miles and at the junction of highways 81 and 16 found some fairly decent cabins and stopped at 2 o'clock to spend the night. There is a short-order eating place here and a mile down 16 is a little town with more food, so we are all right. Tomorrow with good luck we should be at Grace's. We are only about 70 miles from there.

So here we are in South Dakota. Yankton certainly bids us hail and farewell.

You remember the farewell.

We don't like Kansas but are crazy about Nebraska. So far we don't like South Dakota. It is dry and trying to rain by can't. Drove 185 miles today.

EXPENSES

12 gal. gas	$1.97
Breakfast and milk	.35
Cookies	.10
Cabin	1.25
Garage for car	.50
	$4.17

JUNE 11

Left camp at 5:30 A.M. Nice cool morning. Road finely graveled. Can see for miles in every direction. Crops look good in spite of freezing ice three nights last week. Our coats are none too warm this morning. There are lots of pheasants feeding by the roadside, running in the grass, picking bugs, and standing to look at us, gray ones and brown ones and dove-colored and beautiful dark red ones like a bright leghorn cock in color with bright red on their heads.

A 160-acre cornfield. Meadowlarks singing. Nice farmhouse and awfully large farms. The country seems so quiet and peaceful. Houses on the road about 4 miles apart and no cars on the highway. We have driven two hours and met only one truck and two cars. None has passed us. At the side of the road far from any house was a group of signs, one following the other, spaced apart that read "For-the-land's-sake-eat-butter."

This country has the feeling we loved so much in the Ozarks when we first went there, but which it has lost, a feeling of quiet and peacefulness. But then the wind isn't blowing this morning.

Fine Durham cattle in pastures, cows, proving my contention that one doesn't have to sacrifice beef to produce milk.

Left highway 81, turning west on 34 to Howard, 8 miles. Had a wonderful breakfast in Howard. I had bacon and eggs and coffee, bread, and for the land's sake ate the best butter I've tasted in ages. Manly had bacon and eggs, pancakes and syrup and good old northern green tea. Nero had hamburger and a drink of water.

Took highway 25 out at 9:10 A.M., headed for De Smet 26 miles north. Awfully dry wild prairie grass, dried up to the roots. Not a bit of moisture in the fields and the crops just standing. Girls herding some cows along the sides of the road because grass is so short and pastures dead. It is greener in the road ditches.

Came to De Smet from the south, but the town is built out so far and roads are in different places so nothing looked natural. Went through a corner of town and on to Manchester.

Just out of Manchester met a rainstorm from the southwest. Clouds looked quite their old-fashioned way. The rain poured and we dodged into a garage until the shower was over, then drove around the corner to Grace's. She came out to meet us, surprised, for she had got my letter just yesterday. She is the same old Grace, only not looking very well. Arrived at 10:30 A.M.

EXPENSES

Gas	none
Breakfast	$ .90
Shave	.25
Fruit	.25
	$1.40

MANCHESTER, JUNE 12

Grace seems like a stranger only now and then something familiar about her face. I suppose it is the same with me. Nate is nice but his asthma is very bad.

We all went to De Smet today. Manly and Nate went on their own and Grace and I went to Sassee's drugstore. Saw Mrs. Sassee and Merl. Mrs. Sassee is like herself only more so. Strong faced and dispositioned as of yore. She is running the store. Marl talked of Rose and their class in school. Went to Wilmarth's store. They didn't know me of course and I didn't care to know them. Sherwood was at Lake Preston.

Saw his sister whom I don't remember having known though she says I did. Ran around town awhile then sat at the music store waiting for Manly and Nate to show up. Stupid, tiresome, hot. I got tired of it and went by myself up the street. Grace was tired and her feet swollen so it was hard for her to walk. Just as I met Manly, a little, wrinkled old woman came across the street and spoke. It was Jennie Ross Wheat. The same in every way only older. Mr. Wheat is dead. Gaylord Ross is in the north part of the state a helpless cripple. Jennie talked and talked as always. Finally we tore loose, found Nate and Grace and went to supper, dinner at a café. Very good, fine service, seemed a treat to Grace and Nate. Then home to a close, hot bedroom for the night.

JUNE 13

Manly and I went to De Smet by ourselves in the afternoon. I went to the courthouse to examine records in Ma's estate. Found all in Carrie's name as we thought it should be. On the way to Green's law office saw Charley

Dawley and Manly visiting on the sidewalk in the shade. Dawley seems unchanged.

Grace and I called on Mrs. Tinkham. She is a little bit of an old woman but seemed very natural. Called me Laura and kissed me and seemed very glad to see me. Harold is a man and more of a fool than ever. He horrified me. Chatted a bit and went on. Called on Green and heard the story of the estate practically as we knew of it. Then back to Manchester.

JUNE 14

In the morning, Manly took Grace and me to De Smet to the old house, where we looked over Ma's and Mary's things that had been stored in one room. Everything of value left there has disappeared. In the afternoon we all drove out to Nate's farm.

JUNE 15

Manly and I went to De Smet in the afternoon. Called on Florence Garland Dawley. She is quite feeble, not at all well, and going the next day to Rochester to Mayo's [Clinic] with her son who is a doctor. Florence was sweet as could be and we talked of the old days of the hard winter when she taught the school before it was closed for lack of fuel and because it was too dangerous to go to the schoolhouse.

Called upon Mrs. Green who is a very nice person and spoke so sweetly of Ma and Mary. Said Ma was a mother to her when she first came to De Smet and lived in the house with her. I like Mrs. Green.

Then Manly and I drove out past Pa's farm on the road from town across the slough, nearly in the place where Carrie and I walked to school and Manly used to drive Barnum and Skip as he came dashing out to take me on those long Sunday afternoon drives when I was seventeen.

The road is a highway now. The little sand hill south of where the old house used to be was all that looked natural. The highway turns east and runs along beside what used to be Bert Cornwell's tree claim. We went far enough to be opposite Boast's old farm but the crossroad was so bad we did not go over. Drove back to town and out past our old farms. The homestead has no building on it and is all a grain field over the hill. The school land between it and the tree claim is still grass. There are no buildings on the tree claim and only a few trees left. Al and Oll Sheldon's houses across the road still stand with additions. We drove on toward Spirit Lake. Country looks as it used to, but there are houses and barns where the prairie used to sweep unmarked. Crossroads so bad we did not go to the lake.

Back to Manchester and another hot night. No water fit to drink. We all drank weak tea . . .

[The conclusion of Wilder's diary entry for the following day.] It is funny how everyone who never would have been so familiar in the old days calls me Laurie and loves me so much, but in some way I like it. It all makes me miss those who are gone, Pa and Ma and Mary and the Boasts and Cap Garland.

SOURCE

A Little House Traveler: Writings from Laura Ingalls Wilder's Journeys across America. New York: HarperCollins, 2006. Used with permission of Little House Heritage Trust, the copyright holder. All rights reserved.

DOCUMENT **8**

WILSON LIBRARY BULLETIN, VOL. 22, NO. 8: APRIL 1948

In the aftermath of World War II and the conclusion of the *Little House* series, the accolades and awards rolled in for Wilder's work. National media attention intensified, but Wilder continued to maintain her quiet, private, and unpretentious lifestyle at Rocky Ridge Farm in Mansfield, Missouri.

LAURA INGALLS WILDER

Laura Ingalls Wilder presents, in her novels for young people, a picture of pioneer life in the Northwest of extraordinary vividness, simplicity and sensitivity. Her great gifts as a person and writer, honesty, clear vision, understanding of people and the ability to put down what she sees and imagines in simple, interesting and effective prose, have enabled her to draw out of a covered wagon girlhood a lasting record of a significant phase in American social history. Her sympathetic insight into the urgent unrest that impelled men like her father to take part in the westward expansion and into the courageous patience of women like her mother who accompanied them, are but part of the sense of fact that fill this record with the vital breath of full living.

"I was born in the *Little House in the Big Woods* of Wisconsin (Pepin, Pepin County) February 7, 1867," says Mrs. Wilder. "From there, with my parents and sisters, I traveled in a prairie schooner across Minnesota, Iowa, Missouri, and Kansas and into Indian Territory where we lived in the *Little House on the Prairie*. Then traveling back to western Minnesota, we lived for several years *On the Banks of Plum Creek*. From there we went West again *By the Shores of Silver Lake* in Dakota territory. We lived in De Smet, the *Little Town on the Prairie*, and I married Almanzo of *Farmer Boy*, just as I told in *These Happy Golden Years*."

Mrs. Wilder's parents, Charles and Caroline Lake (Quiner) Ingalls (the Pa and Ma of the "Little House" books), were pioneer farmers of English and Scottish descent. She was the second of four daughters. Acquiring her schooling in "the old-fashioned one-room school," at the age of fifteen years young Laura was teaching school herself. She married Almanzo J. Wilder a few years later on August 25, 1885. "After our marriage," writes Mrs. Wilder, "Almanzo and I lived for a while in the little gray house on the tree claim (De Smet, South Dakota). Then with our little daughter, Rose, we went to live in the piney woods of Florida. In 1894 the Wilders went to live in the Ozarks. "There is no other country like the Ozarks in the world . . . it is old old land. On one low hill that in the springtime is covered with a blue carpet of wild violets, there is a white farmhouse. Almanzo and I live in this white farmhouse with our pet bulldog . . . Now Almanzo is in his nineties . . . Pa and Ma and my sisters are all gone; of the family I alone am left. But Pa's fiddle is in the museum of the South Dakota Historical Society, where every year for always someone will play on it the songs he used to play. It has been many years since I beat eggs with a fork, or cleaned a kerosene lamp. Many things have changed since then, but the truths we learned from our parents and the principles they taught us are always true—they can never change."

It was at the insistence of her daughter, Rose Wilder Lane, herself an author, who was eager to preserve a record of her mother's early life that Mrs. Wilder began to write the "Little House" books. Before that she had been for twelve years home editor of the *Missouri Ruralist,* poultry editor of the St. Louis *Star,* and had also contributed to *Country Gentleman* and *McCall's Magazine.*

Little House in the Big Woods was published in 1932. A Literary Guild book, it was immediately acclaimed as a unique bit of Americana. Jessie Herschl wrote in the New York *Herald Tribune Books* "This small saga of pioneer Wisconsin should be read by all Middle Border children—and by many others, to whom its experiences will not be even an echo of word-to-mouth inheritance. Too few nowadays can tell as real and treasurable a story." Next came *Farmer Boy* (1933), a year in the early childhood of Almanzo. Of the *Little House on the Prairie* (1935) which followed, Anne T. Eaton observed, "Mrs. Wilder has caught the very essence of pioneer life . . ."

And so on down the whole list of books, each with its particular personality and flavor. May Lamberton Becker says of *The Long Winter* (1940), "For sheer gallantry, the story can't be beat. It puts iron into the imagination." This story tells of the "hard winter" of 1880–1881 when the little settlement of De Smet was cut off from outside help.

158 • Documents

The last of Mrs. Wilder's books, *These Happy Golden Years* (1943), was awarded a prize in the New York *Herald Tribune* Spring Book Festival. The author was then 76 years old. Anne T. Eaton summing up the entire contribution stated, "These books are based on the author's own life and ring true in every particular. Their authentic background, sensitive characterization, their fine integrity and spirit of sturdy independence make them an invaluable addition to our list of genuinely American stories and as such they have a special significance for us today."

Mrs. Wilder is now eighty-one years old. She is still living in Mansfield, Missouri. Famous throughout the county for her gingerbread, she is "still very busy doing all the work of the home for Almanzo and myself . . . We are not farming now and have sold part of our land leaving us only seventy acres which is a pasture and woodland." The author is described as being five feet two inches tall (her father always called her half-pint), with blue eyes and white hair. She reads widely, is intensely interested in politics and economics. Her hobby is needlework.

Maria Cimino

SOURCE

Maria Cimino, "Laura Ingalls Wilder," *Wilson Library Bulletin* 22, no. 8 (April 1948) p. 582. Courtesy of H. W. Wilson, a division of EBSCO Information Services.

DOCUMENT **9**

LETTERS TO LAURA: "I AM ALWAYS DREAMING ABOUT YOU . . ."

While modern criticism focuses on the cultural legacy of Wilder's work, no children's writer experienced a greater outpouring of affection from her dedicated readers than did Laura Ingalls Wilder. Her powerful and lasting hold on the hearts, minds, and imaginations of her readers is an important aspect of that legacy and a testament to the unique appeal of her work. Many children wrote to Wilder as if she were their own grandmother—or their invisible friend. Until shortly before her death, Wilder personally answered every letter she received from her fans. An oversized mailbox was installed at Rocky Ridge Farm to accommodate the overwhelming volume of mail.

———

Undated

Dear Mrs. Wilder,

I injoyed [sic] your books very much. My teacher just finished reading "These Happy Golden Years" and when she put it up, we all just stared without a sound as if there were more. You could never guess unless I told you that I am always dreaming about you. And I even talk about you in my sleep.

Almanzo must have been a good driver—at least Nellie Olson thought he was just utterly too-too. And she wasn't kidding when she said her tongue was meant to go plipety-plop.

I think I would have stayed awake at night too, if I was afraid of waking up with a knife in front of me. I wouldn't have liked being on that school term. And Clarence made it worse until you used Ma's advice.

160 • Documents

And I don't think Clarence had any right to call Almanzo your beau.

Your Friend,
Greta Walker

***

January 27, 1944

Dear Mrs. Wilder,

I have read all your books except On the Banks of Plum Creek which doesn't seem to be in the 42nd Street Library. I was very excited when I read the book Hard Winter [sic]. I wondered how you lived through all those blizzards. How come the winds didn't blow your house away? How did you feel when you had to be a school teacher because Mary was blind? I feel very sorry for her. My little twin sisters want to know if Grace, Carrie and Mary are still living. Do you still want to get even with you(r) teacher Eliza Jane Wilder because she did those mean things to Carrie? I wish you could write some books about the life of Carrie and Grace later on. I think Grace was cute when she asked if Pa if his nose is frozen. Weren't you afraid when you slid on Silver Lake and saw the big Buffalo Wolf? If I was in your place then I would be so scared that I'd run away without Carrie. I wish I lived with you all through your life.

Yours Truly,
Emily Mazur

***

Kaiulani School
738 North King Street

May, 5, 1948

Dear Mrs. Wilder,

I have read many of your books, which I borrowed from the library of our school. Now I'm reading one of your books called "The Long Winter." I have already finished reading "Little House in the Big Woods," "Little House on the Prairie," "One the Banks of Plum Creek" and "By the Shores of Silver Lake." All of the books were very interesting. I have enjoyed them very much. Many other children are also enjoying reading your books.

I am a Chinese boy. I came from China about two years ago. Now I am in the fifth grade and working hard. I have just started to enjoy reading books.

I like your books the best because they are so interesting and exciting. I hope someday you will come to Hawaii and write a story about us.

Mahalo,
Johnson Yee

SOURCES

Walker Letter: Rose Wilder Lane Papers, Herbert Hoover Presidential Library, West Branch, IA.
Other Letters: Anderson, William. *A Little House Sampler*. Lincoln: University of Nebraska Press, 1988. All used with permission of Little House Heritage Trust, the copyright holder. All rights reserved.

Bibliography

Adam, Kathryn. "Laura, Ma, Mary, Carrie and Grace: Western Women Portrayed by Laura Ingalls Wilder," in *The Women's West,* edited by Susan Armitage and Elizabeth Jameson. University of Oklahoma Press, 1987, pp. 95–110.

Allexan, Sarah S., Carrie L. Byington, Jerome I. Finkelstein, and Beth A. Tarini. "Blindness in Walnut Grove: How Did Mary Ingalls Lose Her Sight?" *American Journal of Pediatrics* 131, no. 3: 404–40 (February 2013).

Anderson, William, ed. *The Horn Book's Laura Ingalls Wilder: Articles about and by Laura Ingalls Wilder, Garth Williams, and the Little House Books.* Boston, MA: Horn Book, 1987.

Anderson, William, ed. *A Little House Sampler.* Lincoln, NE: University of Nebraska Press, 1988.

Barns, Cass G. *The Sod House.* Lincoln, NE: University of Nebraska Press, 1970.

Berkhofer, Robert F. *The White Man's Indian: Images of the American Indian from Columbus to the Present.* New York: Knopf, 1978.

Bettelheim, Bruno. *The Uses of Enchantment: The Meaning and Importance of Fairy Tales.* New York: Knopf, 1976.

Brown, Curt. "In the Footsteps of Little Crow; 150 Years after the U.S.-Dakota War." *Star Tribune* (Minneapolis, MN), August 15, 2012.

Burns, Louis F. *A History of the Osage People.* Tuscaloosa, AL: University of Alabama Press, 2004.

Cather, Willa. *My Antonia.* New York: Houghton Mifflin, 1954.

Cimino, Maria. "Laura Ingalls Wilder." *Wilson Library Bulletin* 22, no. 8 (April 1948), p. 582.

Daily National Pilot, November 22, 1845. Available at Maritime History of the Great Lakes, http://images.maritimehistoryofthegreatlakes.ca/54141/data?n=9.

Dictionary of Wisconsin Biography. Madison, WI: Wisconsin Historical Society Press, 1960.

Favell, Angela Haste. "A Girl Pioneer in the Wisconsin Wilderness." *Milwaukee Journal,* August 7, 1932.

Fellman, Anita Clair. *Little House, Long Shadow: Laura Ingalls Wilder's Impact on American Culture.* Columbia, MO: University of Missouri Press, 2008.

Finkelman, Paul. "I Could Not Afford to Hang Men for Votes." *William Mitchell Law Review* 39, no. 2: 405–49 (2013).

Fraser, Caroline. "Laura Ingalls Wilder and the Wolves," *Los Angeles Review of Books,* October 10, 2012.

Hill, Pamela Smith. *Laura Ingalls Wilder: A Writer's Life.* Pierre, SD: South Dakota State Historical Society Press, 2007.

164 • Bibliography

Hines, Stephen W., ed. *Laura Ingalls Wilder, Farm Journalist: Writings from the Ozarks.* Columbia, MO: University of Missouri Press, 2007.

History of Howard and Chariton Counties, Missouri: Written and Compiled from the Most Official Authentic and Private Sources, Including a History of Its Townships, Towns, and Villages, Together with a Condensed History of Missouri. St. Louis: National Historical, 1883.

Holtz, William V. *The Ghost in the Little House: A Life of Rose Wilder Lane.* Columbia, MO: University of Missouri Press, 1993.

Holy Cross Hospital Records, Accn 588, 1875–1927. Special Collections and Archives. Salt Lake City, UT: University of Utah, J. Willard Marriott.

The Independent Fifth Reader. A. S. Barnes and Company, New York, 1876.

Kaye, Frances W. "Little Squatter on the Osage Diminished Reserve: Reading Laura Ingalls Wilder's Kansas Indians." *Great Plains Quarterly,* University of Nebraska at Lincoln, Paper 23 (2000).

Kirkpatrick, Patricia. "It is Better Farther On: A Journey into the Landscape of Laura Ingalls Wilder," *Minnesota Historical Society Archives* 8, no. 9 (September 1974).

Kirkus, Virginia. "The Discovery of Laura Ingalls Wilder." *The Horn Book Magazine,* December 1953.

Lane, Rose Wilder. *A Little House Traveler: Writings from Laura Ingalls Wilder's Journeys Across America.* New York: HarperCollins, 2006.

Lane, Rose Wilder. *The Rose Wilder Lane Papers.* West Branch, IA: Herbert Hoover Presidential Library.

Laskin, David. *The Children's Blizzard.* New York: HarperCollins, 2004.

Lichty, Irene V. *The Ingalls Family from Plum Creek to Walnut Grove via Burr Oak, Iowa.* Monograph, Minnesota Historical Society Archives. Private printing, 1970.

Limerick, Patricia Nelson. *The Legacy of Conquest: The Unbroken past of the American West.* New York: Norton, 1987.

Linsenmayer, Penny T. "Kansas Settlers on the Osage Diminished Reserve." *Kansas History: A Journal of the Central Plains* 24, no. 3 (2001), 168–85.

Lockwood, Jeffrey Alan. *Locust: The Devastating Rise and Mysterious Disappearance of the Insect That Shaped the American Frontier.* New York: Basic Books, 2004.

Luchetti, Cathy. *Children of the West: Family Life on the Frontier.* New York: Norton, 2001.

Marshall, James M. *Land Fever: Dispossession and the Frontier Myth.* Lexington, KY: University Press of Kentucky, 1986.

McCormick, David. "The Bloody Benders Grim Harvest." *Wild West Magazine,* March 30, 2012. Available at http://www.historynet.com/the-bloody-benders-grim-harvest.htm.

Miller, John E. *Becoming Laura Ingalls Wilder: The Woman behind the Legend.* Columbia, MO: University of Missouri Press, 1998.

Peavy, Linda S., and Ursula Smith. *The Gold Rush Widows of Little Falls: A Story Drawn from the Letters of Pamelia and James Fergus.* St. Paul, MI: Minnesota Historical Society, 1990.

Peavy, Linda S., and Ursula Smith. *Pioneer Women: The Lives of Women on the Frontier.* New York: Smithmark Publishers, 1996.

Riley, Glenda. *Frontierswomen, the Iowa Experience.* Ames, IA: Iowa State University Press, 1981.

Rosenblum, Dolores. "'Intimate Immensity': Mystic Space in the Works of Laura Ingalls Wilder," in *Where the West Begins,* edited by Arthur R. Huseboe and Willian Geyer, 72–79. Sioux Falls, SD: Center for Western Studies Press, 1978.

Sandoz, Mari. *Sandhill Sundays and Other Recollections.* Lincoln, NE: University of Nebraska Press, 1966.

Stevenson, Robert Louis. *Across the Plains with Other Memories and Essays.* New York: C. Scribner's Sons, 1892.

Stratton, Joanna L. *Pioneer Women: Voices from the Kansas Frontier.* New York: Simon and Schuster, 1981.

Turner, Frederick Jackson. *The Frontier in American History.* New York: Holt, Rinehart and Winston, 1962.

Warnock, Alene M. *Laura Ingalls Wilder: The Westville Florida Years.* Leonardtown, MD: Heritage Printing & Graphics, 1979.

Wilder, Laura Ingalls, and Garth Williams. *By the Shores of Silver Lake.* New York: Harper & Bros., 1953.

Wilder, Laura Ingalls, and Garth Williams. *Little House in the Big Woods.* New York: Harper & Bros., 1953.

Wilder, Laura Ingalls, and Garth Williams. *Little House on the Prairie.* New York: Harper & Bros., 1953.

Wilder, Laura Ingalls, and Garth Williams. *The Long Winter.* New York: Harper & Bros., 1953.

Wilder, Laura Ingalls, and Garth Williams. *These Happy Golden Years.* New York: Harper & Bros., 1953.

Wilder, Laura Ingalls, and Garth Williams. *The First Four Years.* New York: Harper & Row, 1971.

Wilder, Laura Ingalls. "Pioneer Girl." Unpublished Manuscript, Brandt Draft, Herbert Hoover Presidential Library.

Women's World. "A Fireside Chat with Rose Wilder Lane," September 1939.

Zinn, Howard. *A People's History of the United States, 1492–Present.* New York: HarperCollins, 1980.

Zochert, Donald. *Laura: The Life of Laura Ingalls Wilder.* New York: Avon Books, 1977.

ADDITIONAL RESOURCES

Anderson, William. *The Iowa Story: Laura Ingalls Wilder's Life in Burr Oak, Iowa.* Burr Oak, IA: Laura Ingalls Wilder Park and Museum, 1990.

Anderson, William. *Laura Wilder of Mansfield: Life on Rocky Ridge Farm and in the Town of Mansfield.* Lapeer, MI: Dixon Graphics, 2012.

Anderson, William, and Leslie A. Kelly. *Laura Ingalls Wilder Country: [the People and Places in Laura Ingalls Wilder's Life and Books].* New York: Harper Perennial, 1990.

Cleaveland, Nancy, and Penny Lisenmayer. *Charles Ingalls and the U.S. Public Land Laws.* 4th ed. SeventhWinter Press, 2010.

Dathe, Mary Jo. *Spring Valley: The Laura Ingalls Wilder Connection.* Revised 4th ed. Private printing, 2001.

Deloria, Philip Joseph. *Playing Indian.* New Haven, CT: Yale University Press, 1998.

Deloria, Vine, and Clifford M. Lytle. *American Indians, American Justice.* Austin, TX: University of Texas Press, 1983.

Draper, Fannie McClurg. *My Ever Dear Charlie: Letters Home from the Dakota Territory.* Guilford, CT: Globe Pequot Press, 2005.

Fatzinger, Amy S. *"Indians in the House": Revisiting American Indians in Laura Ingalls Wilder's Little House Books.* University of Arizona dissertation, 2008.

The Ingalls Family of De Smet. De Smet, SD: Laura Ingalls Wilder Memorial Society, 2001.

Miller, Dwight M. *Laura Ingalls Wilder and the American Frontier: Five Perspectives.* Lanham, MD: University Press of America, 2002.

Miller, John E. *Laura Ingalls Wilder and Rose Wilder Lane: Authorship, Place, Time, and Culture.* Columbia, MO: University of Missouri Press, 2008.

O'Leary, Dorothy Petrucci, and Catherine G. Goddard. Gleanings from Our Past, A History of the Iowa Braille and Sight Saving School, Vinton Iowa, pp. 23–29. Published by The Iowa Braille & Sight Saving School 1984. Copyright 1984 by Iowa Braille & Sight Saving School.

Riley, Glenda. *Women and Indians on the Frontier, 1825–1915.* Albuquerque, NM: University of New Mexico Press, 1984.

Riley, Glenda. *Women and Nature: Saving the "Wild" West.* Lincoln, NE: University of Nebraska Press, 1999.

166 • Bibliography

Romines, Ann. *Constructing the Little House: Gender, Culture, and Laura Ingalls Wilder.* Amherst, MA: University of Massachusetts Press, 1997.

Shlaes, Amity. *The Forgotten Man: A New History of the Great Depression.* New York: HarperCollins Publishers, 2007.

Stauffer, Helen Winter. *Mari Sandoz, Story Catcher of the Plains.* Lincoln, NE: University of Nebraska Press, 1982.

Trachtenberg, Alan. *Shades of Hiawatha: Staging Indians, Making Americans: 1880–1930.* New York: Hill and Wang, 2004.

Wilder, Laura Ingalls. *West from Home: Letters of Laura Ingalls Wilder to Almanzo Wilder, San Francisco, 1915.* New York: Harper & Row, 1974.

INDEX

Alcott, Louisa May 41
Alden, Rev. Edwin 32, 35, 56, 63
Amati violin 87
American Library Association/Wilder Award 109
"As A Farm Woman Thinks" 98, 135

Barnes, Cass G. 30
Beatty, Bessie 91, 96
Bettelheim, Bruno 1, 118
Big Woods 8
Black Hawk War 9
Bloody Benders 22
Boast, Robert and Ella 55, 56, 57, 65
Bouchie ("Brewster") Family and school 66, 67
Boyle, Mildred 108
Boylston, Helen "Troub" 101
Burr Oak House (Masters Hotel) 38, 39, 42
Burr Oak, Iowa 38, 39
Bye, George 102, 107

Carpenter, Martha Quiner (aunt) 9, 10, 18, 37, 103
Cather, Willa 49
Chariton County, Missouri 16
Chicago & North Western Railroad 29, 48, 55, 57, 59, 65
Children's Blizzard, The 61
Comstock "Chastity" Laws 36
Concord, Wisconsin 8
Congregational Church 31, 32, 35, 82, 87
Cooley Family 81, 86
Crowley, Louisiana 88

Dakota Land Boom 57
Dakota Diaspora 15
Dakota War 1862 ("Sioux Uprising") 13
De Smet, South Dakota 57, 61, 62
Domestic pioneer life 12, 19, 31, 39
Dow, Grace Pearl Ingalls 41, 42, 76, 87, 104, 109, 153

Ensign Family 44
Ensign, Howard 44, 45
Exodusters 20

Father Pierre-Jean De Smet 57
Favell, Angela Haste 13
Fergus, Pamelia 29
Fiery, Marion 103
Financial Panic (1873) 44, 45, 54
Forbes, Docia Ingalls (aunt) 48, 49
Forbes, Gene and Lena (cousins) 54, 55
Forbes, Hiram 48, 55
Frontier Thesis/Free Land 114, 115

Garland, Florence 60, 104, 154
Garland, Margaret Frances 60
Garland, Oscar Edmund "Cap" 60, 61, 62, 155
Gibson, Isaac 18, 26n37
Grasshopper invasions 33–6

Hader, Berta 99, 103
Hard Winter, The 59, 60, 61, 62
Harper & Brothers 104, 105, 108
Holbrook, Charlotte Tucker Quiner 9, 10, 37, 43

168 · Index

Holbrook, Frederick 10, 35
Homestead Act 15

Ingalls, Caroline Quiner (mother) 8–11, 14, 18, 28, 30, 33–5, 39, 46, 56, 58, 68, 74, 87, 100, 137
Ingalls, Charles Frederick (Freddie) 35, 36, 38, 39
Ingalls, Charles Philip (father) 7–9, 11, 15–17, 27–30, 33–4, 38, 41, 43, 44, 47, 48, 54–9, 79, 80, 86
Ingalls, Lansford and Laura Colby 8, 9, 11
Ingalls, Mary Amelia 8, 12, 20, 23, 31, 40, 41, 45, 55, 61, 63, 64, 68, 79, 87, 102, 129; loses sight 47–8
Ingalls, Peter (uncle) 9, 27, 28, 34, 37, 43
Ingalls, Peter (cousin) 75, 76, 77
Iowa College for the Blind 63, 64

Johnson, Adamantine 15, 16
Junior Literary Guild 105, 146
Justamere Club 99

Kennedy, Nettie and Sandy 32, 49
Kirkus, Virginia 104

Lane, Claire Gillette 91, 96, 99
Lane, Rose Wilder (daughter): birth 74; in De Smet 78; "malnutrition child" 79; Rocky Ridge childhood 83–4; on Laura as mother 85; leaves home with EJ Wilder 88; marriage 91; death of son 91; early writing career 96; in San Francisco 96–8; divorces Lane 99; on her parents 85, 89, 101; European tours and return to Rocky Ridge 99–101; literary success 98; depression and bipolar disorder 101; works on *Little House* series 103, 106, 107; *Let the Hurricane Roar* 105; libertarianism 107; in Danbury 106; Viet Nam correspondent 112; as guardian of Wilder's work and legacy 112
Libertarian Movement 107
Lichty, Irene 48, 108
Limerick, Patricia Nelson 24, 115, 116
Little House book series 106
Little House on the Prairie (television series) 116
Lockwood, Jeffrey 33, 34, 36
Loftus, Daniel 62
Longcor (Loncher), George 23

Manifest Destiny 3, 114
Mansfield, Missouri 82, 84, 86

Masters, Geneva 65
Masters, George and Maggie 59, 60, 61
Masters, William and Nancy 39, 46
Masterson, Martha Gay 36
McBride, Roger Lea 113
McGregor, Alexander 9
McKee Family 68, 69
Meningoencephalitis (Mary Ingalls) 47
Meta, Rexh 101
Missouri Ruralist, The 95, 96, 97, 98, 99
Moyston, Guy 89
Mr. Bisbee (singing instructor) 39

Nation, Carrie 41, 42
National Farm Loan Association 99
Nelson, Eleck and Olena 29, 32, 34, 35, 44
Nordstrom, Ursula 108

Oleson, Nellie (character) 35, 65, 116, 118
Order of the Eastern Star 86, 99, 108, 123
Osage Diminished Reserve 16, 17
Osage Indians 15–24
Owens, Nellie 35, 45
Ozarks 81, 82, 83

Panama-Pacific International Exposition 140
Panic of 1893 79, 80, 87, 114
Paterson, Isabel 107
People's Party (Populists) 47, 55, 134
Pepin, Wisconsin 11
"Pioneer Girl" manuscript 19, 34, 39, 42, 43, 46, 55, 102, 103, 105, 106
Plum Creek 29, 30, 34, 35
Prairie School architecture 90
Preemption Act (1841) 15

Quiner letters 9, 25n5
Quiner, Edwin Bentley 10
Quiner, Elisha 10
Quiner, Henry N. 9
Quiner, Joseph 9

Rand, Ayn 107
Riley, Glenda 12, 31
Rock Cottage 101
Rocky Ridge Farm 83, 86, 88, 133
Rothville, Missouri 16
Rude, Silas 46

Sandoz, Mari 37
San Francisco 90, 96, 97, 140–5
San Francisco Bulletin 91, 96, 97, 98
San Francisco Call 91

Index · 169

Seal, Neta and Silas 108, 109
Sewall, Helen 108
Sherman Silver Purchase Act 80
Soldat du Chene 18, 23
Spring Valley, Minnesota 66, 77
Steadman Family 36–40
Stevenson, Robert Louis 57
Sturges Treaty (1868) 17
Swanzey, Carrie Celestia Ingalls 20, 41, 48, 60, 62, 65, 87, 102, 105, 109

Tann, Dr. George 20, 21
Thayer, Eliza Jane Wilder (EJ) 64, 65, 66, 69, 70, 88
Turner, Frederick Jackson 114–16

Vinton, Iowa 63, 64

Walnut Grove, Minnesota 28, 29, 32, 44
Westville, Florida 77
Wilder, Almanzo James: childhood 66; moves to Spring Valley 66; homesteads in De Smet 66; local hero in Hard Winter 62; expert horse handler 66; courts Laura 66–7; marriage 70; diphtheria and aftermath 75; loses homestead and tree claim 76; moves to Florida 77; moves to Mansfield 82; buys and clears Rocky Ridge Farm 82–3;

travels with Laura 104; *Farmer Boy* 105; death 109
Wilder, James and Angeline 77, 87
Wilder, Laura Ingalls: birth 8; life in Pepin 11–12; in Kansas, witnesses removal of Osages 19; returns to Pepin 27; moves to Walnut Grove 28; locust invasions 33–4; works in Burr Oak hotel 38; returns to Walnut Grove 43–4; school days 45; and Mary's blindness 47; moves to C & NW railroad camp 52; surveyor's house 55; in De Smet and Hard Winter 59–62; love of prairie 62–3; meets Almanzo 65; teaches at Bouchie School 66–7; marriage 70; birth of Rose 74; death of son 76; loses homestead 76; moves to Florida 77; moves to Missouri 82; in San Francisco 96–7; designs and builds Rocky Ridge Farm 90, 95; as farm journalist 94, 95; runs for local office 99; "Pioneer Girl" 102; relationship with Rose 98–100; *Little House in the Big Woods* 103–5; success and sequence of series 106–7; awards 105, 109; death 110
Wilder, Royal 60, 66, 69, 75, 77
Wilkins School 69, 70
Williams, Garth 108, 112
Winnebago Indians 15
Women's Christian Temperance Union 42
Wright, Frank Lloyd 90